I0458645

Prophetic Propaganda Mentioned In The Quran

Compiled By Gregory Heary

Due to the popularity of unprophetic proselytization of the prophetic religion of Islam I find it necessary to compile the propaganda by the prophets mentioned in the Quran. This is not a biographical work on the prophets nor does it mention everything ever said by a prophet, or even what every prophet is said to have said according to the Quran; rather it is a small collection of *"public statements of prophetic propaganda"* that were so pleasing to God as to merit God quoting them in his speech. The hadith complete our knowledge of the prophetic propaganda but to include all the hadith on the prophets' speech would be too lengthy for most readers and beyond my capabilities. In collecting the Quranically mentioned prophetic propaganda I have limited myself to citing the God-citated best speech of the best people. Surely if any of us were to meet a prophet under time constraints, they would condense their message to us and sensibly choose their words to please God most. Wisely God already chose their words that pleased God most to pass on to us directly, and it is these very God-chosen words of the prophets that I have collected. Thus you have in this book the pinnacle of human propaganda as quoted or commanded by God's speech. You will find the prophets' message was clear and consistent throughout time while their creed and methodology in propagating was identical and uniform. Unfortunately, many who claim to follow their faith do not preach the same message as the prophets nor do they utilize the same mannerisms or methodology. The cure is sincerity and knowledge leading to correct intentions and actions. Only the pure prophetic propaganda will lead to the prophetic faith dominating all satanic falsehoods.

Public Statements of Prophetic Propaganda Mentioned in the Quran

Quran 7:172-173

وَإِذْ أَخَذَ رَبُّكَ مِنۢ بَنِىٓ ءَادَمَ مِن ظُهُورِهِمْ ذُرِّيَّتَهُمْ وَأَشْهَدَهُمْ عَلَىٰٓ أَنفُسِهِمْ أَلَسْتُ بِرَبِّكُمْۖ قَالُوا۟ بَلَىٰۛ شَهِدْنَآۛ أَن تَقُولُوا۟ يَوْمَ ٱلْقِيَٰمَةِ إِنَّا كُنَّا عَنْ هَٰذَا غَٰفِلِينَ (١٧٢) أَوْ تَقُولُوٓا۟ إِنَّمَآ أَشْرَكَ ءَابَآؤُنَا مِن قَبْلُ وَكُنَّا ذُرِّيَّةً مِّنۢ بَعْدِهِمْۖ أَفَتُهْلِكُنَا بِمَا فَعَلَ ٱلْمُبْطِلُونَ (١٧٣)

And (remember) when your Lord brought forth from the Children of Adam, from their loins, their seed (or from Adam's loin his offspring) and made them testify as to themselves (saying): "Am I not your Lord?" They said: "Yes! We testify," lest you should say on the Day of Resurrection: "Verily, we have been unaware of this." (172) Or lest you should say: "It was only our fathers afortime who took others as partners in worship along with Allâh, and we were (merely their) descendants after them; will You then destroy us because of the deeds of men who practiced Al-Bâtil (i.e. polytheism and committing crimes and sins, invoking and worshipping others besides Allâh)?" (173)

Quran 3:81

وَإِذْ أَخَذَ ٱللَّهُ مِيثَـٰقَ ٱلنَّبِيِّـۧنَ لَمَآ ءَاتَيْتُكُم مِّن كِتَـٰبٍ وَحِكْمَةٍ ثُمَّ جَآءَكُمْ رَسُولٌ مُّصَدِّقٌ لِّمَا مَعَكُمْ لَتُؤْمِنُنَّ بِهِۦ وَلَتَنصُرُنَّهُۥ قَالَ ءَأَقْرَرْتُمْ وَأَخَذْتُمْ عَلَىٰ ذَٰلِكُمْ إِصْرِى قَالُوٓا أَقْرَرْنَا قَالَ فَٱشْهَدُوا وَأَنَا۠ مَعَكُم مِّنَ ٱلشَّـٰهِدِينَ

And (remember) when Allâh took the Covenant of the Prophets, saying: "Take whatever I gave you from the Book and Hikmah (understanding of the Laws of Allâh), and afterwards there will come to you a Messenger confirming what is with you; you must, then, believe in him and help him." Allâh said: "Do you agree (to it) and will you take up My Covenant (which I conclude with you)?" They said: "We agree." He said: "Then bear witness; and I am with you among the witnesses (for this)." (81)

Quran 7:23

قَالَا رَبَّنَا ظَلَمْنَآ أَنفُسَنَا وَإِن لَّمْ تَغْفِرْ لَنَا وَتَرْحَمْنَا لَنَكُونَنَّ مِنَ ٱلْخَـٰسِرِينَ

They (Adam and Eve) said: "Our Lord! We have wronged ourselves. If You forgive us not, and bestow not upon us Your Mercy, we shall certainly be of the losers." (23)

Quran 7:59-63

لَقَدْ أَرْسَلْنَا نُوحًا إِلَىٰ قَوْمِهِ فَقَالَ يَـٰقَوْمِ ٱعْبُدُوا۟ ٱللَّهَ مَا لَكُم مِّنْ إِلَـٰهٍ غَيْرُهُۥٓ إِنِّىٓ أَخَافُ عَلَيْكُمْ عَذَابَ يَوْمٍ عَظِيمٍ (٥٩) قَالَ ٱلْمَلَأُ مِن قَوْمِهِ إِنَّا لَنَرَىٰكَ فِى ضَلَـٰلٍ مُّبِينٍ (٦٠) قَالَ يَـٰقَوْمِ لَيْسَ بِى ضَلَـٰلَةٌ وَلَـٰكِنِّى رَسُولٌ

مِّن رَّبِّ ٱلْعَـٰلَمِينَ ﴿٦١﴾ أُبَلِّغُكُمْ رِسَـٰلَـٰتِ رَبِّى وَأَنصَحُ لَكُمْ وَأَعْلَمُ مِنَ ٱللَّهِ مَا لَا تَعْلَمُونَ ﴿٦٢﴾ أَوَعَجِبْتُمْ أَن جَآءَكُمْ ذِكْرٌ مِّن رَّبِّكُمْ عَلَىٰ رَجُلٍ مِّنكُمْ لِيُنذِرَكُمْ وَلِتَتَّقُواْ وَلَعَلَّكُمْ تُرْحَمُونَ ﴿٦٣﴾

Indeed, We sent Nûh (Noah) to his people and he said: "O my people! Worship Allâh! You have no other Ilâh (God) but Him. (Lâ ilâha ill-allâh: none has the right to be worshipped but Allâh). Certainly, I fear for you the torment of a Great Day!" (59) The leaders of his people said: "Verily, we see you in plain error." (60) [Nûh (Noah)] said: "O my people! There is no error in me, but I am a Messenger from the Lord of the 'Alamîn (mankind, jinn and all that exists)! (61) "I convey unto you the Messages of my Lord and give sincere advice to you. And I know from Allâh what you know not. (62) "Do you wonder that there has come to you a Reminder from your Lord through a

man from amongst you, that he may
warn you, so that you may fear Allâh
and that you may receive (His) Mercy?"
(63)

Quran 10:71-72

وَٱتْلُ عَلَيْهِمْ نَبَأَ نُوحٍ إِذْ قَالَ لِقَوْمِهِ يَٰقَوْمِ إِن كَانَ
كَبُرَ عَلَيْكُم مَّقَامِى وَتَذْكِيرِى بِـَٔايَٰتِ ٱللَّهِ فَعَلَى ٱللَّهِ
تَوَكَّلْتُ فَأَجْمِعُوٓا۟ أَمْرَكُمْ وَشُرَكَآءَكُمْ ثُمَّ لَا يَكُنْ
أَمْرُكُمْ عَلَيْكُمْ غُمَّةً ثُمَّ ٱقْضُوٓا۟ إِلَىَّ وَلَا تُنظِرُونِ
(٧١) فَإِن تَوَلَّيْتُمْ فَمَا سَأَلْتُكُم مِّنْ أَجْرٍ إِنْ أَجْرِىَ إِلَّا
عَلَى ٱللَّهِ وَأُمِرْتُ أَنْ أَكُونَ مِنَ ٱلْمُسْلِمِينَ (٧٢)

And recite to them the news of Nûh
(Noah). When he said to his people: "O
my people, if my stay (with you), and
my reminding (you) of the Ayât (proofs,
evidences, verses, lessons, signs,
revelations, etc.) of Allâh is hard on you,
then I put my trust in Allâh. So devise
your plot, you and your partners, and
let not your plot be in doubt for you.
Then pass your sentence on me and give

me no respite. (71) "But if you turn away
[from accepting my doctrine of Islâmic
Monotheism, i.e. to worship none but
Allâh], then no reward have I asked of
you, my reward is only from Allâh, and
I have been commanded to be of the
Muslims (those who submit to Allâh's
Will)." (72)

Quran 11:25-34

وَلَقَدۡ أَرۡسَلۡنَا نُوحًا إِلَىٰ قَوۡمِهِۦٓ إِنِّى لَكُمۡ نَذِيرٌ مُّبِينٌ
(٢٥) أَن لَّا تَعۡبُدُوٓاْ إِلَّا ٱللَّهَۖ إِنِّىٓ أَخَافُ عَلَيۡكُمۡ عَذَابَ
يَوۡمٍ أَلِيمٖ (٢٦) فَقَالَ ٱلۡمَلَأُ ٱلَّذِينَ كَفَرُواْ مِن قَوۡمِهِۦ مَا
نَرَىٰكَ إِلَّا بَشَرٗا مِّثۡلَنَا وَمَا نَرَىٰكَ ٱتَّبَعَكَ إِلَّا ٱلَّذِينَ هُمۡ
أَرَاذِلُنَا بَادِىَ ٱلرَّأۡىِ وَمَا نَرَىٰ لَكُمۡ عَلَيۡنَا مِن فَضۡلِۭ بَلۡ
نَظُنُّكُمۡ كَٰذِبِينَ (٢٧) قَالَ يَٰقَوۡمِ أَرَءَيۡتُمۡ إِن كُنتُ عَلَىٰ
بَيِّنَةٖ مِّن رَّبِّى وَءَاتَىٰنِى رَحۡمَةٗ مِّنۡ عِندِهِۦ فَعُمِّيَتۡ عَلَيۡكُمۡ
أَنُلۡزِمُكُمُوهَا وَأَنتُمۡ لَهَا كَٰرِهُونَ (٢٨) وَيَٰقَوۡمِ لَآ
أَسۡـَٔلُكُمۡ عَلَيۡهِ مَالًاۖ إِنۡ أَجۡرِىَ إِلَّا عَلَى ٱللَّهِۚ وَمَآ أَنَا۠
بِطَارِدِ ٱلَّذِينَ ءَامَنُوٓاْۚ إِنَّهُم مُّلَٰقُواْ رَبِّهِمۡ وَلَٰكِنِّىٓ أَرَىٰكُمۡ
قَوۡمٗا تَجۡهَلُونَ (٢٩) وَيَٰقَوۡمِ مَن يَنصُرُنِى مِنَ ٱللَّهِ إِن
طَرَدتُّهُمۡۚ أَفَلَا تَذَكَّرُونَ (٣٠) وَلَآ أَقُولُ لَكُمۡ عِندِى

خَزَآئِنُ ٱللَّهِ وَلَآ أَعْلَمُ ٱلْغَيْبَ وَلَآ أَقُولُ إِنِّى مَلَكٌ وَلَآ أَقُولُ لِلَّذِينَ تَزْدَرِىٓ أَعْيُنُكُمْ لَن يُؤْتِيَهُمُ ٱللَّهُ خَيْرًا ٱللَّهُ أَعْلَمُ بِمَا فِىٓ أَنفُسِهِمْ إِنِّىٓ إِذًا لَّمِنَ ٱلظَّٰلِمِينَ (٣١) قَالُوا۟ يَٰنُوحُ قَدْ جَٰدَلْتَنَا فَأَكْثَرْتَ جِدَٰلَنَا فَأْتِنَا بِمَا تَعِدُنَآ إِن كُنتَ مِنَ ٱلصَّٰدِقِينَ (٣٢) قَالَ إِنَّمَا يَأْتِيكُم بِهِ ٱللَّهُ إِن شَآءَ وَمَآ أَنتُم بِمُعْجِزِينَ (٣٣) وَلَا يَنفَعُكُمْ نُصْحِىٓ إِنْ أَرَدتُّ أَنْ أَنصَحَ لَكُمْ إِن كَانَ ٱللَّهُ يُرِيدُ أَن يُغْوِيَكُمْ هُوَ رَبُّكُمْ وَإِلَيْهِ تُرْجَعُونَ (٣٤)

And indeed We sent Nûh (Noah) to his people (and he said): "I have come to you as a plain warner." (25) "That you worship none but Allâh, surely, I fear for you the torment of a painful Day." (26) The chiefs who disbelieved among his people said: "We see you but a man like ourselves, nor do we see any follow you but the meanest among us and they (too) followed you without thinking. And we do not see in you any merit above us, in fact we think you are liars." (27) He said: "O my people! Tell me, if I have a clear proof from my Lord, and a

Mercy (Prophethood) has come to me from Him, but that (Mercy) has been obscured from your sight. Shall we compel you to accept it (Islâmic Monotheism) when you have a strong hatred for it? (28) "And O my people! I ask of you no wealth for it, my reward is from none but Allâh. I am not going to drive away those who have believed. Surely, they are going to meet their Lord, but I see that you are a people that are ignorant (29) "And O my people! Who will help me against Allâh, if I drove them away? Will you not then give a thought? (30) "And I do not say to you that with me are the Treasures of Allâh, "Nor that I know the Ghaib (unseen);"nor do I say I am an angel, and I do not say of those whom your eyes look down upon that Allâh will not bestow any good on them. Allâh knows what is in their inner-selves (as regards belief, etc.). In that case, I should, indeed be one of the Zâlimûn (wrong-doers, oppressors)." (31) They said: "O Nûh (Noah)! You have disputed with us and much have you prolonged the dispute with us, now bring upon us what you threaten us with, if you are of the truthful." (32) He said: "Only Allâh will bring it (the punishment) on you, if He wills, and then you will escape not. (33) "And my advice will not profit you, even if I wish to give you good counsel, if Allâh's Will is to keep you astray. He is your Lord! and to Him you shall return." (34)

Quran 26:105-118

كَذَّبَتْ قَوْمُ نُوحٍ ٱلْمُرْسَلِينَ (١٠٥) إِذْ قَالَ لَهُمْ أَخُوهُمْ نُوحٌ أَلَا تَتَّقُونَ (١٠٦) إِنِّى لَكُمْ رَسُولٌ أَمِينٌ (١٠٧) فَٱتَّقُواْ ٱللَّهَ وَأَطِيعُونِ (١٠٨) وَمَآ أَسْـَٔلُكُمْ عَلَيْهِ مِنْ أَجْرٍ إِنْ أَجْرِىَ إِلَّا عَلَىٰ رَبِّ ٱلْعَٰلَمِينَ (١٠٩) فَٱتَّقُواْ ٱللَّهَ وَأَطِيعُونِ (١١٠) ۞ قَالُوٓاْ أَنُؤْمِنُ لَكَ وَٱتَّبَعَكَ ٱلْأَرْذَلُونَ (١١١) قَالَ وَمَا عِلْمِى

13

بِمَا كَانُوا۟ يَعْمَلُونَ ﴿١١٢﴾ إِنْ حِسَابُهُمْ إِلَّا عَلَىٰ رَبِّى لَوْ تَشْعُرُونَ ﴿١١٣﴾ وَمَآ أَنَا۠ بِطَارِدِ ٱلْمُؤْمِنِينَ ﴿١١٤﴾ إِنْ أَنَا۠ إِلَّا نَذِيرٌ مُّبِينٌ ﴿١١٥﴾ قَالُوا۟ لَئِن لَّمْ تَنتَهِ يَٰنُوحُ لَتَكُونَنَّ مِنَ ٱلْمَرْجُومِينَ ﴿١١٦﴾ قَالَ رَبِّ إِنَّ قَوْمِى كَذَّبُونِ ﴿١١٧﴾ فَٱفْتَحْ بَيْنِى وَبَيْنَهُمْ فَتْحًا وَنَجِّنِى وَمَن مَّعِىَ مِنَ ٱلْمُؤْمِنِينَ ﴿١١٨﴾

The people of Nûh (Noah) belied the Messengers. (105) When their brother Nûh (Noah) said to them: "Will you not fear Allâh and obey Him? (106) "I am a trustworthy Messenger to you. (107) "So fear Allâh, keep your duty to Him, and obey me. (108) "No reward do I ask of you for it (my Message of Islâmic Monotheism), my reward is only from the Lord of the 'Alamîn (mankind, jinn and all that exists). (109) "So keep your duty to Allâh, fear Him and obey me." (110) They said: "Shall we believe in you, when the meanest (of the people) follow you?" (111) He said: "And what knowledge have I of what they used to

14

do? (112) "Their account is only with my Lord, if you could (but) know. (113) "And I am not going to drive away the believers. (114) I am only a plain warner." (115) They said: "If you cease not, O Nûh (Noah)! You will surely be among those stoned (to death)." (116) He said: "My Lord! Verily, my people have belied me. (117) Therefore judge You between me and them, and save me and those of the believers who are with me." (118)

Quran 71:1-12

إِنَّآ أَرْسَلْنَا نُوحًا إِلَىٰ قَوْمِهِۦٓ أَنْ أَنذِرْ قَوْمَكَ مِن قَبْلِ أَن يَأْتِيَهُمْ عَذَابٌ أَلِيمٌ (١) قَالَ يَـٰقَوْمِ إِنِّى لَكُمْ نَذِيرٌ مُّبِينٌ (٢) أَنِ ٱعْبُدُوا۟ ٱللَّهَ وَٱتَّقُوهُ وَأَطِيعُونِ (٣) يَغْفِرْ لَكُم مِّن ذُنُوبِكُمْ وَيُؤَخِّرْكُمْ إِلَىٰٓ أَجَلٍ مُّسَمًّى ۚ إِنَّ أَجَلَ ٱللَّهِ إِذَا جَآءَ لَا يُؤَخَّرُ ۘ لَوْ كُنتُمْ تَعْلَمُونَ (٤) قَالَ رَبِّ إِنِّى دَعَوْتُ قَوْمِى لَيْلًا وَنَهَارًا (٥) فَلَمْ يَزِدْهُمْ دُعَآءِىٓ إِلَّا فِرَارًا (٦) وَإِنِّى كُلَّمَا دَعَوْتُهُمْ لِتَغْفِرَ لَهُمْ جَعَلُوٓا۟ أَصَـٰبِعَهُمْ فِىٓ ءَاذَانِهِمْ وَٱسْتَغْشَوْا۟ ثِيَابَهُمْ وَأَصَرُّوا۟

وَٱسْتَكْبَرُواْ ٱسْتِكْبَارًا (٧) ثُمَّ إِنِّى دَعَوْتُهُمْ جِهَارًا (٨) ثُمَّ إِنِّى أَعْلَنتُ لَهُمْ وَأَسْرَرْتُ لَهُمْ إِسْرَارًا (٩) فَقُلْتُ ٱسْتَغْفِرُواْ رَبَّكُمْ إِنَّهُ كَانَ غَفَّارًا (١٠) يُرْسِلِ ٱلسَّمَآءَ عَلَيْكُم مِّدْرَارًا (١١) وَيُمْدِدْكُم بِأَمْوَٰلٍ وَبَنِينَ وَيَجْعَل لَّكُمْ جَنَّٰتٍ وَيَجْعَل لَّكُمْ أَنْهَٰرًا (١٢)

Verily, We sent Nûh (Noah) to his people (Saying): "Warn your people before there comes to them a painful torment." (1) He said: "O my people! Verily, I am a plain warner to you, (2) "That you should worship Allâh (Alone), be dutiful to Him, and obey me, (3) "He (Allâh) will forgive you of your sins and respite you to an appointed term. Verily, the term of Allâh when it comes, cannot be delayed, if you but knew." (4) He said: "O my Lord! Verily, I have called my people night and day (i.e. secretly and openly to accept the doctrine of Islâmic Monotheism) , (5) "But all my calling added nothing but to (their) flight (from the truth) (6) "And verily, every time I called unto them that You might forgive them, they thrust their fingers into their ears, covered themselves up with their garments, and persisted (in their refusal), and magnified themselves in pride. (7) "Then verily, I called to them openly (aloud); (8) "Then verily, I proclaimed to them in public, and I have appealed to them in private, (9) "I said (to them): 'Ask forgiveness from your Lord; Verily, He is Oft-Forgiving; (10) 'He will send rain to you in abundance; (11) 'And give you increase in wealth and children, and bestow on you gardens and bestow on you rivers.' " (12)

Quran 71:21-24

قَالَ نُوحٌ رَّبِّ إِنَّهُمْ عَصَوْنِى وَٱتَّبَعُواْ مَن لَّمْ يَزِدْهُ مَالُهُ وَوَلَدُهُ إِلَّا خَسَارًا (٢١) وَمَكَرُواْ مَكْرًا كُبَّارًا (٢٢) وَقَالُواْ لَا تَذَرُنَّ ءَالِهَتَكُمْ وَلَا تَذَرُنَّ وَدًّا وَلَا

سُوَاعًا وَلَا يَغُوثَ وَيَعُوقَ وَنَسْرًا (٢٣) وَقَدْ أَضَلُّوا۟
كَثِيرًا ۖ وَلَا تَزِدِ ٱلظَّـٰلِمِينَ إِلَّا ضَلَـٰلًا (٢٤)

Nûh (Noah) said: "My Lord! They have
disobeyed me, and followed one whose
wealth and children give him no
increase but loss. (21) "And they have
plotted a mighty plot. (22) "And they
have said: 'You shall not leave your
gods, nor shall you leave Wadd, nor
Suwâ', nor Yaghûth, nor Ya'ûq, nor Nasr
(these are the names of their idols). (23)
"And indeed they have led many astray.
And (O Allâh): 'Grant no increase to the
Zâlimûn (polytheists, wrong-doers, and
disbelievers) save error.' " (24)

Quran 71:26-28

وَقَالَ نُوحٌ رَّبِّ لَا تَذَرْ عَلَى ٱلْأَرْضِ مِنَ ٱلْكَـٰفِرِينَ
دَيَّارًا (٢٦) إِنَّكَ إِن تَذَرْهُمْ يُضِلُّوا۟ عِبَادَكَ وَلَا يَلِدُوٓا۟
إِلَّا فَاجِرًا كَفَّارًا (٢٧) رَّبِّ ٱغْفِرْ لِى وَلِوَٰلِدَىَّ
وَلِمَن دَخَلَ بَيْتِىَ مُؤْمِنًا وَلِلْمُؤْمِنِينَ وَٱلْمُؤْمِنَـٰتِ وَلَا
تَزِدِ ٱلظَّـٰلِمِينَ إِلَّا تَبَارًا (٢٨)

And Nûh (Noah) said: "My Lord! Leave not one of the disbelievers on the earth! (26) "If You leave them, they will mislead Your slaves, and they will beget none but wicked disbelievers." (27) "My Lord! Forgive me, and my parents, and him who enters my home as a believer, and all the believing men and women. And to the Zâlimûn (polytheists, wrong-doers, and disbelievers) grant You no increase but destruction!" (28)

Quran 11:38-43

وَيَصْنَعُ ٱلْفُلْكَ وَكُلَّمَا مَرَّ عَلَيْهِ مَلَأٌ مِّن قَوْمِهِ سَخِرُواْ مِنْهُ قَالَ إِن تَسْخَرُواْ مِنَّا فَإِنَّا نَسْخَرُ مِنكُمْ كَمَا تَسْخَرُونَ (٣٨) فَسَوْفَ تَعْلَمُونَ مَن يَأْتِيهِ عَذَابٌ يُخْزِيهِ وَيَحِلُّ عَلَيْهِ عَذَابٌ مُّقِيمٌ (٣٩) حَتَّىٰ إِذَا جَآءَ أَمْرُنَا وَفَارَ ٱلتَّنُّورُ قُلْنَا ٱحْمِلْ فِيهَا مِن كُلٍّ زَوْجَيْنِ ٱثْنَيْنِ وَأَهْلَكَ إِلَّا مَن سَبَقَ عَلَيْهِ ٱلْقَوْلُ وَمَنْ ءَامَنَ وَمَآ ءَامَنَ مَعَهُۥ إِلَّا قَلِيلٌ (٤٠) ۞ وَقَالَ ٱرْكَبُواْ فِيهَا بِسْمِ ٱللَّهِ مَجْر۪ىٰهَا وَمُرْسَىٰهَآ إِنَّ رَبِّى لَغَفُورٌ رَّحِيمٌ (٤١) وَهِىَ تَجْرِى بِهِمْ فِى مَوْجٍ كَٱلْجِبَالِ وَنَادَىٰ

نُوحٌ ٱبْنَهُ وَكَانَ فِى مَعْزِلٍ يَبُنَىَّ ٱرْكَب مَّعَنَا وَلَا تَكُن مَّعَ ٱلْكَفِرِينَ (٤٢) قَالَ سَـَٔاوِىٓ إِلَىٰ جَبَلٍ يَعْصِمُنِى مِنَ ٱلْمَآءِ قَالَ لَا عَاصِمَ ٱلْيَوْمَ مِنْ أَمْرِ ٱللَّهِ إِلَّا مَن رَّحِمَ وَحَالَ بَيْنَهُمَا ٱلْمَوْجُ فَكَانَ مِنَ ٱلْمُغْرَقِينَ (٤٣)

And as he was constructing the ship, whenever the chiefs of his people passed by him, they mocked at him. He said: "If you mock at us, so do we mock at you likewise for your mocking (38) "And you will know who it is on whom will come a torment that will cover him with disgrace and on whom will fall a lasting torment." (39) (So it was) till when Our Command came and the oven gushed forth (water like fountains from the earth). We said: "Embark therein, of each kind two (male and female), and your family - except him against whom the Word has already gone forth - and those who believe. And none believed with him, except a few."

(40) And he [Nûh (Noah)] said: "Embark therein, in the Name of Allâh will be its (moving) course and its (resting) anchorage. Surely, my Lord is Oft-Forgiving, Most Merciful." (41) So it (the ship) sailed with them amidst the waves like mountains, and Nûh (Noah) called out to his son, who had separated himself (apart), "O my son! Embark with us and be not with the disbelievers." (42) (The son) replied: "I will betake myself to some mountain, it will save me from the water." Nûh (Noah) said: "This day there is no saviour from the Decree of Allâh except him on whom He has mercy." And a wave came in between them, so he (the son) was among the drowned. (43)

Quran 14:9-14

أَلَمْ يَأْتِكُمْ نَبَؤُاْ ٱلَّذِينَ مِن قَبْلِكُمْ قَوْمِ نُوحٍ وَعَادٍ وَثَمُودَ وَٱلَّذِينَ مِنۢ بَعْدِهِمْ لَا يَعْلَمُهُمْ إِلَّا ٱللَّهُ جَآءَتْهُمْ رُسُلُهُم بِٱلْبَيِّنَٰتِ فَرَدُّوٓاْ أَيْدِيَهُمْ فِىٓ أَفْوَٰهِهِمْ وَقَالُوٓاْ إِنَّا كَفَرْنَا

بِمَآ أُرْسِلْتُم بِهِۦ وَإِنَّا لَفِى شَكٍّ مِّمَّا تَدْعُونَنَآ إِلَيْهِ مُرِيبٍ
(٩) ۞ قَالَتْ رُسُلُهُمْ أَفِى ٱللَّهِ شَكٌّ فَاطِرِ ٱلسَّمَـٰوَٰتِ
وَٱلْأَرْضِ يَدْعُوكُمْ لِيَغْفِرَ لَكُم مِّن ذُنُوبِكُمْ
وَيُؤَخِّرَكُمْ إِلَىٰٓ أَجَلٍ مُّسَمًّى قَالُوٓاْ إِنْ أَنتُمْ إِلَّا بَشَرٌ
مِّثْلُنَا تُرِيدُونَ أَن تَصُدُّونَا عَمَّا كَانَ يَعْبُدُ ءَابَآؤُنَا
فَأْتُونَا بِسُلْطَـٰنٍ مُّبِينٍ (١٠) قَالَتْ لَهُمْ رُسُلُهُمْ إِن نَّحْنُ
إِلَّا بَشَرٌ مِّثْلُكُمْ وَلَـٰكِنَّ ٱللَّهَ يَمُنُّ عَلَىٰ مَن يَشَآءُ مِنْ
عِبَادِهِۦ وَمَا كَانَ لَنَآ أَن نَّأْتِيَكُم بِسُلْطَـٰنٍ إِلَّا بِإِذْنِ ٱللَّهِ
وَعَلَى ٱللَّهِ فَلْيَتَوَكَّلِ ٱلْمُؤْمِنُونَ (١١) وَمَا لَنَآ أَلَّا
نَتَوَكَّلَ عَلَى ٱللَّهِ وَقَدْ هَدَىٰنَا سُبُلَنَا وَلَنَصْبِرَنَّ عَلَىٰ مَآ
ءَاذَيْتُمُونَا وَعَلَى ٱللَّهِ فَلْيَتَوَكَّلِ ٱلْمُتَوَكِّلُونَ (١٢) وَقَالَ
ٱلَّذِينَ كَفَرُواْ لِرُسُلِهِمْ لَنُخْرِجَنَّكُم مِّنْ أَرْضِنَآ أَوْ
لَتَعُودُنَّ فِى مِلَّتِنَا فَأَوْحَىٰٓ إِلَيْهِمْ رَبُّهُمْ لَنُهْلِكَنَّ ٱلظَّـٰلِمِينَ
(١٣) وَلَنُسْكِنَنَّكُمُ ٱلْأَرْضَ مِنْ بَعْدِهِمْ ذَٰلِكَ لِمَنْ
خَافَ مَقَامِى وَخَافَ وَعِيدِ (١٤)

Has not the news reached you, of those
before you, the people of Nûh (Noah),
and 'Ad, and Thamud? And those after
them? None knows them but Allâh. To
them came their Messengers with clear
proofs, but they put their hands in their

mouths (biting them from anger) and said: "Verily, we disbelieve in that with which you have been sent, and we are really in grave doubt as to that to which you invite us (i.e. Islâmic Monotheism)." (9) Their Messengers said: "What! Can there be a doubt about Allâh, the Creator of the heavens and the earth? He calls you (to Monotheism and to be obedient to Allâh) that He may forgive you of your sins and give you respite for a term appointed." They said: "You are no more than human beings like us! You wish to turn us away from what our fathers used to worship. Then bring us a clear authority (i.e. a clear proof of what you say)." (10) Their Messengers said to them: "We are no more than human beings like you, but Allâh bestows His Grace to whom He wills of His slaves. It is not ours to bring you an authority (proof) except by the Permission of Allâh. And in Allâh (Alone) let the believers put their trust. (11) "And why should we not put our trust in Allâh while He indeed has guided us our ways? And we shall certainly bear with patience all the hurt you may cause us, and in Allâh (Alone) let those who trust, put their trust." (12) And those who disbelieved, said to their Messengers: "Surely, we shall drive you out of our land, or you shall return to our religion." So their Lord revealed to them: "Truly, We shall destroy the Zâlimûn (polytheists, disbelievers and wrong-doers.). (13) "And indeed, We shall make you dwell in the land after them. This is for him who fears standing before Me (on the Day of Resurrection or fears My Punishment) and also fears My threat." (14)

Quran 23:23-29

وَلَقَدْ أَرْسَلْنَا نُوحًا إِلَىٰ قَوْمِهِ فَقَالَ يَٰقَوْمِ ٱعْبُدُواْ ٱللَّهَ مَا لَكُم مِّنْ إِلَٰهٍ غَيْرُهُۥٓ أَفَلَا تَتَّقُونَ (٢٣) فَقَالَ ٱلْمَلَؤُاْ

ٱلَّذِينَ كَفَرُواْ مِن قَوْمِهِ مَا هَـٰذَآ إِلَّا بَشَرٌ مِّثْلُكُمْ يُرِيدُ أَن يَتَفَضَّلَ عَلَيْكُمْ وَلَوْ شَآءَ ٱللَّهُ لَأَنزَلَ مَلَـٰٓئِكَةً مَّا سَمِعْنَا بِهَـٰذَا فِىٓ ءَابَآئِنَا ٱلْأَوَّلِينَ (٢٤) إِنْ هُوَ إِلَّا رَجُلٌۢ بِهِ جِنَّةٌ فَتَرَبَّصُواْ بِهِ حَتَّىٰ حِينٍ (٢٥) قَالَ رَبِّ ٱنصُرْنِى بِمَا كَذَّبُونِ (٢٦) فَأَوْحَيْنَآ إِلَيْهِ أَنِ ٱصْنَعِ ٱلْفُلْكَ بِأَعْيُنِنَا وَوَحْيِنَا فَإِذَا جَآءَ أَمْرُنَا وَفَارَ ٱلتَّنُّورُ فَٱسْلُكْ فِيهَا مِن كُلٍّ زَوْجَيْنِ ٱثْنَيْنِ وَأَهْلَكَ إِلَّا مَن سَبَقَ عَلَيْهِ ٱلْقَوْلُ مِنْهُمْ وَلَا تُخَـٰطِبْنِى فِى ٱلَّذِينَ ظَلَمُوٓاْ إِنَّهُم مُّغْرَقُونَ (٢٧) فَإِذَا ٱسْتَوَيْتَ أَنتَ وَمَن مَّعَكَ عَلَى ٱلْفُلْكِ فَقُلِ ٱلْحَمْدُ لِلَّهِ ٱلَّذِى نَجَّىٰنَا مِنَ ٱلْقَوْمِ ٱلظَّـٰلِمِينَ (٢٨) وَقُل رَّبِّ أَنزِلْنِى مُنزَلاً مُّبَارَكًا وَأَنتَ خَيْرُ ٱلْمُنزِلِينَ (٢٩)

And indeed We sent Nûh (Noah) to his people, and he said: "O my people! Worship Allâh! You have no other Ilâh (God) but Him. Will you not then be afraid (of Him i.e. of His Punishment because of worshipping others besides Him)?" (23) But the chiefs of his people who disbelieved said: "He is no more than a human being like you, he seeks to make himself superior to you. Had Allâh willed, He surely could have sent down angels; Never did we hear such a thing among our fathers of old. (24) "He is only a man in whom is madness, so wait for him a while." (25) [Nûh (Noah)] said: "O my Lord! Help me because they deny me." (26) So We revealed to him (saying): "Construct the ship under Our Eyes and under Our Revelation (guidance). Then, when Our Command comes, and water gushes forth from the oven, take on board of each kind two (male and female), and your family, except those thereof against whom the Word has already gone forth. And address Me not in favour of those who have done wrong. Verily, they are to be drowned. (27) And when you have embarked on the ship, you and whoever is with you, then say: "All the praises and thanks are to Allâh, Who has saved us from the people who are Zâlimûn (i.e. oppressors, wrong-doers, polytheists, those who join others in worship with Allâh). (28) And say: "My Lord! Cause me to land at a blessed landing-place, for You are the Best of those who bring to land." (29)

Quran 7:65-71

۞ وَإِلَىٰ عَادٍ أَخَاهُمْ هُودًا ۗ قَالَ يَـٰقَوْمِ ٱعْبُدُوا۟ ٱللَّهَ مَا لَكُم مِّنْ إِلَـٰهٍ غَيْرُهُۥٓ ۚ أَفَلَا تَتَّقُونَ (٦٥) قَالَ ٱلْمَلَأُ ٱلَّذِينَ كَفَرُوا۟ مِن قَوْمِهِۦٓ إِنَّا لَنَرَىٰكَ فِى سَفَاهَةٍۢ وَإِنَّا لَنَظُنُّكَ مِنَ ٱلْكَـٰذِبِينَ (٦٦) قَالَ يَـٰقَوْمِ لَيْسَ بِى سَفَاهَةٌۭ وَلَـٰكِنِّى رَسُولٌۭ مِّن رَّبِّ ٱلْعَـٰلَمِينَ (٦٧) أُبَلِّغُكُمْ رِسَـٰلَـٰتِ رَبِّى وَأَنَا۠ لَكُمْ نَاصِحٌ أَمِينٌ (٦٨) أَوَعَجِبْتُمْ أَن جَآءَكُمْ ذِكْرٌۭ مِّن رَّبِّكُمْ عَلَىٰ رَجُلٍۢ مِّنكُمْ لِيُنذِرَكُمْ ۚ وَٱذْكُرُوٓا۟ إِذْ جَعَلَكُمْ خُلَفَآءَ مِنۢ بَعْدِ قَوْمِ نُوحٍۢ وَزَادَكُمْ فِى ٱلْخَلْقِ بَصْۜطَةًۭ ۖ فَٱذْكُرُوٓا۟ ءَالَآءَ ٱللَّهِ لَعَلَّكُمْ تُفْلِحُونَ (٦٩) قَالُوٓا۟ أَجِئْتَنَا لِنَعْبُدَ ٱللَّهَ وَحْدَهُۥ وَنَذَرَ مَا كَانَ يَعْبُدُ ءَابَآؤُنَا ۖ فَأْتِنَا بِمَا تَعِدُنَآ إِن كُنتَ مِنَ ٱلصَّـٰدِقِينَ (٧٠) قَالَ قَدْ وَقَعَ عَلَيْكُم مِّن رَّبِّكُمْ رِجْسٌۭ وَغَضَبٌ ۖ أَتُجَـٰدِلُونَنِى فِىٓ أَسْمَآءٍۢ سَمَّيْتُمُوهَآ أَنتُمْ وَءَابَآؤُكُم مَّا نَزَّلَ ٱللَّهُ بِهَا مِن سُلْطَـٰنٍ ۚ فَٱنتَظِرُوٓا۟ إِنِّى مَعَكُم مِّنَ ٱلْمُنتَظِرِينَ (٧١)

And to 'Ad (people, We sent) their brother Hûd. He said: "O my people! Worship Allâh! You have no other Ilâh (God) but Him. (Lâ ilâha ill-allâh: none has the right to be worshipped but Allâh). Will you not fear (Allâh)?" (65) The leaders of those who disbelieved among his people said: "Verily, we see you in foolishness, and verily, we think you are one of the liars." (66) (Hûd) said: "O my people! There is no foolishness in me, but (I am) a Messenger from the Lord of the 'Alamîn (mankind, jinn and all that exists)! (67) "I convey unto you the Messages of my Lord, and I am a trustworthy adviser (or well-wisher) for you (68) "Do you wonder that there has come to you a Reminder (and an advice) from your Lord through a man from amongst you to warn you? And remember that He made you successors after the people of Nûh (Noah), and increased you amply in stature. So remember the graces (bestowed upon you) from Allâh, so that you may be successful." (69) They said: "You have come to us that we should worship Allâh Alone and forsake that which our fathers used to worship. So bring us that wherewith you have threatened us if you are of the truthful." (70) (Hûd) said: "Torment and wrath have already fallen on you from your Lord. Dispute you with me over names which you have named - you and your fathers, with no authority from Allâh? Then wait, I am with you among those who wait." (71)

Quran 11:50-57

وَإِلَىٰ عَادٍ أَخَاهُمْ هُودًا ۚ قَالَ يَـٰقَوْمِ ٱعْبُدُواْ ٱللَّهَ مَا لَكُم مِّنْ إِلَـٰهٍ غَيْرُهُۥ ۖ إِنْ أَنتُمْ إِلَّا مُفْتَرُونَ (٥٠) يَـٰقَوْمِ لَآ أَسْـَٔلُكُمْ عَلَيْهِ أَجْرًا ۖ إِنْ أَجْرِىَ إِلَّا عَلَى ٱلَّذِى فَطَرَنِىٓ ۚ أَفَلَا تَعْقِلُونَ (٥١) وَيَـٰقَوْمِ ٱسْتَغْفِرُواْ رَبَّكُمْ ثُمَّ تُوبُوٓاْ إِلَيْهِ يُرْسِلِ ٱلسَّمَآءَ عَلَيْكُم مِّدْرَارًا وَيَزِدْكُمْ قُوَّةً إِلَىٰ قُوَّتِكُمْ وَلَا تَتَوَلَّوْاْ مُجْرِمِينَ (٥٢) قَالُواْ يَـٰهُودُ مَا

جِئْنَـٰكَ بِبَيِّنَةٍ وَمَا نَحْنُ بِتَارِكِىٓ ءَالِهَتِنَا عَن قَوْلِكَ وَمَا نَحْنُ لَكَ بِمُؤْمِنِينَ (٥٣) إِن نَّقُولُ إِلَّا ٱعْتَرَىٰكَ بَعْضُ ءَالِهَتِنَا بِسُوٓءٍ ۗ قَالَ إِنِّىٓ أُشْهِدُ ٱللَّهَ وَٱشْهَدُوٓاْ أَنِّى بَرِىٓءٌ مِّمَّا تُشْرِكُونَ (٥٤) مِن دُونِهِۦ ۖ فَكِيدُونِى جَمِيعًا ثُمَّ لَا تُنظِرُونِ (٥٥) إِنِّى تَوَكَّلْتُ عَلَى ٱللَّهِ رَبِّى وَرَبِّكُم ۚ مَّا مِن دَآبَّةٍ إِلَّا هُوَ ءَاخِذٌۢ بِنَاصِيَتِهَآ ۚ إِنَّ رَبِّى عَلَىٰ صِرَٰطٍ مُّسْتَقِيمٍ (٥٦) فَإِن تَوَلَّوْاْ فَقَدْ أَبْلَغْتُكُم مَّآ أُرْسِلْتُ بِهِۦٓ إِلَيْكُمْ ۚ وَيَسْتَخْلِفُ رَبِّى قَوْمًا غَيْرَكُمْ وَلَا تَضُرُّونَهُۥ شَيْـًٔا ۚ إِنَّ رَبِّى عَلَىٰ كُلِّ شَىْءٍ حَفِيظٌ (٥٧)

And to 'Ad (people We sent) their brother Hûd. He said, "O my people! Worship Allâh! You have no other ilâh (god) but Him. Certainly, you do nothing but invent lies! (50) "O my people I ask of you no reward for it (the Message). My reward is only from Him, Who created me. Will you not then understand? (51) "And O my people! Ask forgiveness of your Lord and then repent to Him, He will send you (from the sky) abundant rain, and add strength to your strength, so do not turn away as Mujrimûn (criminals, disbelievers in the Oneness of Allâh)." (52) They said: "O Hûd! No evidence have you brought us, and we shall not leave our gods for your (mere) saying! And we are not believers in you. (53) "All that we say is that some of our gods (false deities) have seized you with evil (madness)." He said: "I call Allâh to witness and bear you witness that I am free from that which you ascribe as partners in worship, — (54) With Him (Allâh). So plot against me, all of you, and give me no respite. (55) "I put my trust in Allâh, my Lord and your Lord! There is not a moving (living) creature but He has grasp of its forelock. Verily, my Lord is on the Straight Path (the truth). (56) "So if you turn away, still I have conveyed the Message with which I was sent to you. My Lord will make another people succeed you, and you will not harm Him in the least. Surely,

my Lord is Guardian over all things."
(57)

Quran 26:123-138

كَذَّبَتْ عَادٌ ٱلْمُرْسَلِينَ (١٢٣) إِذْ قَالَ لَهُمْ أَخُوهُمْ هُودٌ
أَلَا تَتَّقُونَ (١٢٤) إِنِّى لَكُمْ رَسُولٌ أَمِينٌ
(١٢٥) فَٱتَّقُوا ٱللَّهَ وَأَطِيعُونِ (١٢٦) وَمَآ أَسْـَٔلُكُمْ
عَلَيْهِ مِنْ أَجْرٍ إِنْ أَجْرِىَ إِلَّا عَلَىٰ رَبِّ ٱلْعَٰلَمِينَ
(١٢٧) أَتَبْنُونَ بِكُلِّ رِيعٍ ءَايَةً تَعْبَثُونَ
(١٢٨) وَتَتَّخِذُونَ مَصَانِعَ لَعَلَّكُمْ تَخْلُدُونَ
(١٢٩) وَإِذَا بَطَشْتُم بَطَشْتُمْ جَبَّارِينَ (١٣٠) فَٱتَّقُوا
ٱللَّهَ وَأَطِيعُونِ (١٣١) وَٱتَّقُوا ٱلَّذِىَ أَمَدَّكُم بِمَا تَعْلَمُونَ
(١٣٢) أَمَدَّكُم بِأَنْعَٰمٍ وَبَنِينَ (١٣٣) وَجَنَّٰتٍ وَعُيُونٍ
(١٣٤) إِنِّىَ أَخَافُ عَلَيْكُمْ عَذَابَ يَوْمٍ عَظِيمٍ
(١٣٥) قَالُوا سَوَآءٌ عَلَيْنَآ أَوَعَظْتَ أَمْ لَمْ تَكُن مِّنَ
ٱلْوَٰعِظِينَ (١٣٦) إِنْ هَٰذَآ إِلَّا خُلُقُ ٱلْأَوَّلِينَ
(١٣٧) وَمَا نَحْنُ بِمُعَذَّبِينَ (١٣٨)

'Ad (people) belied the Messengers.
(123) When their brother Hûd said to
them: "Will you not fear Allâh and obey
Him? (124) "Verily! I am a trustworthy
Messenger to you. (125) "So fear Allâh,

keep your duty to Him, and obey me. (126) "No reward do I ask of you for it (my Message of Islâmic Monotheism), my reward is only from the Lord of the 'Alamîn (mankind, jinn, and all that exists). (127) "Do you build high palaces on every high place, while you do not live in them? (128) "And do you get for yourselves palaces (fine buildings) as if you will live therein forever (129) "And when you seize (some body), seize you (him) as tyrants? (130) "So fear Allâh, keep your duty to Him, and obey me. (131) "And keep your duty to Him, fear Him Who has aided you with all (good things) that you know. (132) "He has aided you with cattle and children. (133) "And gardens and springs. (134) "Verily, I fear for you the torment of a Great Day." (135) They said: "It is the same to us whether you preach or be not of those who preach. (136) "This is no other than the false-tales and religion of the ancients." (137) "And we are not going to be punished." (138)

Quran 46:21-23

۞ وَٱذْكُرْ أَخَا عَادٍ إِذْ أَنذَرَ قَوْمَهُۥ بِٱلْأَحْقَافِ وَقَدْ خَلَتِ ٱلنُّذُرُ مِنۢ بَيْنِ يَدَيْهِ وَمِنْ خَلْفِهِۦٓ أَلَّا تَعْبُدُوٓا۟ إِلَّا ٱللَّهَ إِنِّىٓ أَخَافُ عَلَيْكُمْ عَذَابَ يَوْمٍ عَظِيمٍ (٢١) قَالُوٓا۟ أَجِئْتَنَا لِتَأْفِكَنَا عَنْ ءَالِهَتِنَا فَأْتِنَا بِمَا تَعِدُنَآ إِن كُنتَ مِنَ ٱلصَّٰدِقِينَ (٢٢) قَالَ إِنَّمَا ٱلْعِلْمُ عِندَ ٱللَّهِ وَأُبَلِّغُكُم مَّآ أُرْسِلْتُ بِهِۦ وَلَٰكِنِّىٓ أَرَىٰكُمْ قَوْمًا تَجْهَلُونَ (٢٣)

And remember (Hûd) the brother of 'Ad, when he warned his people in Al-Ahqâf (the curved sand-hills in the southern part of Arabian Peninsula). And surely, there have passed away warners before him and after him (saying): "Worship none but Allâh; truly, I fear for you the torment of a mighty Day." (i.e. the Day of Resurrection)." (21) They said: "Have you come to turn us away from our âlihah (gods)? Then bring us that with which you threaten us, if you are one of the truthful!" (22) He said: "The knowledge (of the time of its coming) is with Allâh only, And I convey to you that wherewith I have been sent, but I see that you are a people given to ignorance!" (23)

Quran 14:9-14

أَلَمْ يَأْتِكُمْ نَبَؤُاْ ٱلَّذِينَ مِن قَبْلِكُمْ قَوْمِ نُوحٍ وَعَادٍ وَثَمُودَ وَٱلَّذِينَ مِنۢ بَعْدِهِمْ لَا يَعْلَمُهُمْ إِلَّا ٱللَّهُ جَآءَتْهُمْ رُسُلُهُم بِٱلْبَيِّنَـٰتِ فَرَدُّوٓاْ أَيْدِيَهُمْ فِىٓ أَفْوَٰهِهِمْ وَقَالُوٓاْ إِنَّا كَفَرْنَا بِمَآ أُرْسِلْتُم بِهِۦ وَإِنَّا لَفِى شَكٍّ مِّمَّا تَدْعُونَنَآ إِلَيْهِ مُرِيبٍ (٩) ۞ قَالَتْ رُسُلُهُمْ أَفِى ٱللَّهِ شَكٌّ فَاطِرِ ٱلسَّمَٰوَٰتِ وَٱلْأَرْضِ ۖ يَدْعُوكُمْ لِيَغْفِرَ لَكُم مِّن ذُنُوبِكُمْ وَيُؤَخِّرَكُمْ إِلَىٰٓ أَجَلٍ مُّسَمًّى ۚ قَالُوٓاْ إِنْ أَنتُمْ إِلَّا بَشَرٌ مِّثْلُنَا تُرِيدُونَ أَن تَصُدُّونَا عَمَّا كَانَ يَعْبُدُ ءَابَآؤُنَا فَأْتُونَا بِسُلْطَٰنٍ مُّبِينٍ (١٠) قَالَتْ لَهُمْ رُسُلُهُمْ إِن نَّحْنُ إِلَّا بَشَرٌ مِّثْلُكُمْ وَلَٰكِنَّ ٱللَّهَ يَمُنُّ عَلَىٰ مَن يَشَآءُ مِنْ عِبَادِهِۦ ۖ وَمَا كَانَ لَنَآ أَن نَّأْتِيَكُم بِسُلْطَٰنٍ إِلَّا بِإِذْنِ ٱللَّهِ ۚ وَعَلَى ٱللَّهِ فَلْيَتَوَكَّلِ ٱلْمُؤْمِنُونَ (١١) وَمَا لَنَآ أَلَّا نَتَوَكَّلَ عَلَى ٱللَّهِ وَقَدْ هَدَىٰنَا سُبُلَنَا ۚ وَلَنَصْبِرَنَّ عَلَىٰ مَا

35

ءَاذَيْتُمُونَا وَعَلَى ٱللَّهِ فَلْيَتَوَكَّلِ ٱلْمُتَوَكِّلُونَ (١٢) وَقَالَ
ٱلَّذِينَ كَفَرُوا لِرُسُلِهِمْ لَنُخْرِجَنَّكُم مِّنْ أَرْضِنَا أَوْ
لَتَعُودُنَّ فِى مِلَّتِنَا فَأَوْحَىٰ إِلَيْهِمْ رَبُّهُمْ لَنُهْلِكَنَّ ٱلظَّٰلِمِينَ
(١٣) وَلَنُسْكِنَنَّكُمُ ٱلْأَرْضَ مِنْ بَعْدِهِمْ ذَٰلِكَ لِمَنْ
خَافَ مَقَامِى وَخَافَ وَعِيدِ (١٤)

Has not the news reached you, of those
before you, the people of Nûh (Noah),
and 'Ad, and Thamud? And those after
them? None knows them but Allâh. To
them came their Messengers with clear
proofs, but they put their hands in their
mouths (biting them from anger) and
said: "Verily, we disbelieve in that with
which you have been sent, and we are
really in grave doubt as to that to which
you invite us (i.e. Islâmic Monotheism)."
(9) Their Messengers said: "What! Can
there be a doubt about Allâh, the
Creator of the heavens and the earth?
He calls you (to Monotheism and to be
obedient to Allâh) that He may forgive
you of your sins and give you respite for

a term appointed." They said: "You are no more than human beings like us! You wish to turn us away from what our fathers used to worship. Then bring us a clear authority (i.e. a clear proof of what you say)." (10) Their Messengers said to them: "We are no more than human beings like you, but Allâh bestows His Grace to whom He wills of His slaves. It is not ours to bring you an authority (proof) except by the Permission of Allâh. And in Allâh (Alone) let the believers put their trust. (11) "And why should we not put our trust in Allâh while He indeed has guided us our ways? And we shall certainly bear with patience all the hurt you may cause us, and in Allâh (Alone) let those who trust, put their trust." (12) And those who disbelieved, said to their Messengers: "Surely, we shall drive you out of our land, or you shall return to our religion." So their Lord revealed to them: "Truly,

We shall destroy the Zâlimûn (polytheists, disbelievers and wrong-doers.). (13) "And indeed, We shall make you dwell in the land after them. This is for him who fears standing before Me (on the Day of Resurrection or fears My Punishment) and also fears My threat." (14)

Quran 41:13-14

فَإِنْ أَعْرَضُواْ فَقُلْ أَنذَرْتُكُمْ صَـٰعِقَةً مِّثْلَ صَـٰعِقَةِ عَادٍ وَثَمُودَ (١٣) إِذْ جَآءَتْهُمُ ٱلرُّسُلُ مِنۢ بَيْنِ أَيْدِيهِمْ وَمِنْ خَلْفِهِمْ أَلَّا تَعْبُدُوٓاْ إِلَّا ٱللَّهَۖ قَالُواْ لَوْ شَآءَ رَبُّنَا لَأَنزَلَ مَلَـٰٓئِكَةً فَإِنَّا بِمَآ أُرْسِلْتُم بِهِۦ كَـٰفِرُونَ (١٤)

But if they turn away, then say (O Muhammad): "I have warned you of a Sâ'iqah (a destructive awful cry, torment, hit, a thunderbolt) like the Sâ'iqah which overtook 'Ad and Thamûd (people)." (13) When the Messengers came to them, from before them and behind them (saying):

"Worship none but Allâh" They said: "If our Lord had so willed, He would surely have sent down the angels. So indeed we disbelieve in that with which you have been sent." (14)

Quran 26:141-156

كَذَّبَتْ ثَمُودُ ٱلْمُرْسَلِينَ (١٤١) إِذْ قَالَ لَهُمْ أَخُوهُمْ صَٰلِحٌ أَلَا تَتَّقُونَ (١٤٢) إِنِّى لَكُمْ رَسُولٌ أَمِينٌ (١٤٣) فَٱتَّقُوا۟ ٱللَّهَ وَأَطِيعُونِ (١٤٤) وَمَآ أَسْـَٔلُكُمْ عَلَيْهِ مِنْ أَجْرٍ ۖ إِنْ أَجْرِىَ إِلَّا عَلَىٰ رَبِّ ٱلْعَٰلَمِينَ (١٤٥) أَتُتْرَكُونَ فِى مَا هَٰهُنَآ ءَامِنِينَ (١٤٦) فِى جَنَّٰتٍ وَعُيُونٍ (١٤٧) وَزُرُوعٍ وَنَخْلٍ طَلْعُهَا هَضِيمٌ (١٤٨) وَتَنْحِتُونَ مِنَ ٱلْجِبَالِ بُيُوتًا فَٰرِهِينَ (١٤٩) فَٱتَّقُوا۟ ٱللَّهَ وَأَطِيعُونِ (١٥٠) وَلَا تُطِيعُوٓا۟ أَمْرَ ٱلْمُسْرِفِينَ (١٥١) ٱلَّذِينَ يُفْسِدُونَ فِى ٱلْأَرْضِ وَلَا يُصْلِحُونَ (١٥٢) قَالُوٓا۟ إِنَّمَآ أَنتَ مِنَ ٱلْمُسَحَّرِينَ (١٥٣) مَآ أَنتَ إِلَّا بَشَرٌ مِّثْلُنَا فَأْتِ بِـَٔايَةٍ إِن كُنتَ مِنَ ٱلصَّٰدِقِينَ (١٥٤) قَالَ هَٰذِهِۦ نَاقَةٌ لَّهَا شِرْبٌ وَلَكُمْ شِرْبُ يَوْمٍ مَّعْلُومٍ (١٥٥) وَلَا تَمَسُّوهَا بِسُوٓءٍ فَيَأْخُذَكُمْ عَذَابُ يَوْمٍ عَظِيمٍ (١٥٦)

Thamûd (people) belied the Messengers. (141) When their brother Sâlih said to them: "Will you not fear Allâh and obey Him? (142) "I am a trustworthy Messenger to you. (143) "So fear Allâh, keep your duty to Him, and obey me. (144) "No reward do I ask of you for it (my Message of Islâmic Monotheism), my reward is only from the Lord of the 'Alamîn (mankind, jinn and all that exists). (145) "Will you be left secure in that which you have here? (146) "In gardens and springs. (147) And green crops (fields) and date-palms with soft spadix. (148) "And you hew out in the mountains, houses, with great skill. (149) "So fear Allâh, keep your duty to Him, and obey me. (150) "And follow not the command of Al-Musrifûn [i.e. their chiefs, leaders who were polytheists, criminals and sinners], (151) "Who make mischief in the land, and reform not." (152) They said: "You are only of those bewitched! (153) "You are but a human being like us. Then bring us a sign if you are of the truthful." (154) He said: "Here is a she-camel; it has a right to drink (water), and you have a right to drink (water) (each) on a day, known (155) "And touch her not with harm, lest the torment of a Great Day should seize you." (156)

Quran 91:13

فَقَالَ لَهُمْ رَسُولُ ٱللَّهِ نَاقَةَ ٱللَّهِ وَسُقْيَـٰهَا

But the Messenger of Allâh [Sâlih (Saleh)] said to them: "Be cautious! (Fear the evil end). That is the she-camel of Allâh! (Do not harm it) and bar it not from having its drink!" (13)

Quran 7:73-79

وَإِلَىٰ ثَمُودَ أَخَاهُمْ صَـٰلِحًا قَالَ يَـٰقَوْمِ ٱعْبُدُواْ ٱللَّهَ مَا لَكُم مِّنْ إِلَـٰهٍ غَيْرُهُ قَدْ جَآءَتْكُم بَيِّنَةٌ مِّن رَّبِّكُمْ هَـٰذِهِ نَاقَةُ ٱللَّهِ لَكُمْ ءَايَةً فَذَرُوهَا تَأْكُلْ فِىٓ أَرْضِ ٱللَّهِ وَلَا

تَمَسُّوهَا بِسُوٓءٍ فَيَأْخُذَكُمْ عَذَابٌ أَلِيمٌ (٧٣) وَٱذْكُرُوٓاْ
إِذْ جَعَلَكُمْ خُلَفَآءَ مِنۢ بَعْدِ عَادٍ وَبَوَّأَكُمْ فِى ٱلْأَرْضِ
تَتَّخِذُونَ مِن سُهُولِهَا قُصُورًا وَتَنْحِتُونَ ٱلْجِبَالَ بُيُوتًا
فَٱذْكُرُوٓاْ ءَالَآءَ ٱللَّهِ وَلَا تَعْثَوْاْ فِى ٱلْأَرْضِ مُفْسِدِينَ
(٧٤) قَالَ ٱلْمَلَأُ ٱلَّذِينَ ٱسْتَكْبَرُوا مِن قَوْمِهِۦ لِلَّذِينَ
ٱسْتُضْعِفُوا لِمَنْ ءَامَنَ مِنْهُمْ أَتَعْلَمُونَ أَنَّ صَٰلِحًا
مُّرْسَلٌ مِّن رَّبِّهِۦۚ قَالُوٓاْ إِنَّا بِمَآ أُرْسِلَ بِهِۦ مُؤْمِنُونَ
(٧٥) قَالَ ٱلَّذِينَ ٱسْتَكْبَرُوٓاْ إِنَّا بِٱلَّذِىٓ ءَامَنتُم بِهِۦ
كَٰفِرُونَ (٧٦) فَعَقَرُواْ ٱلنَّاقَةَ وَعَتَوْاْ عَنْ أَمْرِ رَبِّهِمْ
وَقَالُواْ يَٰصَٰلِحُ ٱئْتِنَا بِمَا تَعِدُنَآ إِن كُنتَ مِنَ ٱلْمُرْسَلِينَ
(٧٧) فَأَخَذَتْهُمُ ٱلرَّجْفَةُ فَأَصْبَحُواْ فِى دَارِهِمْ جَٰثِمِينَ
(٧٨) فَتَوَلَّىٰ عَنْهُمْ وَقَالَ يَٰقَوْمِ لَقَدْ أَبْلَغْتُكُمْ رِسَالَةَ
رَبِّى وَنَصَحْتُ لَكُمْ وَلَٰكِن لَّا تُحِبُّونَ ٱلنَّٰصِحِينَ
(٧٩)

And to Thamûd (people, We sent) their brother Sâlih (Saleh). He said: "O my people! Worship Allâh! You have no other Ilâh (God) but Him. (Lâ ilâha ill-allâh: none has the right to be worshipped but Allâh). Indeed there has come to you a clear sign (the miracle of the coming out of a huge she-camel from the midst of a rock) from your Lord. This she-camel of Allâh is a sign unto you; so you leave her to graze in Allâh's earth, and touch her not with harm, lest a painful torment should seize you. (73) "And remember when He made you successors after 'Ad (people) and gave you habitations in the land, you build for yourselves palaces in plains, and carve out homes in the mountains. So remember the graces (bestowed upon you) from Allâh, and do not go about making mischief on the earth." (74) The leaders of those who were arrogant among his people said to those who were counted weak - to such of them as believed: "Know you that Sâlih is one sent from his Lord?" They said: "We indeed believe in that with which he has been sent." (75) Those who were arrogant said: "Verily, we disbelieve in that which you believe in." (76) So they killed the she-camel and insolently defied the Commandment of their Lord, and said: "O Sâlih! Bring about your threats if you are indeed one of the Messengers (of Allâh)." (77) So the earthquake seized them, and they lay (dead), prostrate in their homes. (78) Then he (Sâlih) turned from them, and said: "O my people! I have indeed conveyed to you the Message of my Lord, and have given you good advice but you like not good advisers." (79)

Quran 27:45-49

وَلَقَدْ أَرْسَلْنَآ إِلَىٰ ثَمُودَ أَخَاهُمْ صَـٰلِحًا أَنِ ٱعْبُدُوا۟ ٱللَّهَ فَإِذَا هُمْ فَرِيقَانِ يَخْتَصِمُونَ (٤٥) قَالَ يَـٰقَوْمِ لِمَ تَسْتَعْجِلُونَ بِٱلسَّيِّئَةِ قَبْلَ ٱلْحَسَنَةِ ۖ لَوْلَا تَسْتَغْفِرُونَ ٱللَّهَ لَعَلَّكُمْ تُرْحَمُونَ (٤٦) قَالُوا۟ ٱطَّيَّرْنَا بِكَ وَبِمَن مَّعَكَ ۚ قَالَ طَـٰٓئِرُكُمْ عِندَ ٱللَّهِ ۖ بَلْ أَنتُمْ قَوْمٌ تُفْتَنُونَ (٤٧) وَكَانَ فِى ٱلْمَدِينَةِ تِسْعَةُ رَهْطٍ يُفْسِدُونَ فِى ٱلْأَرْضِ وَلَا يُصْلِحُونَ (٤٨) قَالُوا۟ تَقَاسَمُوا۟ بِٱللَّهِ لَنُبَيِّتَنَّهُۥ وَأَهْلَهُۥ ثُمَّ لَنَقُولَنَّ لِوَلِيِّهِۦ مَا شَهِدْنَا مَهْلِكَ أَهْلِهِۦ وَإِنَّا لَصَـٰدِقُونَ (٤٩)

And indeed We sent to Thamûd their brother Sâlih, saying: "Worship Allâh (Alone and none else). Then look! They became two parties (believers and disbelievers) quarreling with each other." (45) He said: "O my people! Why do you seek to hasten the evil (torment) before the good (Allâh's Mercy)? Why seek you not the Forgiveness of Allâh, that you may receive mercy?" (46) They said: "We augur ill omen from you and those with you." He said: "Your ill omen is with Allâh; nay, but you are a people that are being tested." (47) And there were in the city nine men (from the sons of their chiefs), who made mischief in the land, and would not reform. (48) They said: "Swear one to another by Allâh that we shall make a secret night attack on him and his household, and thereafter we will surely say to his near relatives: 'We witnessed not the destruction of his household, and verily, we are telling the truth.'" (49)

Quran 11:61-65

﴿ وَإِلَىٰ ثَمُودَ أَخَاهُمْ صَـٰلِحًا ۚ قَالَ يَـٰقَوْمِ ٱعْبُدُواْ ٱللَّهَ مَا لَكُم مِّنْ إِلَـٰهٍ غَيْرُهُۥ ۖ هُوَ أَنشَأَكُم مِّنَ ٱلْأَرْضِ وَٱسْتَعْمَرَكُمْ فِيهَا فَٱسْتَغْفِرُوهُ ثُمَّ تُوبُوٓاْ إِلَيْهِ ۚ إِنَّ رَبِّى قَرِيبٌ مُّجِيبٌ (٦١) قَالُواْ يَـٰصَـٰلِحُ قَدْ كُنتَ فِينَا مَرْجُوًّا قَبْلَ هَـٰذَآ ۖ أَتَنْهَىٰنَآ أَن نَّعْبُدَ مَا يَعْبُدُ ءَابَآؤُنَا وَإِنَّنَا لَفِى شَكٍّ مِّمَّا تَدْعُونَآ إِلَيْهِ مُرِيبٍ (٦٢) قَالَ يَـٰقَوْمِ أَرَءَيْتُمْ إِن كُنتُ عَلَىٰ بَيِّنَةٍ مِّن رَّبِّى وَءَاتَىٰنِى مِنْهُ رَحْمَةً فَمَن يَنصُرُنِى مِنَ ٱللَّهِ إِنْ عَصَيْتُهُۥ ۖ فَمَا تَزِيدُونَنِى غَيْرَ تَخْسِيرٍ (٦٣) وَيَـٰقَوْمِ هَـٰذِهِۦ نَاقَةُ ٱللَّهِ لَكُمْ ءَايَةً فَذَرُوهَا تَأْكُلْ فِىٓ أَرْضِ ٱللَّهِ وَلَا تَمَسُّوهَا بِسُوٓءٍ فَيَأْخُذَكُمْ عَذَابٌ قَرِيبٌ (٦٤) فَعَقَرُوهَا فَقَالَ تَمَتَّعُواْ فِى دَارِكُمْ ثَلَـٰثَةَ أَيَّامٍ ۖ ذَٰلِكَ وَعْدٌ غَيْرُ مَكْذُوبٍ (٦٥)

And to Thamûd (people, We sent) their brother Sâlih. He said: "O my people! Worship Allâh, you have no other ilâh (god) but Him. He brought you forth from the earth and settled you therein, then ask forgiveness of Him and turn to Him in repentance. Certainly, my Lord is Near (to all by His Knowledge), Responsive." (61) They said: "O Sâlih! You have been among us as a figure of good hope (and we wished for you to be our chief), till this [new thing which you have brought; that we leave our gods and worship your God (Allâh) Alone]! Do you (now) forbid us the worship of what our fathers have worshipped? But we are really in grave doubt as to that which you invite us (monotheism)." (62) He said: "O my people! Tell me, if I have a clear proof from my Lord, and there has come to me a Mercy (Prophethood) from Him, who then can help me against Allâh, if I were to disobey Him? Then you increase me not but in loss. (63) "And O my people! This she-camel of Allâh is a sign to you, leave her to feed (graze) in Allâh's land, and touch her not with evil, lest a near torment should seize you." (64) But they killed her. So he said: "Enjoy yourselves in your homes for three days. This is a promise (i.e. a threat) that will not be belied." (65)

Quran 26:69-89

وَٱتْلُ عَلَيْهِمْ نَبَأَ إِبْرَٰهِيمَ (٦٩) إِذْ قَالَ لِأَبِيهِ وَقَوْمِهِ مَا تَعْبُدُونَ (٧٠) قَالُوا۟ نَعْبُدُ أَصْنَامًا فَنَظَلُّ لَهَا عَٰكِفِينَ (٧١) قَالَ هَلْ يَسْمَعُونَكُمْ إِذْ تَدْعُونَ (٧٢) أَوْ يَنفَعُونَكُمْ أَوْ يَضُرُّونَ (٧٣) قَالُوا۟ بَلْ وَجَدْنَآ ءَابَآءَنَا كَذَٰلِكَ يَفْعَلُونَ (٧٤) قَالَ أَفَرَءَيْتُم مَّا كُنتُمْ تَعْبُدُونَ (٧٥) أَنتُمْ وَءَابَآؤُكُمُ ٱلْأَقْدَمُونَ (٧٦) فَإِنَّهُمْ عَدُوٌّ لِّىَ إِلَّا رَبَّ ٱلْعَٰلَمِينَ (٧٧) ٱلَّذِى خَلَقَنِى فَهُوَ يَهْدِينِ (٧٨) وَٱلَّذِى هُوَ يُطْعِمُنِى وَيَسْقِينِ (٧٩) وَإِذَا مَرِضْتُ فَهُوَ يَشْفِينِ (٨٠) وَٱلَّذِى يُمِيتُنِى ثُمَّ يُحْيِينِ (٨١) وَٱلَّذِىٓ أَطْمَعُ أَن يَغْفِرَ لِى خَطِيٓئَتِى يَوْمَ ٱلدِّينِ (٨٢) رَبِّ هَبْ لِى حُكْمًا وَأَلْحِقْنِى بِٱلصَّٰلِحِينَ (٨٣) وَٱجْعَل لِّى لِسَانَ صِدْقٍ فِى ٱلْءَاخِرِينَ (٨٤) وَٱجْعَلْنِى مِن وَرَثَةِ جَنَّةِ ٱلنَّعِيمِ (٨٥) وَٱغْفِرْ لِأَبِىٓ إِنَّهُۥ كَانَ مِنَ ٱلضَّآلِّينَ (٨٦) وَلَا تُخْزِنِى يَوْمَ

يُبْعَثُونَ (٨٧) يَوْمَ لَا يَنفَعُ مَالٌ وَلَا بَنُونَ (٨٨) إِلَّا
مَنْ أَتَى ٱللَّهَ بِقَلْبٍ سَلِيمٍ (٨٩)

And recite to them the story of Ibrâhim (Abraham). (69) When he said to his father and his people: "What do you worship?" (70) They said: "We worship idols, and to them we are ever devoted." (71) He said: "Do they hear you, when you call on (them)? (72) "Or do they benefit you or do they harm (you)?" (73) They said: "(Nay), but we found our fathers doing so." (74) He said: "Do you observe that which you have been worshipping, — (75) "You and your ancient fathers? (76) "Verily! they are enemies to me, save the Lord of the 'Alamîn (mankind, jinn and all that exists); (77) "Who has created me, and it is He Who guides me; (78) "And it is He Who feeds me and gives me to drink (79) "And when I am ill, it is He who cures me; (80) "And Who will cause me to die, and then will bring me to life (again); (81) "And Who, I hope will forgive me my faults on the Day of Recompense, (the Day of Resurrection)," (82) My Lord! Bestow Hukm (religious knowledge, right judgement of the affairs and Prophethood) on me, and join me with the righteous, (83) And grant me an honourable mention in later generations. (84) And make me one of the inheritors of the Paradise of Delight. (85) And forgive my father, verily he is of the erring. (86) And disgrace me not on the Day when (all the creatures) will be resurrected; (87) The Day whereon neither wealth nor sons will avail, (88) Except him who brings to Allâh a clean heart [clean from Shirk (polytheism) and Nifâq (hypocrisy)]. (89)

Quran 29:16-18

وَإِبْرَاهِيمَ إِذْ قَالَ لِقَوْمِهِ ٱعْبُدُوا۟ ٱللَّهَ وَٱتَّقُوهُۚ ذَٰلِكُمْ خَيْرٌ لَّكُمْ إِن كُنتُمْ تَعْلَمُونَ (١٦) إِنَّمَا تَعْبُدُونَ مِن دُونِ

ٱللَّهِ أَوْثَٰنًا وَتَخْلُقُونَ إِفْكًا إِنَّ ٱلَّذِينَ تَعْبُدُونَ مِن دُونِ ٱللَّهِ لَا يَمْلِكُونَ لَكُمْ رِزْقًا فَٱبْتَغُواْ عِندَ ٱللَّهِ ٱلرِّزْقَ وَٱعْبُدُوهُ وَٱشْكُرُواْ لَهُ إِلَيْهِ تُرْجَعُونَ (١٧) وَإِن تُكَذِّبُواْ فَقَدْ كَذَّبَ أُمَمٌ مِّن قَبْلِكُمْ وَمَا عَلَى ٱلرَّسُولِ إِلَّا ٱلْبَلَٰغُ ٱلْمُبِينُ (١٨)

And (remember) Ibrâhim (Abraham) when he said to his people: "Worship Allâh (Alone), and fear Him, that is better for you if you did but know. (16) "You worship besides Allâh only idols, and you only invent falsehood. Verily, those whom you worship besides Allâh have no power to give you provision, so seek your provision from Allâh (Alone), and worship Him (Alone), and be grateful to Him. To Him (Alone) you will be brought back. (17) "And if you deny, then nations before you have denied (their Messengers). And the duty of the Messenger is only to convey (the Message) plainly." (18)

Quran 43:26-27

وَإِذْ قَالَ إِبْرَاهِيمُ لِأَبِيهِ وَقَوْمِهِ إِنَّنِى بَرَآءٌ مِّمَّا تَعْبُدُونَ
(٢٦) إِلَّا ٱلَّذِى فَطَرَنِى فَإِنَّهُۥ سَيَهْدِينِ (٢٧)

And (remember) when Ibrahîm (Abraham) said to his father and his people: "Verily, I am innocent of what you worship, (26) "Except Him (i.e. but Allâh Alone I worship none) Who did create me, and verily, He will guide me." (27)

Quran 60:4-5

قَدْ كَانَتْ لَكُمْ أُسْوَةٌ حَسَنَةٌ فِىٓ إِبْرَاهِيمَ وَٱلَّذِينَ مَعَهُۥٓ إِذْ
قَالُواْ لِقَوْمِهِمْ إِنَّا بُرَءَآؤُاْ مِنكُمْ وَمِمَّا تَعْبُدُونَ مِن دُونِ
ٱللَّهِ كَفَرْنَا بِكُمْ وَبَدَا بَيْنَنَا وَبَيْنَكُمُ ٱلْعَدَاوَةُ وَٱلْبَغْضَآءُ
أَبَدًا حَتَّىٰ تُؤْمِنُواْ بِٱللَّهِ وَحْدَهُۥٓ إِلَّا قَوْلَ إِبْرَاهِيمَ لِأَبِيهِ
لَأَسْتَغْفِرَنَّ لَكَ وَمَآ أَمْلِكُ لَكَ مِنَ ٱللَّهِ مِن شَىْءٍ ۖ رَّبَّنَا
عَلَيْكَ تَوَكَّلْنَا وَإِلَيْكَ أَنَبْنَا وَإِلَيْكَ ٱلْمَصِيرُ (٤) رَبَّنَا لَا
تَجْعَلْنَا فِتْنَةً لِّلَّذِينَ كَفَرُواْ وَٱغْفِرْ لَنَا رَبَّنَآ ۖ إِنَّكَ أَنتَ
ٱلْعَزِيزُ ٱلْحَكِيمُ (٥)

Indeed there has been an excellent example for you in Ibrâhim (Abraham) and those with him, when they said to their people: "Verily, we are free from you and whatever you worship besides Allâh, we have rejected you, and there has started between us and you, hostility and hatred for ever, until you believe in Allâh Alone," except the saying of Ibrâhim (Abraham) to his father: "Verily, I will ask forgiveness (from Allâh) for you, but I have no power to do anything for you before Allâh." Our Lord! In You (Alone) we put our trust, and to You (Alone) we turn in repentance, and to You (Alone) is (our) final Return, (4) "Our Lord! Make us not a trial for the disbelievers, and forgive us, Our Lord! Verily, You, only You are the All-Mighty, the All-Wise." (5)

Quran 29:24-26

فَمَا كَانَ جَوَابَ قَوْمِهِ إِلَّا أَن قَالُوا اقْتُلُوهُ أَوْ حَرِّقُوهُ فَأَنجَاهُ اللَّهُ مِنَ النَّارِ ۚ إِنَّ فِى ذَٰلِكَ لَآيَٰتٍ لِّقَوْمٍ يُؤْمِنُونَ ﴿٢٤﴾ وَقَالَ إِنَّمَا اتَّخَذْتُم مِّن دُونِ اللَّهِ أَوْثَٰنًا مَّوَدَّةَ بَيْنِكُمْ فِى الْحَيَوٰةِ الدُّنْيَا ۖ ثُمَّ يَوْمَ الْقِيَٰمَةِ يَكْفُرُ بَعْضُكُم بِبَعْضٍ وَيَلْعَنُ بَعْضُكُم بَعْضًا وَمَأْوَىٰكُمُ النَّارُ وَمَا لَكُم مِّن نَّٰصِرِينَ ﴿٢٥﴾ ۞ فَآمَنَ لَهُ لُوطٌ ۘ وَقَالَ إِنِّى مُهَاجِرٌ إِلَىٰ رَبِّى ۚ إِنَّهُ هُوَ الْعَزِيزُ الْحَكِيمُ ﴿٢٦﴾

So nothing was the answer of [Ibrahîm's (Abraham)] people except that they said: "Kill him or burn him." Then Allâh saved him from the fire. Verily, in this are indeed signs for a people who believe (24) And [Ibrâhim (Abraham)] said: "You have taken (for worship) idols instead of Allâh, The love between you is only in the life of this world, but on the Day of Resurrection, you shall disown each other, and curse each other, and your abode will be the Fire, and you shall have no helper." (25) So Lut (Lot) believed in him [Ibrâhim's (Abraham) Message of Islâmic Monotheism]. He

[Ibrâhim (Abraham)] said: "I will emigrate for the sake of my Lord. Verily, He is the All-Mighty, the All-Wise." (26)

Quran 6:74-81

۞ وَإِذْ قَالَ إِبْرَٰهِيمُ لِأَبِيهِ ءَازَرَ أَتَتَّخِذُ أَصْنَامًا ءَالِهَةً إِنِّىٓ أَرَىٰكَ وَقَوْمَكَ فِى ضَلَٰلٍ مُّبِينٍ (٧٤) وَكَذَٰلِكَ نُرِىٓ إِبْرَٰهِيمَ مَلَكُوتَ ٱلسَّمَٰوَٰتِ وَٱلْأَرْضِ وَلِيَكُونَ مِنَ ٱلْمُوقِنِينَ (٧٥) فَلَمَّا جَنَّ عَلَيْهِ ٱلَّيْلُ رَءَا كَوْكَبًا قَالَ هَٰذَا رَبِّى فَلَمَّآ أَفَلَ قَالَ لَآ أُحِبُّ ٱلْءَافِلِينَ (٧٦) فَلَمَّا رَءَا ٱلْقَمَرَ بَازِغًا قَالَ هَٰذَا رَبِّى فَلَمَّآ أَفَلَ قَالَ لَئِن لَّمْ يَهْدِنِى رَبِّى لَأَكُونَنَّ مِنَ ٱلْقَوْمِ ٱلضَّآلِّينَ (٧٧) فَلَمَّا رَءَا ٱلشَّمْسَ بَازِغَةً قَالَ هَٰذَا رَبِّى هَٰذَآ أَكْبَرُ فَلَمَّآ أَفَلَتْ قَالَ يَٰقَوْمِ إِنِّى بَرِىٓءٌ مِّمَّا تُشْرِكُونَ (٧٨) إِنِّى وَجَّهْتُ وَجْهِىَ لِلَّذِى فَطَرَ ٱلسَّمَٰوَٰتِ وَٱلْأَرْضَ حَنِيفًا وَمَآ أَنَا۠ مِنَ ٱلْمُشْرِكِينَ (٧٩) وَحَآجَّهُۥ قَوْمُهُۥ قَالَ أَتُحَٰجُّوٓنِّى فِى ٱللَّهِ وَقَدْ هَدَىٰنِ وَلَآ أَخَافُ مَا تُشْرِكُونَ بِهِۦٓ إِلَّآ أَن يَشَآءَ رَبِّى شَيْـًٔا وَسِعَ رَبِّى كُلَّ شَىْءٍ عِلْمًا أَفَلَا تَتَذَكَّرُونَ (٨٠) وَكَيْفَ أَخَافُ مَآ أَشْرَكْتُمْ وَلَا تَخَافُونَ أَنَّكُمْ أَشْرَكْتُم بِٱللَّهِ مَا لَمْ يُنَزِّلْ بِهِۦ عَلَيْكُمْ سُلْطَٰنًا فَأَىُّ ٱلْفَرِيقَيْنِ أَحَقُّ بِٱلْأَمْنِ إِن كُنتُمْ تَعْلَمُونَ (٨١)

And (remember) when Ibrâhim (Abraham) said to his father Azar: "Do you take idols as âlihâh (gods)? Verily, I see you and your people in manifest error." (74) Thus did we show Ibrâhim (Abraham) the kingdom of the heavens and the earth that he be one of those who have Faith with certainty (75) When the night covered him over with darkness he saw a star. He said: "This is my lord." But when it set, he said: "I like not those that set." (76) When he saw the moon rising up, he said: "This is my lord." But when it set, he said: "Unless my Lord guides me, I shall surely be among the people who went astray." (77) When he saw the sun rising up, he said: "This is my lord. This is greater." But when it set, he said: "O my people! I am indeed free from all that you join as partners (in worship with Allâh). (78) Verily, I have turned my face towards Him Who has created the heavens and the earth Hanifa (Islâmic Monotheism, i.e. worshipping none but Allâh Alone) and I am not of Al-Mushrikûn". (79) His people disputed with him. He said: "Do you dispute with me concerning Allâh while He has guided me, and I fear not those whom you associate with Him (Allâh) in worship. (Nothing can happen to me) except when my Lord (Allâh) wills something. My Lord comprehends in His Knowledge all things. Will you not then remember? (80) And how should I fear those whom you associate in worship with Allâh (though they can neither benefit nor harm), while you fear not that you have joined in worship with Allâh things for which He has not sent down to you any authority. (So) which of the two parties has more right to be in security? If you but know." (81)

Quran 19:41-48

وَٱذْكُرْ فِى ٱلْكِتَٰبِ إِبْرَٰهِيمَ إِنَّهُۥ كَانَ صِدِّيقًا نَّبِيًّا (٤١) إِذْ قَالَ لِأَبِيهِ يَٰٓأَبَتِ لِمَ تَعْبُدُ مَا لَا يَسْمَعُ وَلَا يُبْصِرُ وَلَا يُغْنِى عَنكَ شَيْـًٔا (٤٢) يَٰٓأَبَتِ إِنِّى قَدْ جَآءَنِى مِنَ ٱلْعِلْمِ مَا لَمْ يَأْتِكَ فَٱتَّبِعْنِىٓ أَهْدِكَ صِرَٰطًا سَوِيًّا (٤٣) يَٰٓأَبَتِ لَا تَعْبُدِ ٱلشَّيْطَٰنَ إِنَّ ٱلشَّيْطَٰنَ كَانَ لِلرَّحْمَٰنِ عَصِيًّا (٤٤) يَٰٓأَبَتِ إِنِّىٓ أَخَافُ أَن يَمَسَّكَ عَذَابٌ مِّنَ ٱلرَّحْمَٰنِ فَتَكُونَ لِلشَّيْطَٰنِ وَلِيًّا (٤٥) قَالَ أَرَاغِبٌ أَنتَ عَنْ ءَالِهَتِى يَٰٓإِبْرَٰهِيمُ لَئِن لَّمْ تَنتَهِ لَأَرْجُمَنَّكَ وَٱهْجُرْنِى مَلِيًّا (٤٦) قَالَ سَلَٰمٌ عَلَيْكَ سَأَسْتَغْفِرُ لَكَ رَبِّىٓ إِنَّهُۥ كَانَ بِى حَفِيًّا (٤٧) وَأَعْتَزِلُكُمْ وَمَا تَدْعُونَ مِن دُونِ ٱللَّهِ وَأَدْعُوا۟ رَبِّى عَسَىٰٓ أَلَّآ أَكُونَ بِدُعَآءِ رَبِّى شَقِيًّا (٤٨)

And mention in the Book Ibrâhim (Abraham). Verily! he was a man of truth, a Prophet. (41) When he said to his father: "O my father! Why do you worship that which hears not, sees not and cannot avail you in anything? (42) "O my father! Verily! there has come to me of knowledge that which came not unto you. So follow me. I will guide you to a Straight Path. (43) "O my father! Worship not Shaitân (Satan). Verily! Shaitân (Satan) has been a rebel against the Most Gracious (Allâh) (44) "O my father! Verily! I fear lest a torment from the Most Gracious (Allâh) should overtake you, so that you become a companion of Shaitân (Satan) (in the Hell-fire)." (45) He (the father) said: "Do you reject my gods, O Ibrâhim (Abraham)? If you stop not (this), I will indeed stone you. So get away from me safely (before I punish you)." (46) Ibrâhim (Abraham) said: "Peace be on you! I will ask Forgiveness of my Lord for you. Verily! He is unto me, Ever Most Gracious. (47) "And I shall turn away from you and from those whom you invoke besides Allâh. And I shall call upon my Lord; and I hope that I shall not be unblest in my invocation to my Lord." (48)

Quran 21:51-68

۞ وَلَقَدْ ءَاتَيْنَآ إِبْرَٰهِيمَ رُشْدَهُۥ مِن قَبْلُ وَكُنَّا بِهِۦ عَٰلِمِينَ (٥١) إِذْ قَالَ لِأَبِيهِ وَقَوْمِهِۦ مَا هَٰذِهِ ٱلتَّمَاثِيلُ ٱلَّتِىٓ أَنتُمْ لَهَا عَٰكِفُونَ (٥٢) قَالُوا۟ وَجَدْنَآ ءَابَآءَنَا لَهَا عَٰبِدِينَ (٥٣) قَالَ لَقَدْ كُنتُمْ أَنتُمْ وَءَابَآؤُكُمْ فِى ضَلَٰلٍ مُّبِينٍ (٥٤) قَالُوٓا۟ أَجِئْتَنَا بِٱلْحَقِّ أَمْ أَنتَ مِنَ ٱللَّٰعِبِينَ (٥٥) قَالَ بَل رَّبُّكُمْ رَبُّ ٱلسَّمَٰوَٰتِ وَٱلْأَرْضِ ٱلَّذِى فَطَرَهُنَّ وَأَنَا۠ عَلَىٰ ذَٰلِكُم مِّنَ ٱلشَّٰهِدِينَ (٥٦) وَتَٱللَّهِ لَأَكِيدَنَّ أَصْنَٰمَكُم بَعْدَ أَن تُوَلُّوا۟ مُدْبِرِينَ (٥٧) فَجَعَلَهُمْ جُذَٰذًا إِلَّا كَبِيرًا لَّهُمْ لَعَلَّهُمْ إِلَيْهِ يَرْجِعُونَ (٥٨) قَالُوا۟ مَن فَعَلَ هَٰذَا بِـَٔالِهَتِنَآ إِنَّهُۥ لَمِنَ ٱلظَّٰلِمِينَ (٥٩) قَالُوا۟ سَمِعْنَا فَتًى يَذْكُرُهُمْ يُقَالُ لَهُۥٓ إِبْرَٰهِيمُ (٦٠) قَالُوا۟ فَأْتُوا۟ بِهِۦ عَلَىٰٓ أَعْيُنِ ٱلنَّاسِ لَعَلَّهُمْ يَشْهَدُونَ (٦١) قَالُوٓا۟ ءَأَنتَ فَعَلْتَ هَٰذَا بِـَٔالِهَتِنَا يَٰٓإِبْرَٰهِيمُ (٦٢) قَالَ بَلْ فَعَلَهُۥ كَبِيرُهُمْ هَٰذَا فَسْـَٔلُوهُمْ إِن كَانُوا۟ يَنطِقُونَ (٦٣) فَرَجَعُوٓا۟ إِلَىٰٓ أَنفُسِهِمْ فَقَالُوٓا۟ إِنَّكُمْ أَنتُمُ ٱلظَّٰلِمُونَ (٦٤) ثُمَّ نُكِسُوا۟ عَلَىٰ رُءُوسِهِمْ لَقَدْ عَلِمْتَ مَا هَٰٓؤُلَآءِ يَنطِقُونَ (٦٥) قَالَ أَفَتَعْبُدُونَ مِن دُونِ ٱللَّهِ مَا لَا يَنفَعُكُمْ شَيْـًٔا وَلَا يَضُرُّكُمْ (٦٦) أُفٍّ لَّكُمْ وَلِمَا تَعْبُدُونَ مِن دُونِ ٱللَّهِ أَفَلَا تَعْقِلُونَ

قَالُواْ حَرِّقُوهُ وَٱنصُرُوٓاْ ءَالِهَتَكُمۡ إِن كُنتُمۡ (٦٧) فَـٰعِلِينَ (٦٨)

And indeed We bestowed aforetime on Ibrâhim (Abraham) his (portion of) guidance, and We were Well-Acquainted with him (as to his Belief in the Oneness of Allâh). (51) When he said to his father and his people: "What are these images, to which you are devoted?" (52) They said: "We found our fathers worshipping them." (53) He said: "Indeed you and your fathers have been in manifest error." (54) They said: "Have you brought us the truth, or are you one of those who play about?" (55) He said: "Nay, your Lord is the Lord of the heavens and the earth, Who created them and to that I am one of the witnesses. (56) "And by Allâh, I shall plot a plan (to destroy) your idols after you have gone away and turned your backs." (57) So he broke them to pieces, (all) except the biggest of them, that they might turn to it. (58) They said: "Who has done this to our âlihah (gods)? He must indeed be one of the Zalimun (wrong-doers)." (59) They said: "We heard a young man talking against them, who is called Ibrâhim (Abraham)." (60) They said: "Then bring him before the eyes of the people, that they may testify." (61) They said: "Are you the one who has done this to our gods, O Ibrâhim (Abraham)?" (62) [Ibrâhim (Abraham)] said: "Nay, this one, the biggest of them (idols) did it. Ask them, if they can speak!" (63) So they turned to themselves and said: "Verily, you are the Zâlimûn (polytheists and wrong-doers)." (64) Then they turned to themselves (their first thought and said): "Indeed you [Ibrâhim (Abraham)] know well that these (idols) speak not!" (65) [Ibrâhim (Abraham)] said: "Do you then worship besides Allâh, things that can neither profit you, nor harm you? (66) "Fie upon you, and upon that which you worship besides Allâh! Have you then no sense?" (67) They said: "Burn him and help your âlihah (gods), if you will be doing." (68)

Quran 37:83-102

﴿ وَإِنَّ مِن شِيعَتِهِ لَإِبْرَٰهِيمَ (٨٣) إِذْ جَآءَ رَبَّهُ بِقَلْبٍ سَلِيمٍ (٨٤) إِذْ قَالَ لِأَبِيهِ وَقَوْمِهِ مَاذَا تَعْبُدُونَ (٨٥) أَئِفْكًا ءَالِهَةً دُونَ ٱللَّهِ تُرِيدُونَ (٨٦) فَمَا ظَنُّكُم بِرَبِّ ٱلْعَٰلَمِينَ (٨٧) فَنَظَرَ نَظْرَةً فِى ٱلنُّجُومِ (٨٨) فَقَالَ إِنِّى سَقِيمٌ (٨٩) فَتَوَلَّوْا عَنْهُ مُدْبِرِينَ (٩٠) فَرَاغَ إِلَىٰٓ ءَالِهَتِهِمْ فَقَالَ أَلَا تَأْكُلُونَ (٩١) مَا لَكُمْ لَا تَنطِقُونَ (٩٢) فَرَاغَ عَلَيْهِمْ ضَرْبًا بِٱلْيَمِينِ (٩٣) فَأَقْبَلُوٓا إِلَيْهِ يَزِفُّونَ (٩٤) قَالَ أَتَعْبُدُونَ مَا تَنْحِتُونَ (٩٥) وَٱللَّهُ خَلَقَكُمْ وَمَا تَعْمَلُونَ (٩٦) قَالُوا ٱبْنُوا لَهُ بُنْيَٰنًا فَأَلْقُوهُ فِى ٱلْجَحِيمِ (٩٧) فَأَرَادُوا بِهِ كَيْدًا فَجَعَلْنَٰهُمُ ٱلْأَسْفَلِينَ (٩٨) وَقَالَ إِنِّى ذَاهِبٌ إِلَىٰ رَبِّى سَيَهْدِينِ (٩٩) رَبِّ هَبْ لِى مِنَ ٱلصَّٰلِحِينَ (١٠٠) فَبَشَّرْنَٰهُ بِغُلَٰمٍ حَلِيمٍ (١٠١) فَلَمَّا بَلَغَ مَعَهُ ٱلسَّعْىَ قَالَ يَٰبُنَىَّ إِنِّىٓ أَرَىٰ فِى ٱلْمَنَامِ أَنِّىٓ أَذْبَحُكَ

فَٱنظُرْ مَاذَا تَرَىٰ قَالَ يَـٰٓأَبَتِ ٱفۡعَلۡ مَا تُؤۡمَرُ سَتَجِدُنِىٓ إِن شَآءَ ٱللَّهُ مِنَ ٱلصَّـٰبِرِينَ (١٠٢)

And, verily, among those who followed his [Nûh's (Noah)] way (Islâmic Monotheism) was Ibrâhim (Abraham). (83) When he came to his Lord with a pure heart [attached to Allâh Alone - and none else, worshipping none but Allâh Alone true Islâmic Monotheism, pure from the filth of polytheism]. (84) When he said to his father and to his people: "What is it that which you worship? (85) "Is it a falsehood âlihah (gods) other than Allâh that you desire? (86) "Then what think you about the Lord of the 'Alamîn (mankind, jinn, and all that exists)?" (87) Then he cast a glance at the stars, (88) And he said: "Verily, I am sick (with plague). [He did this trick to remain in their temple of idols to destroy them and not to accompany them to the pagan feast]."

(89) So they turned away from him, and departed (for fear of the disease). (90) Then he turned to their âlihah (gods) and said: "Will you not eat (of the offering before you)? (91) "What is the matter with you that you speak not?" (92) Then he turned upon them, striking (them) with (his) right hand. (93) Then they (the worshippers of idols) came, towards him, hastening. (94) He said: "Worship you that which you (yourselves) carve? (95) "While Allâh has created you and what you make!" (96) They said: "Build for him a building (it is said that the building was like a furnace) and throw him into the blazing fire!" (97) So they plotted a plot against him, but We made them the lowest. (98) And he said (after his rescue from the fire): "Verily, I am going to my Lord. He will guide me!" (99) "My Lord! Grant me (offspring) from the righteous." (100) So We gave him the glad tidings of a

forbearing boy. (101) And, when he (his son) was old enough to walk with him, he said: "O my son! I have seen in a dream that I am slaughtering you (offer you in sacrifice to Allâh), so look what you think!" He said: "O my father! Do that which you are commanded, Inshâ' Allâh (if Allâh will), you shall find me of As-Sâbirun (the patient)." (102)

Quran 2:258

أَلَمْ تَرَ إِلَى ٱلَّذِى حَاجَّ إِبْرَٰهِـۧمَ فِى رَبِّهِۦٓ أَنْ ءَاتَىٰهُ ٱللَّهُ ٱلْمُلْكَ إِذْ قَالَ إِبْرَٰهِـۧمُ رَبِّىَ ٱلَّذِى يُحْىِۦ وَيُمِيتُ قَالَ أَنَا۠ أُحْىِۦ وَأُمِيتُ ۖ قَالَ إِبْرَٰهِـۧمُ فَإِنَّ ٱللَّهَ يَأْتِى بِٱلشَّمْسِ مِنَ ٱلْمَشْرِقِ فَأْتِ بِهَا مِنَ ٱلْمَغْرِبِ فَبُهِتَ ٱلَّذِى كَفَرَ ۗ وَٱللَّهُ لَا يَهْدِى ٱلْقَوْمَ ٱلظَّٰلِمِينَ

Have you not looked at him who disputed with Ibrâhim (Abraham) about his Lord (Allâh), because Allâh had given him the kingdom? When Ibrâhim (Abraham) said (to him): "My Lord (Allâh) is He Who gives life and causes death." He said, "I give life and cause death." Ibrâhim (Abraham) said, "Verily! Allâh causes the sun to rise from the east; then cause it you to rise from the west." So the disbeliever was utterly defeated. And Allâh guides not the people, who are Zâlimûn (wrong-doers). (258)

Quran 14:35-41

وَإِذْ قَالَ إِبْرَاهِيمُ رَبِّ ٱجْعَلْ هَٰذَا ٱلْبَلَدَ ءَامِنًا وَٱجْنُبْنِى وَبَنِىَّ أَن نَّعْبُدَ ٱلْأَصْنَامَ (٣٥) رَبِّ إِنَّهُنَّ أَضْلَلْنَ كَثِيرًا مِّنَ ٱلنَّاسِ فَمَن تَبِعَنِى فَإِنَّهُۥ مِنِّى وَمَنْ عَصَانِى فَإِنَّكَ غَفُورٌ رَّحِيمٌ (٣٦) رَّبَّنَآ إِنِّىٓ أَسْكَنتُ مِن ذُرِّيَّتِى بِوَادٍ غَيْرِ ذِى زَرْعٍ عِندَ بَيْتِكَ ٱلْمُحَرَّمِ رَبَّنَا لِيُقِيمُوا۟ ٱلصَّلَوٰةَ فَٱجْعَلْ أَفْـِٔدَةً مِّنَ ٱلنَّاسِ تَهْوِىٓ إِلَيْهِمْ وَٱرْزُقْهُم مِّنَ ٱلثَّمَرَٰتِ لَعَلَّهُمْ يَشْكُرُونَ (٣٧) رَبَّنَآ إِنَّكَ تَعْلَمُ مَا نُخْفِى وَمَا نُعْلِنُ وَمَا يَخْفَىٰ عَلَى ٱللَّهِ مِن شَىْءٍ فِى ٱلْأَرْضِ وَلَا فِى ٱلسَّمَآءِ (٣٨) ٱلْحَمْدُ لِلَّهِ ٱلَّذِى وَهَبَ لِى عَلَى ٱلْكِبَرِ إِسْمَٰعِيلَ وَإِسْحَٰقَ إِنَّ رَبِّى لَسَمِيعُ ٱلدُّعَآءِ (٣٩) رَبِّ ٱجْعَلْنِى مُقِيمَ ٱلصَّلَوٰةِ وَمِن ذُرِّيَّتِى

67

رَبَّنَا وَتَقَبَّلْ دُعَآءِ (٤٠) رَبَّنَا ٱغْفِرْ لِى وَلِوَٰلِدَىَّ وَلِلْمُؤْمِنِينَ يَوْمَ يَقُومُ ٱلْحِسَابُ (٤١)

And (remember) when Ibrâhim (Abraham) said: "O my Lord! Make this city (Makkah) one of peace and security, and keep me and my sons away from worshipping idols. (35) "O my Lord! They have indeed led astray many among mankind. But whoso follows me, he verily is of me. And whoso disobeys me, - still You are indeed Oft-Forgiving, Most Merciful. (36) "O our Lord! I have made some of my offspring to dwell in an uncultivable valley by Your Sacred House (the Ka'bah at Makkah); in order, O our Lord, that they may perform As-Salât (Iqâmat-as-Salât), so fill some hearts among men with love towards them, and (O Allâh) provide them with fruits so that they may give thanks. (37) "O our Lord! Certainly, You know what we conceal and what we reveal.

Nothing on the earth or in the heaven is hidden from Allâh (38) "All the praises and thanks are to Allâh, Who has given me in old age Ismâ'il (Ishmael) and Ishâq (Isaac). Verily! My Lord is indeed the All-Hearer of invocations. (39) "O my Lord! Make me one who performs As-Salât (Iqâmat-as-Salât), and (also) from my offspring, our Lord! And accept my invocation. (40) "Our Lord! Forgive me and my parents, and (all) the believers on the Day when the reckoning will be established." (41)

Quran 2:124-132

وَإِذِ ٱبْتَلَىٰٓ إِبْرَٰهِـۧمَ رَبُّهُۥ بِكَلِمَـٰتٍ فَأَتَمَّهُنَّ ۖ قَالَ إِنِّى جَاعِلُكَ لِلنَّاسِ إِمَامًا ۖ قَالَ وَمِن ذُرِّيَّتِى ۖ قَالَ لَا يَنَالُ عَهْدِى ٱلظَّـٰلِمِينَ (١٢٤) وَإِذْ جَعَلْنَا ٱلْبَيْتَ مَثَابَةً لِّلنَّاسِ وَأَمْنًا وَٱتَّخِذُوا۟ مِن مَّقَامِ إِبْرَٰهِـۧمَ مُصَلًّى ۖ وَعَهِدْنَآ إِلَىٰٓ إِبْرَٰهِـۧمَ وَإِسْمَـٰعِيلَ أَن طَهِّرَا بَيْتِىَ لِلطَّآئِفِينَ وَٱلْعَـٰكِفِينَ وَٱلرُّكَّعِ ٱلسُّجُودِ (١٢٥) وَإِذْ قَالَ إِبْرَٰهِـۧمُ رَبِّ ٱجْعَلْ هَـٰذَا بَلَدًا ءَامِنًا وَٱرْزُقْ أَهْلَهُۥ

69

مِنَ ٱلثَّمَرَٰتِ مَنْ ءَامَنَ مِنْهُم بِٱللَّهِ وَٱلْيَوْمِ ٱلْءَاخِرِۖ قَالَ
وَمَن كَفَرَ فَأُمَتِّعُهُ قَلِيلًا ثُمَّ أَضْطَرُّهُ إِلَىٰ عَذَابِ ٱلنَّارِۖ
وَبِئْسَ ٱلْمَصِيرُ (١٢٦) وَإِذْ يَرْفَعُ إِبْرَٰهِ‍ۧمُ ٱلْقَوَاعِدَ
مِنَ ٱلْبَيْتِ وَإِسْمَٰعِيلُ رَبَّنَا تَقَبَّلْ مِنَّآۖ إِنَّكَ أَنتَ ٱلسَّمِيعُ
ٱلْعَلِيمُ (١٢٧) رَبَّنَا وَٱجْعَلْنَا مُسْلِمَيْنِ لَكَ وَمِن ذُرِّيَّتِنَآ
أُمَّةً مُّسْلِمَةً لَّكَ وَأَرِنَا مَنَاسِكَنَا وَتُبْ عَلَيْنَآۖ إِنَّكَ أَنتَ
ٱلتَّوَّابُ ٱلرَّحِيمُ (١٢٨) رَبَّنَا وَٱبْعَثْ فِيهِمْ رَسُولًا
مِّنْهُمْ يَتْلُواْ عَلَيْهِمْ ءَايَٰتِكَ وَيُعَلِّمُهُمُ ٱلْكِتَٰبَ وَٱلْحِكْمَةَ
وَيُزَكِّيهِمْۚ إِنَّكَ أَنتَ ٱلْعَزِيزُ ٱلْحَكِيمُ (١٢٩) وَمَن
يَرْغَبُ عَن مِّلَّةِ إِبْرَٰهِ‍ۧمَ إِلَّا مَن سَفِهَ نَفْسَهُۥۚ وَلَقَدِ
ٱصْطَفَيْنَٰهُ فِى ٱلدُّنْيَاۖ وَإِنَّهُۥ فِى ٱلْءَاخِرَةِ لَمِنَ ٱلصَّٰلِحِينَ
(١٣٠) إِذْ قَالَ لَهُۥ رَبُّهُۥٓ أَسْلِمْۖ قَالَ أَسْلَمْتُ لِرَبِّ
ٱلْعَٰلَمِينَ (١٣١) وَوَصَّىٰ بِهَآ إِبْرَٰهِ‍ۧمُ بَنِيهِ وَيَعْقُوبُ
يَٰبَنِىَّ إِنَّ ٱللَّهَ ٱصْطَفَىٰ لَكُمُ ٱلدِّينَ فَلَا تَمُوتُنَّ إِلَّا وَأَنتُم
مُّسْلِمُونَ (١٣٢)

And (remember) when the Lord of
Ibrâhim (Abraham) [i.e., Allâh] tried
him with (certain) Commands, which he
fulfilled. He (Allâh) said (to him),
"Verily, I am going to make you Imam
(a leader) for mankind (to follow you)."

[Ibrâhim (Abraham)] said, "And of my offspring (to make leaders)." (Allâh) said, "My Covenant (Prophethood) includes not Zâlimûn (polytheists and wrong-doers)." (124) And (remember) when We made the House (the Ka'bah at Makkah) a place of resort for mankind and a place of safety. And take you (people) the Maqâm (place) of Ibrâhim (Abraham) [or the stone on which Ibrâhim (Abraham) stood while he was building the Ka'bah] as a place of prayer (for some of your prayers, e.g. two Rak'at after the Tawâf of the Ka'bah at Makkah), and We commanded Ibrâhim (Abraham) and Ismâ'il (Ishmael) that they should purify My House (the Ka'bah at Makkah) for those who are circumambulating it, or staying (I'tikâf), or bowing or prostrating themselves (there, in prayer). (125) And (remember) when Ibrâhim (Abraham) said, "My Lord, make this city (Makkah) a place of security and provide its people with fruits, such of them as believe in Allâh and the Last Day." He (Allâh) answered: "As for him who disbelieves, I shall leave him in contentment for a while, then I shall compel him to the torment of the Fire, and worst indeed is that destination!" (126) And (remember) when Ibrâhim (Abraham) and (his son) Ismâ'il (Ishmael) were raising the foundations of the House (the Ka'bah at Makkah), (saying), "Our Lord! Accept (this service) from us. Verily! You are the All-Hearer, the All-Knower." (127) "Our Lord! And make us submissive unto You and of our offspring a nation submissive unto You, and show us our Manâsik (all the ceremonies of pilgrimage - Hajj and 'Umrah), and accept our repentance. Truly, You are the One Who accepts repentance, the Most Merciful. (128) "Our Lord! Send

amongst them a Messenger of their own
(and indeed Allâh answered their
invocation by sending Muhammad),
who shall recite unto them Your Verses
and instruct them in the Book (this
Qur'ân) and Al-Hikmah (full knowledge
of the Islâmic laws and jurisprudence or
wisdom or Prophethood), and purify
them. Verily! You are the All-Mighty,
the All-Wise." (129) And who turns
away from the religion of Ibrâhim
(Abraham) (i.e. Islâmic Monotheism)
except him who befools himself? Truly,
We chose him in this world and verily,
in the Hereafter he will be among the
righteous. (130) When his Lord said to
him, "Submit (i.e. be a Muslim)!" He
said, "I have submitted myself (as a
Muslim) to the Lord of the 'Alamîn
(mankind, jinn and all that exists)." (131)
And this (submission to Allâh, Islâm)
was enjoined by Ibrâhim (Abraham)
upon his sons and by Ya'qûb (Jacob),

(saying), "O my sons! Allâh has chosen for you the (true) religion, then die not except in the Faith of Islâm (as Muslims - Islâmic Monotheism)." (132)

Quran 29:28-30

وَلُوطًا إِذْ قَالَ لِقَوْمِهِ إِنَّكُمْ لَتَأْتُونَ ٱلْفَٰحِشَةَ مَا سَبَقَكُم بِهَا مِنْ أَحَدٍ مِّنَ ٱلْعَٰلَمِينَ (٢٨) أَئِنَّكُمْ لَتَأْتُونَ ٱلرِّجَالَ وَتَقْطَعُونَ ٱلسَّبِيلَ وَتَأْتُونَ فِى نَادِيكُمُ ٱلْمُنكَرَ ۖ فَمَا كَانَ جَوَابَ قَوْمِهِ إِلَّآ أَن قَالُوا۟ ٱئْتِنَا بِعَذَابِ ٱللَّهِ إِن كُنتَ مِنَ ٱلصَّٰدِقِينَ (٢٩) قَالَ رَبِّ ٱنصُرْنِى عَلَى ٱلْقَوْمِ ٱلْمُفْسِدِينَ (٣٠)

And (remember) Lut (Lot), when he said to his people: "You commit Al-Fâhishah (sodomy the worst sin) which none has preceded you in (committing) it in the 'Alamîn (mankind and jinn)." (28) "Verily, you practice sodomy with men, and rob the wayfarer (travellers)! And practice Al-Munkar (disbelief and polytheism and every kind of evil wicked deed) in your meetings." But his people gave no answer except, that they said: "Bring Allâh's Torment upon us if you are one of the truthful." (29) He said: "My Lord! Give me victory over the people who are Mufsidûn (those who commit great crimes and sins, oppressors, tyrants, mischief-makers, corrupters). (30)

Quran 26:160-169

كَذَّبَتْ قَوْمُ لُوطٍ ٱلْمُرْسَلِينَ (١٦٠) إِذْ قَالَ لَهُمْ أَخُوهُمْ لُوطٌ أَلَا تَتَّقُونَ (١٦١) إِنِّى لَكُمْ رَسُولٌ أَمِينٌ (١٦٢) فَٱتَّقُواْ ٱللَّهَ وَأَطِيعُونِ (١٦٣) وَمَآ أَسْـَٔلُكُمْ عَلَيْهِ مِنْ أَجْرٍ إِنْ أَجْرِىَ إِلَّا عَلَىٰ رَبِّ ٱلْعَٰلَمِينَ (١٦٤) أَتَأْتُونَ ٱلذُّكْرَانَ مِنَ ٱلْعَٰلَمِينَ (١٦٥) وَتَذَرُونَ مَا خَلَقَ لَكُمْ رَبُّكُم مِّنْ أَزْوَٰجِكُمْ بَلْ أَنتُمْ قَوْمٌ عَادُونَ (١٦٦) قَالُواْ لَئِن لَّمْ تَنتَهِ يَٰلُوطُ لَتَكُونَنَّ مِنَ ٱلْمُخْرَجِينَ (١٦٧) قَالَ إِنِّى لِعَمَلِكُم مِّنَ ٱلْقَالِينَ (١٦٨) رَبِّ نَجِّنِى وَأَهْلِى مِمَّا يَعْمَلُونَ (١٦٩)

The people of Lut (Lot) (who dwelt in the town of Sodom in Palestine) belied the Messengers. (160) When their brother Lut (Lot) said to them: "Will you not fear Allâh and obey Him? (161) "Verily! I am a trustworthy Messenger to you. (162) "So fear Allâh, keep your duty to Him, and obey me. (163) "No reward do I ask of you for it (my Message of Islâmic Monotheism), my reward is only from the Lord of the 'Alamîn (mankind, jinn and all that exists). (164) "Go you in unto the males of the 'Alamîn (mankind), (165) "And leave those whom Allâh has created for you to be your wives? Nay, you are a trespassing people!" (166) They said: "If you cease not. O Lut (Lot)! Verily, you will be one of those who are driven out!" (167) He said: "I am, indeed, of those who disapprove with severe anger and fury your (this evil) action (of sodomy). (168) "My Lord! Save me and my family from what they do." (169)

Quran 27:54-56

وَلُوطًا إِذْ قَالَ لِقَوْمِهِ أَتَأْتُونَ ٱلْفَٰحِشَةَ وَأَنتُمْ تُبْصِرُونَ
(٥٤) أَئِنَّكُمْ لَتَأْتُونَ ٱلرِّجَالَ شَهْوَةً مِّن دُونِ ٱلنِّسَآءِ ۚ بَلْ
أَنتُمْ قَوْمٌ تَجْهَلُونَ (٥٥) ۞ فَمَا كَانَ جَوَابَ قَوْمِهِ
إِلَّا أَن قَالُوٓا۟ أَخْرِجُوٓا۟ ءَالَ لُوطٍ مِّن قَرْيَتِكُمْ ۖ إِنَّهُمْ أُنَاسٌ
يَتَطَهَّرُونَ (٥٦)

And (remember) Lut (Lot)! When he
said to his people. "Do you commit
Al¬Fâhishah (evil, great sin, every kind
of unlawful sexual intercourse, sodomy)
while you see (one another doing evil
without any screen)?" (54) "Do you
practice your lusts on men instead of
women? Nay, but you are a people who
behave senselessly." (55) There was no
other answer given by his people except
that they said: "Drive out the family of
Lut (Lot) from your city. Verily, these
are men who want to be clean and
pure!" (56)

Quran 7:80-83

77

وَلُوطًا إِذْ قَالَ لِقَوْمِهِ أَتَأْتُونَ ٱلْفَٰحِشَةَ مَا سَبَقَكُم بِهَا مِنْ أَحَدٍ مِّنَ ٱلْعَٰلَمِينَ (٨٠) إِنَّكُمْ لَتَأْتُونَ ٱلرِّجَالَ شَهْوَةً مِّن دُونِ ٱلنِّسَاءِ ۚ بَلْ أَنتُمْ قَوْمٌ مُّسْرِفُونَ (٨١) وَمَا كَانَ جَوَابَ قَوْمِهِ إِلَّآ أَن قَالُوٓاْ أَخْرِجُوهُم مِّن قَرْيَتِكُمْ ۖ إِنَّهُمْ أُنَاسٌ يَتَطَهَّرُونَ (٨٢) فَأَنجَيْنَٰهُ وَأَهْلَهُ إِلَّا ٱمْرَأَتَهُ كَانَتْ مِنَ ٱلْغَٰبِرِينَ (٨٣)

And (remember) Lût (Lot), when he said to his people: "Do you commit the worst sin such as none preceding you has committed in the 'Alamîn (mankind and jinn)? (80) "Verily, you practise your lusts on men instead of women. Nay, but you are a people transgressing beyond bounds (by committing great sins)." (81) And the answer of his people was only that they said: "Drive them out of your town, these are indeed men who want to be pure (from sins)!" (82) Then We saved him and his family, except his wife; she was of those who remained behind (in the torment) (83)

Quran 11:77-81

وَلَمَّا جَآءَتْ رُسُلُنَا لُوطًا سِىٓءَ بِهِمْ وَضَاقَ بِهِمْ ذَرْعًا وَقَالَ هَٰذَا يَوْمٌ عَصِيبٌ (٧٧) وَجَآءَهُۥ قَوْمُهُۥ يُهْرَعُونَ إِلَيْهِ وَمِن قَبْلُ كَانُوا۟ يَعْمَلُونَ ٱلسَّيِّـَٔاتِ قَالَ يَٰقَوْمِ هَٰٓؤُلَآءِ بَنَاتِى هُنَّ أَطْهَرُ لَكُمْ فَٱتَّقُوا۟ ٱللَّهَ وَلَا تُخْزُونِ فِى ضَيْفِىٓ أَلَيْسَ مِنكُمْ رَجُلٌ رَّشِيدٌ (٧٨) قَالُوا۟ لَقَدْ عَلِمْتَ مَا لَنَا فِى بَنَاتِكَ مِنْ حَقٍّ وَإِنَّكَ لَتَعْلَمُ مَا نُرِيدُ (٧٩) قَالَ لَوْ أَنَّ لِى بِكُمْ قُوَّةً أَوْ ءَاوِىٓ إِلَىٰ رُكْنٍ شَدِيدٍ (٨٠) قَالُوا۟ يَٰلُوطُ إِنَّا رُسُلُ رَبِّكَ لَن يَصِلُوٓا۟ إِلَيْكَ فَأَسْرِ بِأَهْلِكَ بِقِطْعٍ مِّنَ ٱلَّيْلِ وَلَا يَلْتَفِتْ مِنكُمْ أَحَدٌ إِلَّا ٱمْرَأَتَكَ إِنَّهُۥ مُصِيبُهَا مَآ أَصَابَهُمْ إِنَّ مَوْعِدَهُمُ ٱلصُّبْحُ أَلَيْسَ ٱلصُّبْحُ بِقَرِيبٍ (٨١)

And when Our Messengers came to Lut (Lot), he was grieved on for them and felt himself straitened for them (lest the town people should approach them to commit sodomy with them). He said: "This is a distressful day." (77) And his people came rushing towards him, and since aforetime they used to commit crimes (sodomy), he said: "O my people! Here are my daughters (i.e. the women of nation), they are purer for you (if you marry them lawfully). So fear Allâh and disgrace me not with regards to my guests! Is there not among you a single right-minded man?" (78) They said: "Surely you know that we have neither any desire nor need of your daughters, and indeed you know well what we want!" (79) He said: "Would that I had strength (men) to overpower you, or that I could betake myself to some powerful support (to resist you)." (80) They (Messengers) said: "O Lut (Lot)! Verily, we are the Messengers from your Lord! They shall not reach you! So travel with your family in a part of the night, and let not any of you look back, but your wife (will remain behind), verily, the punishment which will afflict them, will afflict her. Indeed, morning is their appointed time. Is not the morning near?" (81)

Quran 15:68-71

قَالَ إِنَّ هَـٰٓؤُلَآءِ ضَيْفِى فَلَا تَفْضَحُونِ (٦٨) وَٱتَّقُواْ
ٱللَّهَ وَلَا تُخْزُونِ (٦٩) قَالُوٓاْ أَوَلَمْ نَنْهَكَ عَنِ ٱلْعَـٰلَمِينَ
(٧٠) قَالَ هَـٰٓؤُلَآءِ بَنَاتِىٓ إِن كُنتُمْ فَـٰعِلِينَ (٧١)

[Lut (Lot)] said: "Verily! these are my guests, so shame me not. (68) "And fear Allâh and disgrace me not." (69) They (people of the city) said: "Did we not forbid you to entertaining (or protecting) any of the 'Alamîn (people, foreigners, strangers from us)?" (70) [Lut (Lot)] said: "These (the girls of the nation) are my daughters (to marry lawfully), if you must act (so)." (71)

Quran 2:127-129

وَإِذْ يَرْفَعُ إِبْرَاهِـۧمُ ٱلْقَوَاعِدَ مِنَ ٱلْبَيْتِ وَإِسْمَـٰعِيلُ رَبَّنَا
تَقَبَّلْ مِنَّآ إِنَّكَ أَنتَ ٱلسَّمِيعُ ٱلْعَلِيمُ (١٢٧) رَبَّنَا وَٱجْعَلْنَا
مُسْلِمَيْنِ لَكَ وَمِن ذُرِّيَّتِنَآ أُمَّةً مُّسْلِمَةً لَّكَ وَأَرِنَا
مَنَاسِكَنَا وَتُبْ عَلَيْنَآ إِنَّكَ أَنتَ ٱلتَّوَّابُ ٱلرَّحِيمُ
(١٢٨) رَبَّنَا وَٱبْعَثْ فِيهِمْ رَسُولاً مِّنْهُمْ يَتْلُواْ عَلَيْهِمْ
ءَايَـٰتِكَ وَيُعَلِّمُهُمُ ٱلْكِتَـٰبَ وَٱلْحِكْمَةَ وَيُزَكِّيهِمْ إِنَّكَ أَنتَ
ٱلْعَزِيزُ ٱلْحَكِيمُ (١٢٩)

81

And (remember) when Ibrâhim (Abraham) and (his son) Ismâ'il (Ishmael) were raising the foundations of the House (the Ka'bah at Makkah), (saying), "Our Lord! Accept (this service) from us. Verily! You are the All-Hearer, the All-Knower." (127) "Our Lord! And make us submissive unto You and of our offspring a nation submissive unto You, and show us our Manâsik (all the ceremonies of pilgrimage - Hajj and 'Umrah), and accept our repentance. Truly, You are the One Who accepts repentance, the Most Merciful. (128) "Our Lord! Send amongst them a Messenger of their own, who shall recite unto them Your Verses and instruct them in the Book (this Qur'ân) and Al-Hikmah (full knowledge of the Islâmic laws and jurisprudence or wisdom or Prophethood), and purify them. Verily!

You are the All-Mighty, the All-Wise."
(129)

Quran 2:132-133

وَوَصَّىٰ بِهَآ إِبْرَٰهِۦمُ بَنِيهِ وَيَعْقُوبُ يَٰبَنِىَّ إِنَّ ٱللَّهَ ٱصْطَفَىٰ لَكُمُ ٱلدِّينَ فَلَا تَمُوتُنَّ إِلَّا وَأَنتُم مُّسْلِمُونَ (١٣٢) أَمْ كُنتُمْ شُهَدَآءَ إِذْ حَضَرَ يَعْقُوبَ ٱلْمَوْتُ إِذْ قَالَ لِبَنِيهِ مَا تَعْبُدُونَ مِنۢ بَعْدِى قَالُواْ نَعْبُدُ إِلَٰهَكَ وَإِلَٰهَ ءَابَآئِكَ إِبْرَٰهِۦمَ وَإِسْمَٰعِيلَ وَإِسْحَٰقَ إِلَٰهًا وَٰحِدًا وَنَحْنُ لَهُۥ مُسْلِمُونَ (١٣٣)

And this (submission to Allâh, Islâm) was enjoined by Ibrâhim (Abraham) upon his sons and by Ya'qûb (Jacob), (saying), "O my sons! Allâh has chosen for you the (true) religion, then die not except in the Faith of Islâm (as Muslims - Islâmic Monotheism)." (132) Or were you witnesses when death approached Ya'qûb (Jacob)? When he said unto his sons, "What will you worship after me?" They said, "We shall worship your Ilâh (God - Allâh), the Ilâh (God) of your fathers, Ibrâhim (Abraham), Ismâ'il (Ishmael), Ishâq (Isaac), One Ilâh (God), and to Him we submit (in Islâm)." (133)

Quran 12:4-6

إِذْ قَالَ يُوسُفُ لِأَبِيهِ يَـٰٓأَبَتِ إِنِّى رَأَيْتُ أَحَدَ عَشَرَ كَوْكَبًا وَٱلشَّمْسَ وَٱلْقَمَرَ رَأَيْتُهُمْ لِى سَـٰجِدِينَ (٤) قَالَ يَـٰبُنَىَّ لَا تَقْصُصْ رُءْيَاكَ عَلَىٰٓ إِخْوَتِكَ فَيَكِيدُواْ لَكَ كَيْدًا ۖ إِنَّ ٱلشَّيْطَـٰنَ لِلْإِنسَـٰنِ عَدُوٌّ مُّبِينٌ (٥) وَكَذَٰلِكَ يَجْتَبِيكَ رَبُّكَ وَيُعَلِّمُكَ مِن تَأْوِيلِ ٱلْأَحَادِيثِ وَيُتِمُّ نِعْمَتَهُۥ عَلَيْكَ وَعَلَىٰٓ ءَالِ يَعْقُوبَ كَمَآ أَتَمَّهَا عَلَىٰٓ أَبَوَيْكَ مِن قَبْلُ إِبْرَٰهِيمَ وَإِسْحَـٰقَ ۚ إِنَّ رَبَّكَ عَلِيمٌ حَكِيمٌ (٦)

(Remember) when Yûsuf (Joseph) said to his father: "O my father! Verily, I saw (in a dream) eleven stars and the sun and the moon, — I saw them prostrating themselves to me." (4) He (Ya'qub/Jacob) said: "O my son! Relate not your vision to your brothers, lest they arrange a plot against you. Verily! Shaitân (Satan) is to man an open enemy! (5) "Thus will your Lord choose you and teach you the interpretation of dreams (and other things) and perfect His Favour on you and on the offspring of Ya'qûb (Jacob), as He perfected it on your fathers, Ibrahîm (Abraham) and Ishâq (Isaac) aforetime! Verily, your Lord is All-Knowing, All-Wise." (6)

Quran 12:17-18

قَالُواْ يَـٰٓأَبَانَآ إِنَّا ذَهَبْنَا نَسْتَبِقُ وَتَرَكْنَا يُوسُفَ عِندَ مَتَـٰعِنَا فَأَكَلَهُ ٱلذِّئْبُ وَمَآ أَنتَ بِمُؤْمِنٍ لَّنَا وَلَوْ كُنَّا صَـٰدِقِينَ (١٧) وَجَآءُو عَلَىٰ قَمِيصِهِ بِدَمٍ كَذِبٍ قَالَ بَلْ سَوَّلَتْ لَكُمْ أَنفُسُكُمْ أَمْرًا فَصَبْرٌ جَمِيلٌ وَٱللَّهُ ٱلْمُسْتَعَانُ عَلَىٰ مَا تَصِفُونَ (١٨)

They said:"O our father! We went racing with one another, and left Yûsuf (Joseph) by our belongings and a wolf devoured him; but you will never believe us even when we speak the truth." (17) And they brought his shirt stained with false blood. He

(Yaqub/Jacob) said: "Nay, but your
ownselves have made up a tale. So (for
me) patience is most fitting. And it is
Allâh (Alone) Whose help can be sought
against that (lie) which you describe."
(18)

Quran 12:63-64

فَلَمَّا رَجَعُوٓاْ إِلَىٰٓ أَبِيهِمْ قَالُواْ يَـٰٓأَبَانَا مُنِعَ مِنَّا ٱلْكَيْلُ
فَأَرْسِلْ مَعَنَآ أَخَانَا نَكْتَلْ وَإِنَّا لَهُۥ لَحَـٰفِظُونَ
(٦٣) قَالَ هَلْ ءَامَنُكُمْ عَلَيْهِ إِلَّا كَمَآ أَمِنتُكُمْ عَلَىٰٓ
أَخِيهِ مِن قَبْلُ فَٱللَّهُ خَيْرٌ حَـٰفِظًا وَهُوَ أَرْحَمُ ٱلرَّٰحِمِينَ
(٦٤)

So, when they returned to their father,
they said: "O our father! No more
measure of grain shall we get (unless we
take our brother). So send our brother
with us, and we shall get our measure
and truly we will guard him." (63) He
(Ya'qub/Joseph) said: "Can I entrust
him to you except as I entrusted his
brother [Yûsuf (Joseph)] to you

aforetime? But Allâh is the Best to guard, and He is the Most Merciful of those who show mercy." (64)

Quran 12:66-67

قَالَ لَنْ أُرْسِلَهُ مَعَكُمْ حَتَّىٰ تُؤْتُونِ مَوْثِقًا مِّنَ ٱللَّهِ لَتَأْتُنَّنِى بِهِۦٓ إِلَّآ أَن يُحَاطَ بِكُمْۖ فَلَمَّآ ءَاتَوْهُ مَوْثِقَهُمْ قَالَ ٱللَّهُ عَلَىٰ مَا نَقُولُ وَكِيلٌ (٦٦) وَقَالَ يَٰبَنِىَّ لَا تَدْخُلُواْ مِنۢ بَابٍ وَٰحِدٍ وَٱدْخُلُواْ مِنْ أَبْوَٰبٍ مُّتَفَرِّقَةٍۖ وَمَآ أُغْنِى عَنكُم مِّنَ ٱللَّهِ مِن شَىْءٍۖ إِنِ ٱلْحُكْمُ إِلَّا لِلَّهِۖ عَلَيْهِ تَوَكَّلْتُۖ وَعَلَيْهِ فَلْيَتَوَكَّلِ ٱلْمُتَوَكِّلُونَ (٦٧)

He [Ya'qûb (Jacob)] said: "I will not send him with you until you swear a solemn oath to me in Allâh's Name, that you will bring him back to me unless you are yourselves surrounded (by enemies)," And when they had sworn their solemn oath, he said: "Allâh is the Witness over what we have said." (66) And he said: "O my sons! Do not enter by one gate, but enter by different gates, and I cannot avail you against Allâh at all. Verily! The decision rests only with Allâh. In him, I put my trust and let all those that trust, put their trust in Him." (67)

Quran 12:83-87

قَالَ بَلْ سَوَّلَتْ لَكُمْ أَنفُسُكُمْ أَمْرًا ۖ فَصَبْرٌ جَمِيلٌ ۖ عَسَى ٱللَّهُ أَن يَأْتِيَنِى بِهِمْ جَمِيعًا ۚ إِنَّهُۥ هُوَ ٱلْعَلِيمُ ٱلْحَكِيمُ (٨٣) وَتَوَلَّىٰ عَنْهُمْ وَقَالَ يَـٰٓأَسَفَىٰ عَلَىٰ يُوسُفَ وَٱبْيَضَّتْ عَيْنَاهُ مِنَ ٱلْحُزْنِ فَهُوَ كَظِيمٌ (٨٤) قَالُواْ تَٱللَّهِ تَفْتَؤُاْ تَذْكُرُ يُوسُفَ حَتَّىٰ تَكُونَ حَرَضًا أَوْ تَكُونَ مِنَ ٱلْهَـٰلِكِينَ (٨٥) قَالَ إِنَّمَآ أَشْكُواْ بَثِّى وَحُزْنِىَ إِلَى ٱللَّهِ وَأَعْلَمُ مِنَ ٱللَّهِ مَا لَا تَعْلَمُونَ (٨٦) يَـٰبَنِىَّ ٱذْهَبُواْ فَتَحَسَّسُواْ مِن يُوسُفَ وَأَخِيهِ وَلَا تَا۟يْـَٔسُواْ مِن رَّوْحِ ٱللَّهِ ۖ إِنَّهُۥ لَا يَا۟يْـَٔسُ مِن رَّوْحِ ٱللَّهِ إِلَّا ٱلْقَوْمُ ٱلْكَـٰفِرُونَ (٨٧)

He [Ya'qûb (Jacob)] said: "Nay, but your ownselves have beguiled you into something. So patience is most fitting (for me). Maybe Allâh will bring them (back) all to me. Truly He! only He is All-Knowing, All-Wise." (83) And he turned away from them and said: "Alas, my grief for Yûsuf (Joseph)!" And he lost his sight because of the sorrow that he was suppressing. (84) They said: "By Allâh! You will never cease remembering Yûsuf (Joseph) until you become weak with old age, or until you be of the dead." (85) He said: "I only complain of my grief and sorrow to Allâh, and I know from Allâh that which you know not. (86) "O my sons! Go you and enquire about Yûsuf (Joseph) and his brother, and never give up hope of Allâh's Mercy. Certainly no one despairs of Allâh's Mercy, except the people who disbelieve." (87)

Quran 12:94-98

وَلَمَّا فَصَلَتِ ٱلْعِيرُ قَالَ أَبُوهُمْ إِنِّى لَأَجِدُ رِيحَ يُوسُفَ لَوْلَآ أَن تُفَنِّدُونِ (٩٤) قَالُواْ تَٱللَّهِ إِنَّكَ لَفِى ضَلَٰلِكَ ٱلْقَدِيمِ (٩٥) فَلَمَّآ أَن جَآءَ ٱلْبَشِيرُ أَلْقَىٰهُ عَلَىٰ وَجْهِهِ فَٱرْتَدَّ بَصِيرًا قَالَ أَلَمْ أَقُل لَّكُمْ إِنِّىٓ أَعْلَمُ مِنَ ٱللَّهِ مَا لَا تَعْلَمُونَ (٩٦) قَالُواْ يَٰٓأَبَانَا ٱسْتَغْفِرْ لَنَا ذُنُوبَنَآ إِنَّا

كُنَّا خَٰطِـِينَ (٩٧) قَالَ سَوْفَ أَسْتَغْفِرُ لَكُمْ رَبِّيٓ إِنَّهُ
هُوَ ٱلْغَفُورُ ٱلرَّحِيمُ (٩٨)

And when the caravan departed, their father said: "I do indeed feel the smell of Yûsuf (Joseph), if only you think me not a dotard (a person who has weakness of mind because of old age)." (94) They said: "By Allâh! Certainly, you are in your old error." (95) Then, when the bearer of the glad tidings arrived, he cast it (the shirt) over his face, and he became clear-sighted. He said: "Did I not say to you, 'I know from Allâh that which you know not.' " (96) They said: "O our father! Ask forgiveness (from Allâh) for our sins, indeed we have been sinners." (97) He said: "I will ask my Lord for forgiveness for you, verily He! Only He is the Oft-Forgiving, the Most Merciful." (98)

Quran 12:22-23

وَلَمَّا بَلَغَ أَشُدَّهُ ءَاتَيْنَـٰهُ حُكْمًا وَعِلْمًا ۚ وَكَذَٰلِكَ نَجْزِى
ٱلْمُحْسِنِينَ (٢٢) وَرَٰوَدَتْهُ ٱلَّتِى هُوَ فِى بَيْتِهَا عَن
نَّفْسِهِ ۚ وَغَلَّقَتِ ٱلْأَبْوَٰبَ وَقَالَتْ هَيْتَ لَكَ ۚ قَالَ مَعَاذَ ٱللَّهِ ۖ
إِنَّهُ رَبِّى أَحْسَنَ مَثْوَاىَ ۖ إِنَّهُۥ لَا يُفْلِحُ ٱلظَّـٰلِمُونَ (٢٣)

And when he [Yûsuf (Joseph)] attained his full manhood, We gave him wisdom and knowledge (the Prophethood), thus We reward the Muhsinûn (doers of good). (22) And she, in whose house he was, sought to seduce him (to do an evil act), and she closed the doors and said: "Come on, O you." He said: "I seek refuge in Allâh (or Allâh forbid)! Truly, he (your husband) is my master! He made my living in a great comfort! (So I will never betray him). Verily, the Zâlimûn (wrong and evil-doers) will never be successful." (23)

Quran 12:30-33

۞ وَقَالَ نِسْوَةٌ فِى ٱلْمَدِينَةِ ٱمْرَأَتُ ٱلْعَزِيزِ تُرَٰوِدُ
فَتَىٰهَا عَن نَّفْسِهِ ۖ قَدْ شَغَفَهَا حُبًّا ۖ إِنَّا لَنَرَىٰهَا فِى ضَلَـٰلٍ

مُّبِينٍ ﴿٣٠﴾ فَلَمَّا سَمِعَتْ بِمَكْرِهِنَّ أَرْسَلَتْ إِلَيْهِنَّ
وَأَعْتَدَتْ لَهُنَّ مُتَّكَـًٔا وَءَاتَتْ كُلَّ وَاحِدَةٍ مِّنْهُنَّ سِكِّينًا
وَقَالَتِ ٱخْرُجْ عَلَيْهِنَّ ۖ فَلَمَّا رَأَيْنَهُۥٓ أَكْبَرْنَهُۥ وَقَطَّعْنَ
أَيْدِيَهُنَّ وَقُلْنَ حَـٰشَ لِلَّهِ مَا هَـٰذَا بَشَرًا إِنْ هَـٰذَآ إِلَّا مَلَكٌ
كَرِيمٌ ﴿٣١﴾ قَالَتْ فَذَٰلِكُنَّ ٱلَّذِى لُمْتُنَّنِى فِيهِ ۖ وَلَقَدْ
رَٰوَدتُّهُۥ عَن نَّفْسِهِۦ فَٱسْتَعْصَمَ ۖ وَلَئِن لَّمْ يَفْعَلْ مَآ ءَامُرُهُۥ
لَيُسْجَنَنَّ وَلَيَكُونًا مِّنَ ٱلصَّـٰغِرِينَ ﴿٣٢﴾ قَالَ رَبِّ
ٱلسِّجْنُ أَحَبُّ إِلَيَّ مِمَّا يَدْعُونَنِىٓ إِلَيْهِ ۖ وَإِلَّا تَصْرِفْ
عَنِّى كَيْدَهُنَّ أَصْبُ إِلَيْهِنَّ وَأَكُن مِّنَ ٱلْجَـٰهِلِينَ ﴿٣٣﴾

And women in the city said: "The wife
of Al-'Azîz is seeking to seduce her
(slave) young man, indeed she loves
him violently; verily we see her in plain
error." (30) So when she heard of their
accusation, she sent for them and
prepared a banquet for them; she gave
each one of them a knife (to cut the
foodstuff with), and she said [(to Yûsuf
(Joseph)]: "Come out before them."
Then, when they saw him, they exalted
him (at his beauty) and (in their
astonishment) cut their hands. They

said: "How perfect is Allâh (or Allâh forbid)! No man is this! This is none other than a noble angel!" (31) She said: "This is he (the young man) about whom you did blame me, and I did seek to seduce him, but he refused. And now if he refuses to obey my order, he shall certainly be cast into prison, and will be one of those who are disgraced." (32) He said: "O my Lord! Prison is dearer to me than that to which they invite me. Unless You turn away their plot from me, I will feel inclined towards them and be one (of those who commit sin and deserve blame or those who do deeds) of the ignorant." (33)

Quran 12:36-40

وَدَخَلَ مَعَهُ ٱلسِّجْنَ فَتَيَانِ ۖ قَالَ أَحَدُهُمَآ إِنِّىٓ أَرَىٰنِىٓ أَعْصِرُ خَمْرًا ۖ وَقَالَ ٱلْءَاخَرُ إِنِّىٓ أَرَىٰنِىٓ أَحْمِلُ فَوْقَ رَأْسِى خُبْزًا تَأْكُلُ ٱلطَّيْرُ مِنْهُ ۖ نَبِّئْنَا بِتَأْوِيلِهِۦ ۖ إِنَّا نَرَىٰكَ مِنَ ٱلْمُحْسِنِينَ (٣٦) قَالَ لَا يَأْتِيكُمَا طَعَامٌ تُرْزَقَانِهِۦٓ إِلَّا

نَبَّأْتُكُمَا بِتَأْوِيلِهِ قَبْلَ أَن يَأْتِيَكُمَا ذَٰلِكُمَا مِمَّا عَلَّمَنِى رَبِّىٓ إِنِّى تَرَكْتُ مِلَّةَ قَوْمٍ لَّا يُؤْمِنُونَ بِٱللَّهِ وَهُم بِٱلْءَاخِرَةِ هُمْ كَٰفِرُونَ (٣٧) وَٱتَّبَعْتُ مِلَّةَ ءَابَآءِئَ إِبْرَٰهِيمَ وَإِسْحَٰقَ وَيَعْقُوبَ مَا كَانَ لَنَآ أَن نُّشْرِكَ بِٱللَّهِ مِن شَىْءٍ ذَٰلِكَ مِن فَضْلِ ٱللَّهِ عَلَيْنَا وَعَلَى ٱلنَّاسِ وَلَٰكِنَّ أَكْثَرَ ٱلنَّاسِ لَا يَشْكُرُونَ (٣٨) يَٰصَٰحِبَىِ ٱلسِّجْنِ ءَأَرْبَابٌ مُّتَفَرِّقُونَ خَيْرٌ أَمِ ٱللَّهُ ٱلْوَٰحِدُ ٱلْقَهَّارُ (٣٩) مَا تَعْبُدُونَ مِن دُونِهِ إِلَّآ أَسْمَآءً سَمَّيْتُمُوهَآ أَنتُمْ وَءَابَآؤُكُم مَّآ أَنزَلَ ٱللَّهُ بِهَا مِن سُلْطَٰنٍ إِنِ ٱلْحُكْمُ إِلَّا لِلَّهِ أَمَرَ أَلَّا تَعْبُدُوٓا۟ إِلَّآ إِيَّاهُ ذَٰلِكَ ٱلدِّينُ ٱلْقَيِّمُ وَلَٰكِنَّ أَكْثَرَ ٱلنَّاسِ لَا يَعْلَمُونَ (٤٠)

And there entered with him two young men in the prison. One of them said: "Verily, I saw myself (in a dream) pressing wine." The other said: "Verily, I saw myself (in a dream) carrying bread on my head and birds were eating thereof." (They said): "Inform us of the interpretation of this. Verily, we think you are one of the Muhsinûn (doers of good)." (36) He said: "No food will come to you (in wakefulness or in dream) as your provision, but I will inform (in wakefulness) its interpretation before it (the food) comes. This is of that which my Lord has taught me. Verily, I have abandoned the religion of a people that believe not in Allâh and are disbelievers in the Hereafter. (37) "And I have followed the religion of my fathers, - Ibrahîm (Abraham), Ishâq (Isaac) and Ya'qûb (Jacob), and never could we attribute any partners whatsoever to Allâh. This is from the Grace of Allâh to us and to mankind, but most men thank not (i.e. they neither believe in Allâh, nor worship Him). (38) "O two companions of the prison! Are many different lords (gods) better or Allâh, the One, the Irresistible? (39) "You do not worship besides Him but only names which you have named (forged), you and your fathers, — for which Allâh has sent down no authority. The command (or the judgement) is for none but Allâh.

He has commanded that you worship none but Him (i.e. His Monotheism), that is the (true) straight religion, but most men know not. (40)

Quran 12:45-55

وَقَالَ ٱلَّذِى نَجَا مِنْهُمَا وَٱدَّكَرَ بَعْدَ أُمَّةٍ أَنَا۠ أُنَبِّئُكُم بِتَأْوِيلِهِ فَأَرْسِلُونِ (٤٥) يُوسُفُ أَيُّهَا ٱلصِّدِّيقُ أَفْتِنَا فِى سَبْعِ بَقَرَٰتٍ سِمَانٍ يَأْكُلُهُنَّ سَبْعٌ عِجَافٌ وَسَبْعِ سُنۢبُلَٰتٍ خُضْرٍ وَأُخَرَ يَابِسَٰتٍ لَّعَلِّى أَرْجِعُ إِلَى ٱلنَّاسِ لَعَلَّهُمْ يَعْلَمُونَ (٤٦) قَالَ تَزْرَعُونَ سَبْعَ سِنِينَ دَأَبًا فَمَا حَصَدتُّمْ فَذَرُوهُ فِى سُنۢبُلِهِ إِلَّا قَلِيلًا مِّمَّا تَأْكُلُونَ (٤٧) ثُمَّ يَأْتِى مِنۢ بَعْدِ ذَٰلِكَ سَبْعٌ شِدَادٌ يَأْكُلْنَ مَا قَدَّمْتُمْ لَهُنَّ إِلَّا قَلِيلًا مِّمَّا تُحْصِنُونَ (٤٨) ثُمَّ يَأْتِى مِنۢ بَعْدِ ذَٰلِكَ عَامٌ فِيهِ يُغَاثُ ٱلنَّاسُ وَفِيهِ يَعْصِرُونَ (٤٩) وَقَالَ ٱلْمَلِكُ ٱئْتُونِى بِهِ فَلَمَّا جَاءَهُ ٱلرَّسُولُ قَالَ ٱرْجِعْ إِلَىٰ رَبِّكَ فَسْـَٔلْهُ مَا بَالُ ٱلنِّسْوَةِ ٱلَّٰتِى قَطَّعْنَ أَيْدِيَهُنَّ إِنَّ رَبِّى بِكَيْدِهِنَّ عَلِيمٌ (٥٠) قَالَ مَا خَطْبُكُنَّ إِذْ رَٰوَدتُّنَّ يُوسُفَ عَن نَّفْسِهِ قُلْنَ حَٰشَ لِلَّهِ مَا عَلِمْنَا عَلَيْهِ مِن سُوءٍ قَالَتِ ٱمْرَأَتُ ٱلْعَزِيزِ ٱلْـَٰٔنَ حَصْحَصَ ٱلْحَقُّ أَنَا۠ رَٰوَدتُّهُ عَن نَّفْسِهِ وَإِنَّهُ لَمِنَ ٱلصَّٰدِقِينَ (٥١) ذَٰلِكَ لِيَعْلَمَ أَنِّى لَمْ أَخُنْهُ بِٱلْغَيْبِ وَأَنَّ ٱللَّهَ لَا

96

يَهْدِى كَيْدَ ٱلْخَآئِنِينَ (٥٢) ۞ وَمَآ أُبَرِّئُ نَفْسِىٓ إِنَّ ٱلنَّفْسَ لَأَمَّارَةُۢ بِٱلسُّوٓءِ إِلَّا مَا رَحِمَ رَبِّىٓ إِنَّ رَبِّى غَفُورٌ رَّحِيمٌ (٥٣) وَقَالَ ٱلْمَلِكُ ٱئْتُونِى بِهِۦٓ أَسْتَخْلِصْهُ لِنَفْسِىۖ فَلَمَّا كَلَّمَهُۥ قَالَ إِنَّكَ ٱلْيَوْمَ لَدَيْنَا مَكِينٌ أَمِينٌ (٥٤) قَالَ ٱجْعَلْنِى عَلَىٰ خَزَآئِنِ ٱلْأَرْضِۖ إِنِّى حَفِيظٌ عَلِيمٌ (٥٥)

Then the man who was released (one of the two who were in prison), now at length remembered and said: "I will tell you its interpretation, so send me forth." (45) (He said): "O Yûsuf (Joseph), the man of truth! Explain to us (the dream) of seven fat cows whom seven lean ones were devouring, and of seven green ears of corn, and (seven) others dry, that I may return to the people, and that they may know." (46) [(Yûsuf (Joseph)] said: "For seven consecutive years, you shall sow as usual and that (the harvest) which you reap you shall leave it in ears, (all) - except a little of it which you may eat. (47) "Then will come after that,

seven hard (years), which will devour
what you have laid by in advance for
them, (all) except a little of that which
you have guarded (stored) (48) "Then
thereafter will come a year in which
people will have abundant rain and in
which they will press (wine and oil)."
(49) And the king said: "Bring him to
me." But when the messenger came to
him, [Yûsuf (Joseph)] said: "Return to
your lord and ask him, 'What happened
to the women who cut their hands?
Surely, my Lord (Allâh) is Well-Aware
of their plot.'" (50) (The King) said (to
the women): "What was your affair
when you did seek to seduce Yûsuf
(Joseph)?" The women said: "Allâh
forbid! No evil know we against him!"
The wife of Al-'Azîz said: "Now the
truth is manifest (to all), it was I who
sought to seduce him, and he is surely
of the truthful." (51) [Then Yûsuf
(Joseph) said: "I asked for this enquiry]

in order that he (Al-'Azîz) may know that I betrayed him not in his (absence). And, verily! Allâh guides not the plot of the betrayers. (52) "And I free not myself (from the blame). Verily, the (human) self is inclined to evil, except when my Lord bestows His Mercy (upon whom He wills). Verily, my Lord is Oft-Forgiving, Most Merciful." (53) And the king said: "Bring him to me that I may attach him to my person." Then, when he spoke to him, he said: "Verily, this day, you are with us high in rank and fully trusted." (54) [Yûsuf (Joseph)] said: "Set me over the storehouses of the land; I will indeed guard them with full knowledge" (as a minister of finance in Egypt). (55)

Quran 12:88-92

فَلَمَّا دَخَلُواْ عَلَيْهِ قَالُواْ يَـٰٓأَيُّهَا ٱلْعَزِيزُ مَسَّنَا وَأَهْلَنَا ٱلضُّرُّ وَجِئْنَا بِبِضَـٰعَةٍ مُّزْجَىٰةٍ فَأَوْفِ لَنَا ٱلْكَيْلَ وَتَصَدَّقْ عَلَيْنَآ إِنَّ ٱللَّهَ يَجْزِى ٱلْمُتَصَدِّقِينَ (٨٨) قَالَ

هَلْ عَلِمْتُم مَّا فَعَلْتُم بِيُوسُفَ وَأَخِيهِ إِذْ أَنتُمْ جَـٰهِلُونَ
(٨٩) قَالُوٓاْ أَءِنَّكَ لَأَنتَ يُوسُفُ قَالَ أَنَاْ يُوسُفُ وَهَـٰذَآ
أَخِى قَدْ مَنَّ ٱللَّهُ عَلَيْنَآ إِنَّهُۥ مَن يَتَّقِ وَيَصْبِرْ فَإِنَّ ٱللَّهَ لَا
يُضِيعُ أَجْرَ ٱلْمُحْسِنِينَ (٩٠) قَالُواْ تَٱللَّهِ لَقَدْ ءَاثَرَكَ ٱللَّهُ
عَلَيْنَا وَإِن كُنَّا لَخَـٰطِـِٔينَ (٩١) قَالَ لَا تَثْرِيبَ عَلَيْكُمُ
ٱلْيَوْمَ يَغْفِرُ ٱللَّهُ لَكُمْ وَهُوَ أَرْحَمُ ٱلرَّٰحِمِينَ (٩٢)

Then, when they entered unto him
[Yûsuf (Joseph)], they said: "O ruler of
the land! A hard time has hit us and our
family, and we have brought but poor
capital, so pay us full measure and be
charitable to us. Truly, Allâh does
reward the charitable." (88) He said: "Do
you know what you did with Yûsuf
(Joseph) and his brother, when you
were ignorant?" (89) They said: "Are you
indeed Yûsuf (Joseph)?" He said: "I am
Yûsuf (Joseph), and this is my brother
(Benjamin). Allâh has indeed been
gracious to us. Verily, he who fears
Allâh with obedience to Him (by
abstaining from sins and evil deeds, and

by performing righteous good deeds),
and is patient, then surely, Allâh makes
not the reward of the Muhsinûn (good-
doers) to be lost." (90) They said: "By
Allâh! Indeed Allâh has preferred you
above us, and we certainly have been
sinners." (91) He said: "No reproach on
you this day, may Allâh forgive you,
and He is the Most Merciful of those
who show mercy! (92)

Quran 12:99-101

فَلَمَّا دَخَلُوا۟ عَلَىٰ يُوسُفَ ءَاوَىٰٓ إِلَيْهِ أَبَوَيْهِ وَقَالَ ٱدْخُلُوا۟
مِصْرَ إِن شَآءَ ٱللَّهُ ءَامِنِينَ (٩٩) وَرَفَعَ أَبَوَيْهِ عَلَى
ٱلْعَرْشِ وَخَرُّوا۟ لَهُۥ سُجَّدًا ۖ وَقَالَ يَـٰٓأَبَتِ هَـٰذَا تَأْوِيلُ
رُءْيَـٰىَ مِن قَبْلُ قَدْ جَعَلَهَا رَبِّى حَقًّا ۖ وَقَدْ أَحْسَنَ بِىَ إِذْ
أَخْرَجَنِى مِنَ ٱلسِّجْنِ وَجَآءَ بِكُم مِّنَ ٱلْبَدْوِ مِنۢ بَعْدِ أَن
نَّزَغَ ٱلشَّيْطَـٰنُ بَيْنِى وَبَيْنَ إِخْوَتِىٓ ۚ إِنَّ رَبِّى لَطِيفٌ لِّمَا
يَشَآءُ ۚ إِنَّهُۥ هُوَ ٱلْعَلِيمُ ٱلْحَكِيمُ (١٠٠) ۞ رَبِّ قَدْ
ءَاتَيْتَنِى مِنَ ٱلْمُلْكِ وَعَلَّمْتَنِى مِن تَأْوِيلِ ٱلْأَحَادِيثِ ۚ
فَاطِرَ ٱلسَّمَـٰوَٰتِ وَٱلْأَرْضِ أَنتَ وَلِىِّۦ فِى ٱلدُّنْيَا
وَٱلْـَٔاخِرَةِ ۖ تَوَفَّنِى مُسْلِمًا وَأَلْحِقْنِى بِٱلصَّـٰلِحِينَ (١٠١)

Then, when they came in before Yûsuf (Joseph), he betook his parents to himself and said: "Enter Egypt, if Allâh wills, in security." (99) And he raised his parents to the throne and they fell down before him prostrate. And he said: "O my father! This is the interpretation of my dream aforetime! My Lord has made it come true! He was indeed good to me, when He took me out of the prison, and brought you (all here) out of the bedouin-life, after Shaitân (Satan) had sown enmity between me and my brothers. Certainly, my Lord is the Most Courteous and Kind unto whom He wills. Truly He! Only He is the All-Knowing, the All-Wise. (100) "My Lord! You have indeed bestowed on me of the sovereignty, and taught me something of the interpretation of dreams - the (Only) Creator of the heavens and the earth! You are my Walî (Protector, Helper, Supporter, Guardian, God,

Lord.) in this world and in the Hereafter. Cause me to die as a Muslim (the one submitting to Your Will), and join me with the righteous." (101)

Quran 29:36

وَإِلَىٰ مَدْيَنَ أَخَاهُمْ شُعَيْبًا فَقَالَ يَـٰقَوْمِ ٱعْبُدُوا۟ ٱللَّهَ وَٱرْجُوا۟ ٱلْيَوْمَ ٱلْءَاخِرَ وَلَا تَعْثَوْا۟ فِى ٱلْأَرْضِ مُفْسِدِينَ

And to (the people of) Madyan (Midian), We sent their brother Shu'aib (Shuaib). He said: "O my people! Worship Allâh, and hope for (the reward of good deeds by worshipping Allâh Alone, on) the last Day (i.e. the Day of Resurrection), and commit no mischief on the earth as Mufsidûn (those who commit great crimes, oppressors, tyrants, mischief-makers, corrupters). (36)

Quran 26:176-188

كَذَّبَ أَصْحَٰبُ لْئَيْكَةِ ٱلْمُرْسَلِينَ (١٧٦) إِذْ قَالَ لَهُمْ شُعَيْبٌ أَلَا تَتَّقُونَ (١٧٧) إِنِّى لَكُمْ رَسُولٌ أَمِينٌ (١٧٨) فَٱتَّقُوا۟ ٱللَّهَ وَأَطِيعُونِ (١٧٩) وَمَآ أَسْـَٔلُكُمْ عَلَيْهِ مِنْ أَجْرٍ إِنْ أَجْرِىَ إِلَّا عَلَىٰ رَبِّ ٱلْعَٰلَمِينَ (١٨٠) أَوْفُوا۟ ٱلْكَيْلَ وَلَا تَكُونُوا۟ مِنَ ٱلْمُخْسِرِينَ (١٨١) وَزِنُوا۟ بِٱلْقِسْطَاسِ ٱلْمُسْتَقِيمِ (١٨٢) وَلَا تَبْخَسُوا۟ ٱلنَّاسَ أَشْيَآءَهُمْ وَلَا تَعْثَوْا۟ فِى ٱلْأَرْضِ مُفْسِدِينَ (١٨٣) وَٱتَّقُوا۟ ٱلَّذِى خَلَقَكُمْ وَٱلْجِبِلَّةَ ٱلْأَوَّلِينَ (١٨٤) قَالُوٓا۟ إِنَّمَآ أَنتَ مِنَ ٱلْمُسَحَّرِينَ (١٨٥) وَمَآ أَنتَ إِلَّا بَشَرٌ مِّثْلُنَا وَإِن نَّظُنُّكَ لَمِنَ ٱلْكَٰذِبِينَ (١٨٦) فَأَسْقِطْ عَلَيْنَا كِسَفًا مِّنَ ٱلسَّمَآءِ إِن كُنتَ مِنَ ٱلصَّٰدِقِينَ (١٨٧) قَالَ رَبِّىٓ أَعْلَمُ بِمَا تَعْمَلُونَ (١٨٨)

The dwellers of Al-Aikah [near Madyan (Midian)] belied the Messengers. (176) When Shu'âib said to them: "Will you not fear Allâh (and obey Him)? (177) "I am a trustworthy Messenger to you. (178) "So fear Allâh, keep your duty to Him, and obey me. (179) "No reward do I ask of you for it (my Message of Islâmic Monotheism), my reward is only from the Lord of the 'Alamîn (mankind, jinn and all that exists). (180) "Give full measure, and cause no loss (to others). (181) "And weigh with the true and straight balance. (182) "And defraud not people by reducing their things, nor do evil, making corruption and mischief in the land. (183) "And fear Him Who created you and the generations of the men of old." (184) They said: "You are only one of those bewitched! (185) "You are but a human being like us and verily, we think that you are one of the liars! (186) "So cause a piece of the heaven to fall on us, if you are of the truthful!" (187) He said: "My Lord is the Best Knower of what you do." (188)

Quran 11:84-93

﴿۞ وَإِلَىٰ مَدْيَنَ أَخَاهُمْ شُعَيْبًا ۚ قَالَ يَـٰقَوْمِ ٱعْبُدُوا۟ ٱللَّهَ مَا لَكُم مِّنْ إِلَـٰهٍ غَيْرُهُۥ ۖ وَلَا تَنقُصُوا۟ ٱلْمِكْيَالَ وَٱلْمِيزَانَ ۚ إِنِّىٓ أَرَىٰكُم بِخَيْرٍ وَإِنِّىٓ أَخَافُ عَلَيْكُمْ عَذَابَ يَوْمٍ مُّحِيطٍ (٨٤) وَيَـٰقَوْمِ أَوْفُوا۟ ٱلْمِكْيَالَ وَٱلْمِيزَانَ

بِٱلْقِسْطِ وَلَا تَبْخَسُوا۟ ٱلنَّاسَ أَشْيَآءَهُمْ وَلَا تَعْثَوْا۟ فِى ٱلْأَرْضِ مُفْسِدِينَ (٨٥) بَقِيَّتُ ٱللَّهِ خَيْرٌ لَّكُمْ إِن كُنتُم مُّؤْمِنِينَ وَمَآ أَنَا۠ عَلَيْكُم بِحَفِيظٍ (٨٦) قَالُوا۟ يَٰشُعَيْبُ أَصَلَوٰتُكَ تَأْمُرُكَ أَن نَّتْرُكَ مَا يَعْبُدُ ءَابَآؤُنَآ أَوْ أَن نَّفْعَلَ فِىٓ أَمْوَٰلِنَا مَا نَشَٰٓؤُا۟ إِنَّكَ لَأَنتَ ٱلْحَلِيمُ ٱلرَّشِيدُ (٨٧) قَالَ يَٰقَوْمِ أَرَءَيْتُمْ إِن كُنتُ عَلَىٰ بَيِّنَةٍ مِّن رَّبِّى وَرَزَقَنِى مِنْهُ رِزْقًا حَسَنًا وَمَآ أُرِيدُ أَنْ أُخَالِفَكُمْ إِلَىٰ مَآ أَنْهَىٰكُمْ عَنْهُ إِنْ أُرِيدُ إِلَّا ٱلْإِصْلَٰحَ مَا ٱسْتَطَعْتُ وَمَا تَوْفِيقِىٓ إِلَّا بِٱللَّهِ عَلَيْهِ تَوَكَّلْتُ وَإِلَيْهِ أُنِيبُ (٨٨) وَيَٰقَوْمِ لَا يَجْرِمَنَّكُمْ شِقَاقِىٓ أَن يُصِيبَكُم مِّثْلُ مَآ أَصَابَ قَوْمَ نُوحٍ أَوْ قَوْمَ هُودٍ أَوْ قَوْمَ صَٰلِحٍ وَمَا قَوْمُ لُوطٍ مِّنكُم بِبَعِيدٍ (٨٩) وَٱسْتَغْفِرُوا۟ رَبَّكُمْ ثُمَّ تُوبُوٓا۟ إِلَيْهِ إِنَّ رَبِّى رَحِيمٌ وَدُودٌ (٩٠) قَالُوا۟ يَٰشُعَيْبُ مَا نَفْقَهُ كَثِيرًا مِّمَّا تَقُولُ وَإِنَّا لَنَرَىٰكَ فِينَا ضَعِيفًا وَلَوْلَا رَهْطُكَ لَرَجَمْنَٰكَ وَمَآ أَنتَ عَلَيْنَا بِعَزِيزٍ (٩١) قَالَ يَٰقَوْمِ أَرَهْطِىٓ أَعَزُّ عَلَيْكُم مِّنَ ٱللَّهِ وَٱتَّخَذْتُمُوهُ وَرَآءَكُمْ ظِهْرِيًّا إِنَّ رَبِّى بِمَا تَعْمَلُونَ مُحِيطٌ (٩٢) وَيَٰقَوْمِ ٱعْمَلُوا۟ عَلَىٰ مَكَانَتِكُمْ إِنِّى عَٰمِلٌ سَوْفَ تَعْلَمُونَ مَن يَأْتِيهِ عَذَابٌ يُخْزِيهِ وَمَنْ هُوَ كَٰذِبٌ وَٱرْتَقِبُوٓا۟ إِنِّى مَعَكُمْ رَقِيبٌ (٩٣)

And to the Madyan (Midian) people (We sent) their brother Shu'aib. He said: "O my people! Worship Allâh, you have no other ilâh (god) but Him, and give not short measure or weight, I see you in prosperity; and verily I fear for you the torment of a Day encompassing. (84) "And O my people! Give full measure and weight in justice and reduce not the things that are due to the people, and do not commit mischief in the land, causing corruption. (85) "That which is left by Allâh for you (after giving the rights of the people) is better for you, if you are believers. And I am not a guardian over you." (86) They said: "O Shu'aib! Does your Salât (prayer) command that we give up what our fathers used to worship, or that we give up doing what we like with our property? Verily, you are the forbearer, right-minded!" (They said this sarcastically). (87) He said: "O my people! Tell me, if I have a clear evidence from my Lord, and He has given me a good sustenance from Himself (shall I corrupt it by mixing it with the unlawfully earned money). I wish not, in contradiction to you, to do that which I forbid you. I only desire reform to the best of my power. And my guidance cannot come except from Allâh, in Him I trust and unto Him I repent. (88) "And O my people! Let not my Shiqâq cause you to suffer the fate similar to that of the people of Nûh (Noah) or of Hûd or of Sâlih, and the people of Lut (Lot) are not far off from you! (89) "And ask forgiveness of your Lord and turn unto Him in repentance. Verily, my Lord is Most Merciful, Most Loving." (90) They said: "O Shuaib! We do not understand much of what you say, and we see you weak (it is said that he was a blind man) among us. Were it not for your family, we should certainly have stoned you and you are not powerful against us." (91) He said: "O my people! Is then my family of more weight with you than Allâh? And you have cast Him away behind your backs. Verily, my Lord is surrounding all that you do (92) "And O my people! Act according to your ability and way, and I am acting (on my way). You will come to know who it is on whom descends the torment that will cover him with ignominy, and who is a liar! And watch you! Verily, I too am watching with you." (93)

Quran 7:85-93

وَإِلَىٰ مَدْيَنَ أَخَاهُمْ شُعَيْبًا ۗ قَالَ يَـٰقَوْمِ ٱعْبُدُوا۟ ٱللَّهَ مَا لَكُم مِّنْ إِلَـٰهٍ غَيْرُهُ ۖ قَدْ جَآءَتْكُم بَيِّنَةٌ مِّن رَّبِّكُمْ ۖ فَأَوْفُوا۟ ٱلْكَيْلَ وَٱلْمِيزَانَ وَلَا تَبْخَسُوا۟ ٱلنَّاسَ أَشْيَآءَهُمْ وَلَا تُفْسِدُوا۟ فِى ٱلْأَرْضِ بَعْدَ إِصْلَـٰحِهَا ۚ ذَٰلِكُمْ خَيْرٌ لَّكُمْ إِن كُنتُم مُّؤْمِنِينَ (٨٥) وَلَا تَقْعُدُوا۟ بِكُلِّ صِرَٰطٍ تُوعِدُونَ وَتَصُدُّونَ عَن سَبِيلِ ٱللَّهِ مَنْ ءَامَنَ بِهِۦ وَتَبْغُونَهَا عِوَجًا ۚ وَٱذْكُرُوٓا۟ إِذْ كُنتُمْ قَلِيلاً

فَكَثَّرَكُمْ وَٱنظُرُواْ كَيْفَ كَانَ عَٰقِبَةُ ٱلْمُفْسِدِينَ (٨٦) وَإِن كَانَ طَآئِفَةٌ مِّنكُمْ ءَامَنُواْ بِٱلَّذِىٓ أُرْسِلْتُ بِهِۦ وَطَآئِفَةٌ لَّمْ يُؤْمِنُواْ فَٱصْبِرُواْ حَتَّىٰ يَحْكُمَ ٱللَّهُ بَيْنَنَا ۚ وَهُوَ خَيْرُ ٱلْحَٰكِمِينَ (٨٧) ۞ قَالَ ٱلْمَلَأُ ٱلَّذِينَ ٱسْتَكْبَرُواْ مِن قَوْمِهِۦ لَنُخْرِجَنَّكَ يَٰشُعَيْبُ وَٱلَّذِينَ ءَامَنُواْ مَعَكَ مِن قَرْيَتِنَآ أَوْ لَتَعُودُنَّ فِى مِلَّتِنَا ۚ قَالَ أَوَلَوْ كُنَّا كَٰرِهِينَ (٨٨) قَدِ ٱفْتَرَيْنَا عَلَى ٱللَّهِ كَذِبًا إِنْ عُدْنَا فِى مِلَّتِكُم بَعْدَ إِذْ نَجَّىٰنَا ٱللَّهُ مِنْهَا ۚ وَمَا يَكُونُ لَنَآ أَن نَّعُودَ فِيهَآ إِلَّآ أَن يَشَآءَ ٱللَّهُ رَبُّنَا ۚ وَسِعَ رَبُّنَا كُلَّ شَىْءٍ عِلْمًا ۚ عَلَى ٱللَّهِ تَوَكَّلْنَا ۚ رَبَّنَا ٱفْتَحْ بَيْنَنَا وَبَيْنَ قَوْمِنَا بِٱلْحَقِّ وَأَنتَ خَيْرُ ٱلْفَٰتِحِينَ (٨٩) وَقَالَ ٱلْمَلَأُ ٱلَّذِينَ كَفَرُواْ مِن قَوْمِهِۦ لَئِنِ ٱتَّبَعْتُمْ شُعَيْبًا إِنَّكُمْ إِذًا لَّخَٰسِرُونَ (٩٠) فَأَخَذَتْهُمُ ٱلرَّجْفَةُ فَأَصْبَحُواْ فِى دَارِهِمْ جَٰثِمِينَ (٩١) ٱلَّذِينَ كَذَّبُواْ شُعَيْبًا كَأَن لَّمْ يَغْنَوْاْ فِيهَا ۚ ٱلَّذِينَ كَذَّبُواْ شُعَيْبًا كَانُواْ هُمُ ٱلْخَٰسِرِينَ (٩٢) فَتَوَلَّىٰ عَنْهُمْ وَقَالَ يَٰقَوْمِ لَقَدْ أَبْلَغْتُكُمْ رِسَٰلَٰتِ رَبِّى وَنَصَحْتُ لَكُمْ ۖ فَكَيْفَ ءَاسَىٰ عَلَىٰ قَوْمٍ كَٰفِرِينَ (٩٣)

And to (the people of) Madyan (Midian), (We sent) their brother Shu'aib. He said: "O my people! Worship Allâh! You have no other Ilâh

(God) but Him. [Lâ ilâha ill-allâh (none has the right to be worshipped but Allâh)]." Verily, a clear proof (sign) from your Lord has come unto you; so give full measure and full weight and wrong not men in their things, and do not mischief on the earth after it has been set in order, that will be better for you, if you are believers. (85) "And sit not on every road, threatening, and hindering from the Path of Allâh those who believe in Him. and seeking to make it crooked. And remember when you were but few, and He multiplied you. And see what was the end of the Mufsidûn (mischief-makers, corrupters, liars). (86) "And if there is a party of you who believes in that with which I have been sent and a party who do not believe, so be patient until Allâh judges between us, and He is the Best of judges." (87) The chiefs of those who were arrogant among his people said: "We shall certainly drive you out, O Shu'aib, and those who have believed with you from our town, or else you (all) shall return to our religion." He said: "Even though we hate it?". (88) "We should have invented a lie against Allâh if we returned to your religion, after Allâh has rescued us from it. And it is not for us to return to it unless Allâh, our Lord, should will. Our Lord comprehends all things in His Knowledge. In Allâh (Alone) we put our trust. Our Lord! Judge between us and our people in truth, for You are the Best of those who give judgment." (89) The chiefs of those who disbelieved among his people said (to their people): "If you follow Shu'aib, be sure then you will be the losers!" (90) So the earthquake seized them and they lay (dead), prostrate in their homes (91) Those who belied Shu'aib, became as if they had never dwelt there (in their homes). Those who belied Shu'aib, they were the losers. (92)

Then he (Shu'aib) turned from them and said: "O my people! I have indeed conveyed my Lord's Messages unto you and I have given you good advice. Then how can I sorrow for the disbelieving people's (destruction)." (93)

Quran 79:15-19

هَلْ أَتَىٰكَ حَدِيثُ مُوسَىٰٓ (١٥) إِذْ نَادَىٰهُ رَبُّهُ بِٱلْوَادِ ٱلْمُقَدَّسِ طُوًى (١٦) ٱذْهَبْ إِلَىٰ فِرْعَوْنَ إِنَّهُۥ طَغَىٰ (١٧) فَقُلْ هَل لَّكَ إِلَىٰٓ أَن تَزَكَّىٰ (١٨) وَأَهْدِيَكَ إِلَىٰ رَبِّكَ فَتَخْشَىٰ (١٩)

Has there come to you the story of Mûsa (Moses)? (15) When his Lord called him in the sacred valley of Tûwa. (16) Go to Fir'aun (Pharaoh), verily, he has transgressed all bounds (in crimes, sins, polytheism, disbelief). (17) And say to him: "Would you purify yourself (from the sin of disbelief by becoming a believer)", (18) And that I guide you to your Lord, so you should fear Him? (19)

قَالَ لَا تَخَافَآ إِنَّنِى مَعَكُمَآ أَسْمَعُ وَأَرَىٰ (٤٦) فَأْتِيَاهُ
فَقُولَآ إِنَّا رَسُولَا رَبِّكَ فَأَرْسِلْ مَعَنَا بَنِىٓ إِسْرَٰٓءِيلَ وَلَا
تُعَذِّبْهُمْ قَدْ جِئْنَٰكَ بِـَٔايَةٍ مِّن رَّبِّكَ وَٱلسَّلَٰمُ عَلَىٰ مَنِ ٱتَّبَعَ
ٱلْهُدَىٰٓ (٤٧) إِنَّا قَدْ أُوحِىَ إِلَيْنَآ أَنَّ ٱلْعَذَابَ عَلَىٰ مَن
كَذَّبَ وَتَوَلَّىٰ (٤٨) قَالَ فَمَن رَّبُّكُمَا يَٰمُوسَىٰ
(٤٩) قَالَ رَبُّنَا ٱلَّذِىٓ أَعْطَىٰ كُلَّ شَىْءٍ خَلْقَهُۥ ثُمَّ هَدَىٰ
(٥٠) قَالَ فَمَا بَالُ ٱلْقُرُونِ ٱلْأُولَىٰ (٥١) قَالَ عِلْمُهَا
عِندَ رَبِّى فِى كِتَٰبٍ لَّا يَضِلُّ رَبِّى وَلَا يَنسَى
(٥٢) ٱلَّذِى جَعَلَ لَكُمُ ٱلْأَرْضَ مَهْدًا وَسَلَكَ لَكُمْ فِيهَا
سُبُلًا وَأَنزَلَ مِنَ ٱلسَّمَآءِ مَآءً فَأَخْرَجْنَا بِهِۦٓ أَزْوَٰجًا مِّن
نَّبَاتٍ شَتَّىٰ (٥٣) كُلُوا۟ وَٱرْعَوْا۟ أَنْعَٰمَكُمْ إِنَّ فِى ذَٰلِكَ
لَءَايَٰتٍ لِّأُو۟لِى ٱلنُّهَىٰ (٥٤) ۞ مِنْهَا خَلَقْنَٰكُمْ وَفِيهَا
نُعِيدُكُمْ وَمِنْهَا نُخْرِجُكُمْ تَارَةً أُخْرَىٰ (٥٥) وَلَقَدْ أَرَيْنَٰهُ
ءَايَٰتِنَا كُلَّهَا فَكَذَّبَ وَأَبَىٰ (٥٦) قَالَ أَجِئْتَنَا لِتُخْرِجَنَا
مِنْ أَرْضِنَا بِسِحْرِكَ يَٰمُوسَىٰ (٥٧) فَلَنَأْتِيَنَّكَ بِسِحْرٍ
مِّثْلِهِۦ فَٱجْعَلْ بَيْنَنَا وَبَيْنَكَ مَوْعِدًا لَّا نُخْلِفُهُۥ نَحْنُ وَلَآ
أَنتَ مَكَانًا سُوًى (٥٨) قَالَ مَوْعِدُكُمْ يَوْمُ ٱلزِّينَةِ وَأَن
يُحْشَرَ ٱلنَّاسُ ضُحًى (٥٩) فَتَوَلَّىٰ فِرْعَوْنُ فَجَمَعَ
كَيْدَهُۥ ثُمَّ أَتَىٰ (٦٠) قَالَ لَهُم مُّوسَىٰ وَيْلَكُمْ لَا تَفْتَرُوا۟
عَلَى ٱللَّهِ كَذِبًا فَيُسْحِتَكُم بِعَذَابٍ وَقَدْ خَابَ مَنِ ٱفْتَرَىٰ

فَتَنَزَعُوٓاْ أَمْرَهُم بَيْنَهُمْ وَأَسَرُّواْ ٱلنَّجْوَىٰ (٦١) قَالُوٓاْ إِنْ هَٰذَانِ لَسَٰحِرَانِ يُرِيدَانِ أَن يُخْرِجَاكُم مِّنْ أَرْضِكُم بِسِحْرِهِمَا وَيَذْهَبَا بِطَرِيقَتِكُمُ ٱلْمُثْلَىٰ (٦٢) فَأَجْمِعُواْ كَيْدَكُمْ ثُمَّ ٱئْتُواْ صَفًّا وَقَدْ أَفْلَحَ ٱلْيَوْمَ مَنِ ٱسْتَعْلَىٰ (٦٣) قَالُواْ يَٰمُوسَىٰٓ إِمَّآ أَن تُلْقِيَ وَإِمَّآ أَن نَّكُونَ أَوَّلَ مَنْ أَلْقَىٰ (٦٥) قَالَ بَلْ أَلْقُواْ فَإِذَا حِبَالُهُمْ وَعِصِيُّهُمْ يُخَيَّلُ إِلَيْهِ مِن سِحْرِهِمْ أَنَّهَا تَسْعَىٰ (٦٦)

He (Allâh) said: "Fear not, verily! I am with you both, hearing and seeing. (46) "So go you both to him, and say: 'Verily, we are Messengers of your Lord, so let the Children of Israel go with us, and torment them not; indeed, we have come with a sign from your Lord! And peace will be upon him who follows the guidance! (47) 'Truly, it has been revealed to us that the torment will be for him who denies [believes not in the Oneness of Allâh, and in His Messengers], and turns away.'(from the truth and obedience of Allâh)" (48) Fir'aun (Pharaoh) said: "Who then, O

Mûsa (Moses), is the Lord of you two?"
(49) [Mûsa (Moses)] said: "Our Lord is
He Who gave to each thing its form and
nature, then guided it aright." (50)
[Fir'aun (Pharaoh)] said: "What about
the generations of old?" (51) [Mûsa
(Moses)] said: "The knowledge thereof is
with my Lord, in a Record. My Lord is
neither unaware nor He forgets, " (52)
Who has made earth for you like a bed
(spread out); and has opened roads
(ways and paths etc.) for you therein;
and has sent down water (rain) from the
sky. And We have brought forth with it
various kinds of vegetation. (53) Eat and
pasture your cattle, (therein); verily, in
this are Ayat (proofs and signs) for men
of understanding (54) Thereof (the
earth) We created you, and into it We
shall return you, and from it We shall
bring you out once again. (55) And
indeed We showed him [Fir'aun
(Pharaoh)] all Our Ayat (Signs and

Evidences), but he denied and refused.
(56) He [Fir'aun (Pharaoh)] said: "Have
you come to drive us out of our land
with your magic, O Mûsa (Moses)? (57)
"Then verily, we can produce magic the
like thereof; so appoint a meeting
between us and you, which neither we,
nor you shall fail to keep, in an open
wide place where both shall have a just
and equal chance (and beholders could
witness the competition)." (58) [Mûsa
(Moses)] said: "Your appointed meeting
is the day of the festival, and let the
people assemble when the sun has risen
(forenoon)." (59) So Fir'aun (Pharaoh)
withdrew, devised his plot and then
came back. (60) Mûsa (Moses) said to
them: "Woe unto you! Invent not a lie
against Allâh, lest He should destroy
you completely by a torment. And
surely, he who invents a lie (against
Allâh) will fail miserably." (61) Then
they debated one with another what

they must do, and they kept their talk secret. (62) They said: "Verily! these are two magicians. Their object is to drive you out from your land with magic, and overcome your chiefs and nobles. (63) "So devise your plot, and then assemble in line. And whoever overcomes this day will be indeed successful." (64) They said: "O Mûsa (Moses)! Either you throw first or we be the first to throw?" (65) [Mûsa (Moses)] said: "Nay, throw you (first)!" Then behold, their ropes and their sticks, by their magic, appeared to him as though they moved fast. (66)

Quran 43:46-50

وَلَقَدْ أَرْسَلْنَا مُوسَىٰ بِـَٔايَـٰتِنَآ إِلَىٰ فِرْعَوْنَ وَمَلَإِيْهِۦ فَقَالَ إِنِّى رَسُولُ رَبِّ ٱلْعَـٰلَمِينَ (٤٦) فَلَمَّا جَآءَهُم بِـَٔايَـٰتِنَآ إِذَا هُم مِّنْهَا يَضْحَكُونَ (٤٧) وَمَا نُرِيهِم مِّنْ ءَايَةٍ إِلَّا هِىَ أَكْبَرُ مِنْ أُخْتِهَاۖ وَأَخَذْنَـٰهُم بِٱلْعَذَابِ لَعَلَّهُمْ يَرْجِعُونَ (٤٨) وَقَالُوا۟ يَـٰٓأَيُّهَ ٱلسَّاحِرُ ٱدْعُ لَنَا رَبَّكَ بِمَا

عَهِدَ عِندَكَ إِنَّنَا لَمُهْتَدُونَ ﴿٤٩﴾ فَلَمَّا كَشَفْنَا عَنْهُمُ
ٱلْعَذَابَ إِذَا هُمْ يَنكُثُونَ ﴿٥٠﴾

And indeed We did send Mûsa (Moses)
with Our Ayât (proofs, evidences,
verses, lessons, signs, revelations, etc.)
to Fir'aun (Pharaoh) and his chiefs
(inviting them to Allâh's religion of
Islâm) He said: "Verily, I am a
Messenger of the Lord of the 'Alamîn
(mankind, jinn and all that exists)." (46)
But when he came to them with Our
Ayât (proofs, evidences, verses, lessons,
signs, revelations) behold, they laughed
at them. (47) And not an Ayâh (sign,
etc.) We showed them but it was greater
than its fellow, and We seized them
with torment, in order that they might
turn [from their polytheism to Allâh's
religion (Islâmic Monotheism)]. (48)
And they said [to Mûsa (Moses)]: "O
you sorcerer! Invoke your Lord for us
according to what He has covenanted

with you. Verily, We shall guide ourselves (aright)." (49) But when We removed the torment from them, behold, they broke their covenant (that they will believe if We remove the torment from them). (50)

Quran 17:101-102

وَلَقَدْ ءَاتَيْنَا مُوسَىٰ تِسْعَ ءَايَـٰتٍ بَيِّنَـٰتٍ فَسْـَٔلْ بَنِىٓ إِسْرَٰٓءِيلَ إِذْ جَاءَهُمْ فَقَالَ لَهُۥ فِرْعَوْنُ إِنِّى لَأَظُنُّكَ يَـٰمُوسَىٰ مَسْحُورًا (١٠١) قَالَ لَقَدْ عَلِمْتَ مَآ أَنزَلَ هَـٰٓؤُلَآءِ إِلَّا رَبُّ ٱلسَّمَـٰوَٰتِ وَٱلْأَرْضِ بَصَآئِرَ وَإِنِّى لَأَظُنُّكَ يَـٰفِرْعَوْنُ مَثْبُورًا (١٠٢)

And indeed We gave Mûsa (Moses) nine clear signs. Ask then the Children of Israel, when he came to them, then Fir'aun (Pharaoh) said to him: "O Mûsa (Moses)! I think you are indeed bewitched." (101) [Mûsa (Moses)] said: "Verily, you know that these signs have been sent down by none but the Lord of the heavens and the earth (as clear evidences i.e. proofs of Allâh's Oneness and His Omnipotence). And I think you are, indeed, O Fir'aun (Pharaoh) doomed to destruction (away from all good)!" (102)

Quran 26:15-62

قَالَ كَلَّا ۖ فَٱذْهَبَا بِـَٔايَـٰتِنَآ ۖ إِنَّا مَعَكُم مُّسْتَمِعُونَ (١٥) فَأْتِيَا فِرْعَوْنَ فَقُولَآ إِنَّا رَسُولُ رَبِّ ٱلْعَـٰلَمِينَ (١٦) أَنْ أَرْسِلْ مَعَنَا بَنِىٓ إِسْرَٰٓءِيلَ (١٧) قَالَ أَلَمْ نُرَبِّكَ فِينَا وَلِيدًا وَلَبِثْتَ فِينَا مِنْ عُمُرِكَ سِنِينَ (١٨) وَفَعَلْتَ فَعْلَتَكَ ٱلَّتِى فَعَلْتَ وَأَنتَ مِنَ ٱلْكَـٰفِرِينَ (١٩) قَالَ فَعَلْتُهَآ إِذًا وَأَنَا۠ مِنَ ٱلضَّآلِّينَ (٢٠) فَفَرَرْتُ مِنكُمْ لَمَّا خِفْتُكُمْ فَوَهَبَ لِى رَبِّى حُكْمًا وَجَعَلَنِى مِنَ ٱلْمُرْسَلِينَ (٢١) وَتِلْكَ نِعْمَةٌ تَمُنُّهَا عَلَىَّ أَنْ عَبَّدتَّ بَنِىٓ إِسْرَٰٓءِيلَ (٢٢) قَالَ فِرْعَوْنُ وَمَا رَبُّ ٱلْعَـٰلَمِينَ (٢٣) قَالَ رَبُّ ٱلسَّمَـٰوَٰتِ وَٱلْأَرْضِ وَمَا بَيْنَهُمَآ ۖ إِن كُنتُم مُّوقِنِينَ (٢٤) قَالَ لِمَنْ حَوْلَهُۥٓ أَلَا تَسْتَمِعُونَ (٢٥) قَالَ رَبُّكُمْ وَرَبُّ ءَابَآئِكُمُ ٱلْأَوَّلِينَ (٢٦) قَالَ إِنَّ رَسُولَكُمُ ٱلَّذِىٓ أُرْسِلَ إِلَيْكُمْ لَمَجْنُونٌ (٢٧) قَالَ رَبُّ ٱلْمَشْرِقِ وَٱلْمَغْرِبِ وَمَا بَيْنَهُمَآ ۖ إِن كُنتُمْ تَعْقِلُونَ (٢٨) قَالَ لَئِنِ ٱتَّخَذْتَ إِلَـٰهًا غَيْرِى لَأَجْعَلَنَّكَ مِنَ ٱلْمَسْجُونِينَ

121

(٢٩) قَالَ أَوَلَوْ جِئْتُكَ بِشَىْءٍ مُّبِينٍ (٣٠) قَالَ فَأْتِ بِهِ
إِن كُنتَ مِنَ ٱلصَّٰدِقِينَ (٣١) فَأَلْقَىٰ عَصَاهُ فَإِذَا هِىَ
ثُعْبَانٌ مُّبِينٌ (٣٢) وَنَزَعَ يَدَهُ فَإِذَا هِىَ بَيْضَآءُ
لِلنَّٰظِرِينَ (٣٣) قَالَ لِلْمَلَإِ حَوْلَهُ إِنَّ هَٰذَا لَسَٰحِرٌ
عَلِيمٌ (٣٤) يُرِيدُ أَن يُخْرِجَكُم مِّنْ أَرْضِكُم بِسِحْرِهِ
فَمَاذَا تَأْمُرُونَ (٣٥) قَالُوٓاْ أَرْجِهْ وَأَخَاهُ وَٱبْعَثْ فِى
ٱلْمَدَآئِنِ حَٰشِرِينَ (٣٦) يَأْتُوكَ بِكُلِّ سَحَّارٍ عَلِيمٍ
(٣٧) فَجُمِعَ ٱلسَّحَرَةُ لِمِيقَٰتِ يَوْمٍ مَّعْلُومٍ (٣٨) وَقِيلَ
لِلنَّاسِ هَلْ أَنتُم مُّجْتَمِعُونَ (٣٩) لَعَلَّنَا نَتَّبِعُ ٱلسَّحَرَةَ
إِن كَانُواْ هُمُ ٱلْغَٰلِبِينَ (٤٠) فَلَمَّا جَآءَ ٱلسَّحَرَةُ قَالُواْ
لِفِرْعَوْنَ أَئِنَّ لَنَا لَأَجْرًا إِن كُنَّا نَحْنُ ٱلْغَٰلِبِينَ
(٤١) قَالَ نَعَمْ وَإِنَّكُمْ إِذًا لَّمِنَ ٱلْمُقَرَّبِينَ (٤٢) قَالَ لَهُم
مُّوسَىٰٓ أَلْقُواْ مَآ أَنتُم مُّلْقُونَ (٤٣) فَأَلْقَوْاْ حِبَالَهُمْ
وَعِصِيَّهُمْ وَقَالُواْ بِعِزَّةِ فِرْعَوْنَ إِنَّا لَنَحْنُ ٱلْغَٰلِبُونَ
(٤٤) فَأَلْقَىٰ مُوسَىٰ عَصَاهُ فَإِذَا هِىَ تَلْقَفُ مَا يَأْفِكُونَ
(٤٥) فَأُلْقِىَ ٱلسَّحَرَةُ سَٰجِدِينَ (٤٦) قَالُوٓاْ ءَامَنَّا بِرَبِّ
ٱلْعَٰلَمِينَ (٤٧) رَبِّ مُوسَىٰ وَهَٰرُونَ (٤٨) قَالَ
ءَامَنتُمْ لَهُ قَبْلَ أَنْ ءَاذَنَ لَكُمْ إِنَّهُ لَكَبِيرُكُمُ ٱلَّذِى عَلَّمَكُمُ
ٱلسِّحْرَ فَلَسَوْفَ تَعْلَمُونَ لَأُقَطِّعَنَّ أَيْدِيَكُمْ وَأَرْجُلَكُم مِّنْ
خِلَٰفٍ وَلَأُصَلِّبَنَّكُمْ أَجْمَعِينَ (٤٩) قَالُواْ لَا ضَيْرَ إِنَّآ
إِلَىٰ رَبِّنَا مُنقَلِبُونَ (٥٠) إِنَّا نَطْمَعُ أَن يَغْفِرَ لَنَا رَبُّنَا

خَطَـٰیَـٰنَآ أَن كُنَّآ أَوَّلَ ٱلْمُؤْمِنِینَ ﴿٥١﴾ ۞ وَأَوْحَیْنَآ إِلَىٰ مُوسَىٰٓ أَنْ أَسْرِ بِعِبَادِىٓ إِنَّكُم مُّتَّبَعُونَ ﴿٥٢﴾ فَأَرْسَلَ فِرْعَوْنُ فِى ٱلْمَدَآئِنِ حَـٰشِرِینَ ﴿٥٣﴾ إِنَّ هَـٰٓؤُلَآءِ لَشِرْذِمَةٌ قَلِیلُونَ ﴿٥٤﴾ وَإِنَّهُمْ لَنَا لَغَآئِظُونَ ﴿٥٥﴾ وَإِنَّا لَجَمِیعٌ حَـٰذِرُونَ ﴿٥٦﴾ فَأَخْرَجْنَـٰهُم مِّن جَنَّـٰتٍ وَعُیُونٍ ﴿٥٧﴾ وَكُنُوزٍ وَمَقَامٍ كَرِیمٍ ﴿٥٨﴾ كَذَٰلِكَ وَأَوْرَثْنَـٰهَا بَنِىٓ إِسْرَٰٓءِیلَ ﴿٥٩﴾ فَأَتْبَعُوهُم مُّشْرِقِینَ ﴿٦٠﴾ فَلَمَّا تَرَٰٓءَا ٱلْجَمْعَانِ قَالَ أَصْحَـٰبُ مُوسَىٰٓ إِنَّا لَمُدْرَكُونَ ﴿٦١﴾ قَالَ كَلَّآ ۖ إِنَّ مَعِىَ رَبِّى سَیَهْدِینِ ﴿٦٢﴾

(Allâh) said: "Nay! Go you both with Our Signs. Verily! We shall be with you, listening. (15) "And go both of you to Fir'aun (Pharaoh), and say: 'We are the Messengers of the Lord of the 'Alamîn (mankind, jinn and all that exists), (16) "So allow the Children of Israel to go with us.' " (17) [Fir'aun (Pharaoh)] said [to Mûsa (Moses)]: "Did we not bring you up among us as a child? And you did dwell many years of your life with us. (18) "And you did your deed, which

you did (i.e. the crime of killing a man).
And you are one of the ingrates." (19)
Mûsa (Moses) said: "I did it then, when I
was an ignorant (as regards my Lord
and His Message). (20) "So I fled from
you when I feared you. But my Lord has
granted me Hukm (i.e. religious
knowledge, right judgement of the
affairs and Prophethood), and
appointed me one of the Messengers.
(21) "And this is the past favor with
which you reproach me, that you have
enslaved the Children of Israel." (22)
[Fir'aun (Pharaoh)] said: "And what is
the Lord of the 'Alamîn (mankind, jinn
and all that exists)?" (23) [Mûsa (Moses)]
said: "The Lord of the heavens and the
earth, and all that is between them, if
you seek to be convinced with
certainty." (24) [Fir'aun (Pharaoh)] said
to those around: "Do you not hear (what
he says)?" (25) [Mûsa (Moses)] said:
"Your Lord and the Lord of your ancient

fathers!" (26) [Fir'aun (Pharaoh)] said: "Verily, your Messenger who has been sent to you is a madman!" (27) [Mûsa (Moses)] said: "Lord of the east and the west, and all that is between them, if you did but understand!" (28) [Fir'aun (Pharaoh)] said: "If you choose an ilâh (god) other than me, I will certainly put you among the prisoners." (29) [Mûsa (Moses)] said: "Even if I bring you something manifest (and convincing)?" (30) [Fir'aun (Pharaoh)] said: "Bring it forth then, if you are of the truthful!" (31) So [Mûsa (Moses)] threw his stick, and behold, it was a serpent, manifest (32) And he drew out his hand, and behold, it was white to all beholders! (33) [Fir'aun (Pharaoh)] said to the chiefs around him: "Verily! This is indeed a well-versed sorcerer. (34) "He wants to drive you out of your land by his sorcery: what is it then that you command?" (35) They said: "Put him off and his brother (for a while), and send callers to the cities; (36) "To bring up to you every well-versed sorcerer." (37) So the sorcerers were assembled at a fixed time on a day appointed (38) And it was said to the people: "Are you (too) going to assemble? (39) "That we may follow the sorcerers [who were on Fir'aun's (Pharaoh) religion of disbelief] if they are the winners." (40) So when the sorcerers arrived, they said to Fir'aun (Pharaoh): "Will there surely be a reward for us if we are the winners?" (41) He said: "Yes, and you shall then verily be of those brought near (to myself)." (42) Mûsa (Moses) said to them: "Throw what you are going to throw!" (43) So they threw their ropes and their sticks, and said: "By the might of Fir'aun (Pharaoh), it is we who will certainly win!" (44) Then Mûsa (Moses) threw his stick, and behold, it swallowed up all that they falsely showed! (45) And the sorcerers fell down prostrate. (46) Saying: "We believe in the Lord of the 'Alamîn (mankind, jinn and all that exists). (47) "The Lord of Mûsa (Moses) and Hârûn (Aaron)." (48) [Fir'aun (Pharaoh)] said: "You have believed in him before I give you leave. Surely, he indeed is your chief, who has taught you magic! So verily, you shall come to know. Verily, I will cut off your hands and your feet on opposite sides, and I will crucify you all." (49) They said: "No harm! Surely, to our Lord (Allâh) we are to return; (50) "Verily! We really hope that our Lord will forgive us our sins, as we are the first of the believers [in Mûsa (Moses) and in the Monotheism which he has brought from Allâh]." (51) And We revealed to Mûsa (Moses), saying: "Depart by night with My slaves , verily, you will be pursued." (52) Then Fir'aun (Pharaoh) sent callers to (all) the cities. (53) (Saying): "Verily!

these indeed are but a small band. (54) "And verily, they have done what has enraged us; (55) "But we are host all assembled, amply fore-warned." (56) So, We expelled them from gardens and springs, (57) Treasures, and every kind of honorable place. (58) Thus [We turned them (Pharaoh's people) out] and We caused the Children of Israel to inherit them. (59) So they pursued them at sunrise. (60) And when the two hosts saw each other, the companions of Mûsa (Moses) said: "We are sure to be overtaken." (61) [Mûsa (Moses)] said: "Nay, verily! With me is my Lord, He will guide me." (62)

Quran 28:36-37

فَلَمَّا جَآءَهُم مُّوسَىٰ بِـَٔايَـٰتِنَا بَيِّنَـٰتٍ قَالُوا۟ مَا هَـٰذَآ إِلَّا سِحْرٌ مُّفْتَرًى وَمَا سَمِعْنَا بِهَـٰذَا فِىٓ ءَابَآئِنَا ٱلْأَوَّلِينَ (٣٦) وَقَالَ مُوسَىٰ رَبِّىٓ أَعْلَمُ بِمَن جَآءَ بِٱلْهُدَىٰ مِنْ

عِندِهِ وَمَن تَكُونُ لَهُ عَـٰقِبَةُ ٱلدَّارِ ۗ إِنَّهُ لَا يُفْلِحُ ٱلظَّـٰلِمُونَ (٣٧)

Then when Mûsa (Moses) came to them with Our Clear Ayât (proofs, evidences, verses, lessons, signs, revelations, etc.), they said: "This is nothing but invented magic. Never did we hear of this among our fathers of old." (36) Mûsa (Moses) said: "My Lord knows best him who came with guidance from Him, and whose will be the happy end in the Hereafter. Verily, the Zâlimûn (wrong-doers, polytheists and disbelievers in the Oneness of Allâh) will not be successful." (37)

Quran 40:26-27

وَقَالَ فِرْعَوْنُ ذَرُونِىٓ أَقْتُلْ مُوسَىٰ وَلْيَدْعُ رَبَّهُ ۖ إِنِّىٓ أَخَافُ أَن يُبَدِّلَ دِينَكُمْ أَوْ أَن يُظْهِرَ فِى ٱلْأَرْضِ ٱلْفَسَادَ (٢٦) وَقَالَ مُوسَىٰٓ إِنِّى عُذْتُ بِرَبِّى وَرَبِّكُم مِّن كُلِّ مُتَكَبِّرٍ لَّا يُؤْمِنُ بِيَوْمِ ٱلْحِسَابِ (٢٧)

Fir'aun (Pharaoh) said: "Leave me to kill Mûsa (Moses), and let him call his Lord (to stop me from killing him)! I fear that he may change your religion, or that he may cause mischief to appear in the land!" (26) Mûsa (Moses) said: "Verily, I seek refuge in my Lord and your Lord from every arrogant who believes not in the Day of Reckoning!" (27)

Quran 44:17-22

۞ وَلَقَدْ فَتَنَّا قَبْلَهُمْ قَوْمَ فِرْعَوْنَ وَجَآءَهُمْ رَسُولٌ كَرِيمٌ (١٧) أَنْ أَدُّوٓاْ إِلَىَّ عِبَادَ ٱللَّهِ إِنِّى لَكُمْ رَسُولٌ أَمِينٌ (١٨) وَأَن لَّا تَعْلُواْ عَلَى ٱللَّهِ إِنِّىٓ ءَاتِيكُم بِسُلْطَٰنٍ مُّبِينٍ (١٩) وَإِنِّى عُذْتُ بِرَبِّى وَرَبِّكُمْ أَن تَرْجُمُونِ (٢٠) وَإِن لَّمْ تُؤْمِنُواْ لِى فَٱعْتَزِلُونِ (٢١) فَدَعَا رَبَّهُۥٓ أَنَّ هَٰٓؤُلَآءِ قَوْمٌ مُّجْرِمُونَ (٢٢)

And indeed We tried before them Fir'aun's (Pharaoh) people, when there came to them a noble Messenger [i.e. Mûsa (Moses)], (17) Saying: "Deliver to me the slaves of Allâh (i.e. the Children

of Israel). Verily! I am to you a
Messenger worthy of all trust, (18) "And
exalt not yourselves against Allâh.
Truly, I have come to you with a
manifest authority. (19) "And truly, I
seek refuge with my Lord and your
Lord, lest you should stone me (or call
me a sorcerer or kill me). (20) "But if you
believe me not, then keep away from me
and leave me alone." (21) (But they were
aggressive), so he [Mûsa (Moses)] called
upon his Lord (saying): "These are
indeed the people who are Mujrimûn
(disbelievers, polytheists, sinners,
criminals)." (22)

Quran 10:75-89

ثُمَّ بَعَثْنَا مِنۢ بَعْدِهِم مُّوسَىٰ وَهَٰرُونَ إِلَىٰ فِرْعَوْنَ
وَمَلَإِيْهِۦ بِـَٔايَٰتِنَا فَٱسْتَكْبَرُوا۟ وَكَانُوا۟ قَوْمًا مُّجْرِمِينَ
(٧٥) فَلَمَّا جَآءَهُمُ ٱلْحَقُّ مِنْ عِندِنَا قَالُوٓا۟ إِنَّ هَٰذَا
لَسِحْرٌ مُّبِينٌ (٧٦) قَالَ مُوسَىٰٓ أَتَقُولُونَ لِلْحَقِّ لَمَّا
جَآءَكُمْ أَسِحْرٌ هَٰذَا وَلَا يُفْلِحُ ٱلسَّٰحِرُونَ (٧٧) قَالُوٓا۟

أَجِئْتَنَا لِتَلْفِتَنَا عَمَّا وَجَدْنَا عَلَيْهِ ءَابَآءَنَا وَتَكُونَ لَكُمَا
الْكِبْرِيَآءُ فِى الْأَرْضِ وَمَا نَحْنُ لَكُمَا بِمُؤْمِنِينَ
(٧٨) وَقَالَ فِرْعَوْنُ ائْتُونِى بِكُلِّ سَٰحِرٍ عَلِيمٍ
(٧٩) فَلَمَّا جَآءَ السَّحَرَةُ قَالَ لَهُم مُّوسَىٰٓ أَلْقُوا۟ مَآ أَنتُم
مُّلْقُونَ (٨٠) فَلَمَّآ أَلْقَوْا۟ قَالَ مُوسَىٰ مَا جِئْتُم بِهِ السِّحْرُ
إِنَّ اللَّهَ سَيُبْطِلُهُۥٓ إِنَّ اللَّهَ لَا يُصْلِحُ عَمَلَ الْمُفْسِدِينَ
(٨١) وَيُحِقُّ اللَّهُ الْحَقَّ بِكَلِمَٰتِهِۦ وَلَوْ كَرِهَ الْمُجْرِمُونَ
(٨٢) فَمَآ ءَامَنَ لِمُوسَىٰٓ إِلَّا ذُرِّيَّةٌ مِّن قَوْمِهِۦ عَلَىٰ
خَوْفٍ مِّن فِرْعَوْنَ وَمَلَإِيْهِمْ أَن يَفْتِنَهُمْ وَإِنَّ فِرْعَوْنَ
لَعَالٍ فِى الْأَرْضِ وَإِنَّهُۥ لَمِنَ الْمُسْرِفِينَ (٨٣) وَقَالَ
مُوسَىٰ يَٰقَوْمِ إِن كُنتُمْ ءَامَنتُم بِاللَّهِ فَعَلَيْهِ تَوَكَّلُوا۟ إِن
كُنتُم مُّسْلِمِينَ (٨٤) فَقَالُوا۟ عَلَى اللَّهِ تَوَكَّلْنَا رَبَّنَا لَا
تَجْعَلْنَا فِتْنَةً لِّلْقَوْمِ الظَّٰلِمِينَ (٨٥) وَنَجِّنَا بِرَحْمَتِكَ مِنَ
الْقَوْمِ الْكَٰفِرِينَ (٨٦) وَأَوْحَيْنَآ إِلَىٰ مُوسَىٰ وَأَخِيهِ أَن
تَبَوَّءَا لِقَوْمِكُمَا بِمِصْرَ بُيُوتًا وَاجْعَلُوا۟ بُيُوتَكُمْ قِبْلَةً
وَأَقِيمُوا۟ الصَّلَوٰةَ وَبَشِّرِ الْمُؤْمِنِينَ (٨٧) وَقَالَ مُوسَىٰ
رَبَّنَآ إِنَّكَ ءَاتَيْتَ فِرْعَوْنَ وَمَلَأَهُۥ زِينَةً وَأَمْوَٰلًا فِى
الْحَيَوٰةِ الدُّنْيَا رَبَّنَا لِيُضِلُّوا۟ عَن سَبِيلِكَ رَبَّنَا اطْمِسْ
عَلَىٰٓ أَمْوَٰلِهِمْ وَاشْدُدْ عَلَىٰ قُلُوبِهِمْ فَلَا يُؤْمِنُوا۟ حَتَّىٰ
يَرَوُا۟ الْعَذَابَ الْأَلِيمَ (٨٨) قَالَ قَدْ أُجِيبَت دَّعْوَتُكُمَا
فَاسْتَقِيمَا وَلَا تَتَّبِعَآنِّ سَبِيلَ الَّذِينَ لَا يَعْلَمُونَ (٨٩)

Then after them We sent Mûsa (Moses) and Hârûn (Aaron) to Fir'aun (Pharaoh) and his chiefs with Our Ayât (proofs, evidences, verses, lessons, signs, revelations, etc.). But they behaved arrogantly and were Mujrimûn (disbelievers, sinners, polytheists, criminals, etc.) folk. (75) So when came to them the truth from Us, they said: "This is indeed clear magic." (76) Mûsa (Moses) said: "Say you (this) about the truth when it has come to you? Is this magic? But the magicians will never be successful." (77) They said: "Have you come to us to turn us away from that (Faith) we found our fathers following, - and that you two may have greatness in the land? We are not going to believe you two!" (78) And Fir'aun (Pharaoh) said: "Bring me every well-versed sorcerer." (79) And when the sorcerers came, Mûsa (Moses) said to them: "Cast down what you want to cast!" (80) Then when they had cast down, Mûsa (Moses) said: "What you have brought is sorcery, Allâh will surely make it of no effect. Verily, Allâh does not set right the work of Al-Mufsidûn (the evil-doers, corrupters). (81) "And Allâh will establish and make apparent the truth by His Words, however much the Mujrimûn (criminals, disbelievers, polytheists, sinners) may hate it." (82) But none believed in Mûsa (Moses) except the offspring of his people, because of the fear of Fir'aun (Pharaoh) and his chiefs, lest they should persecute them; and verily, Fir'aun (Pharaoh) was an arrogant tyrant on the earth, he was indeed one of the Musrifûn (polytheists, sinners and transgressors, those who give up the truth and follow the evil, and commit all kinds of great sins). (83) And Mûsa (Moses) said: "O my people! If you have believed in Allâh, then put your trust in

Him if you are Muslims (those who submit to Allâh's Will)." (84) They said: "In Allâh we put our trust. Our Lord! Make us not a trial for the folk who are Zâlimûn (polytheists and wrong-doing) (i.e. do not make them overpower us) (85) "And save us by Your Mercy from the disbelieving folk." (86) And We revealed to Mûsa (Moses) and his brother (saying): "Provide dwellings for your people in Egypt, and make your dwellings as places for your worship, and perform As-Salât (Iqâmat-as-Salât), and give glad tidings to the believers." (87) And Mûsa (Moses) said: "Our Lord! You have indeed bestowed on Fir'aun (Pharaoh) and his chiefs splendour and wealth in the life of this world, our Lord! that they may lead men astray from Your Path. Our Lord! Destroy their wealth, and harden their hearts, so that they will not believe until they see the painful torment." (88) Allâh said:

"Verily, the invocation of you both is accepted. So you both keep to the Straight Way (i.e. keep on doing good deeds and preaching Allâh's Message with patience), and follow not the path of those who know not (the truth i.e. to believe in the Oneness of Allâh, and also to believe in the Reward of Allâh: Paradise)." (89)

Quran 20:86-98

فَرَجَعَ مُوسَىٰ إِلَىٰ قَوْمِهِ غَضْبَـٰنَ أَسِفًۭا قَالَ يَـٰقَوْمِ أَلَمْ يَعِدْكُمْ رَبُّكُمْ وَعْدًا حَسَنًا أَفَطَالَ عَلَيْكُمُ ٱلْعَهْدُ أَمْ أَرَدتُّمْ أَن يَحِلَّ عَلَيْكُمْ غَضَبٌۭ مِّن رَّبِّكُمْ فَأَخْلَفْتُم مَّوْعِدِى (٨٦) قَالُوا۟ مَآ أَخْلَفْنَا مَوْعِدَكَ بِمَلْكِنَا وَلَـٰكِنَّا حُمِّلْنَآ أَوْزَارًۭا مِّن زِينَةِ ٱلْقَوْمِ فَقَذَفْنَـٰهَا فَكَذَٰلِكَ أَلْقَى ٱلسَّامِرِئُ (٨٧) فَأَخْرَجَ لَهُمْ عِجْلًۭا جَسَدًۭا لَّهُۥ خُوَارٌۭ فَقَالُوا۟ هَـٰذَآ إِلَـٰهُكُمْ وَإِلَـٰهُ مُوسَىٰ فَنَسِىَ (٨٨) أَفَلَا يَرَوْنَ أَلَّا يَرْجِعُ إِلَيْهِمْ قَوْلًۭا وَلَا يَمْلِكُ لَهُمْ ضَرًّۭا وَلَا نَفْعًۭا (٨٩) وَلَقَدْ قَالَ لَهُمْ هَـٰرُونُ مِن قَبْلُ يَـٰقَوْمِ إِنَّمَا فُتِنتُم بِهِۦ ۖ وَإِنَّ رَبَّكُمُ ٱلرَّحْمَـٰنُ فَٱتَّبِعُونِى وَأَطِيعُوٓا۟ أَمْرِى (٩٠) قَالُوا۟ لَن نَّبْرَحَ عَلَيْهِ عَـٰكِفِينَ حَتَّىٰ يَرْجِعَ

إِلَيْنَا مُوسَىٰ (٩١) قَالَ يَـٰهَـٰرُونُ مَا مَنَعَكَ إِذْ رَأَيْتَهُمْ ضَلُّوٓا۟ (٩٢) أَلَّا تَتَّبِعَنِّ ۖ أَفَعَصَيْتَ أَمْرِى (٩٣) قَالَ يَبْنَؤُمَّ لَا تَأْخُذْ بِلِحْيَتِى وَلَا بِرَأْسِىٓ ۖ إِنِّى خَشِيتُ أَن تَقُولَ فَرَّقْتَ بَيْنَ بَنِىٓ إِسْرَٰٓءِيلَ وَلَمْ تَرْقُبْ قَوْلِى (٩٤) قَالَ فَمَا خَطْبُكَ يَـٰسَـٰمِرِىُّ (٩٥) قَالَ بَصُرْتُ بِمَا لَمْ يَبْصُرُوا۟ بِهِ فَقَبَضْتُ قَبْضَةً مِّنْ أَثَرِ ٱلرَّسُولِ فَنَبَذْتُهَا وَكَذَٰلِكَ سَوَّلَتْ لِى نَفْسِى (٩٦) قَالَ فَٱذْهَبْ فَإِنَّ لَكَ فِى ٱلْحَيَوٰةِ أَن تَقُولَ لَا مِسَاسَ ۖ وَإِنَّ لَكَ مَوْعِدًا لَّن تُخْلَفَهُۥ ۖ وَٱنظُرْ إِلَىٰٓ إِلَـٰهِكَ ٱلَّذِى ظَلْتَ عَلَيْهِ عَاكِفًا ۖ لَّنُحَرِّقَنَّهُۥ ثُمَّ لَنَنسِفَنَّهُۥ فِى ٱلْيَمِّ نَسْفًا (٩٧) إِنَّمَآ إِلَـٰهُكُمُ ٱللَّهُ ٱلَّذِى لَآ إِلَـٰهَ إِلَّا هُوَ ۚ وَسِعَ كُلَّ شَىْءٍ عِلْمًا (٩٨)

Then Mûsa (Moses) returned to his people in a state of anger and sorrow. He said: "O my people! Did not your Lord promise you a fair promise? Did then the promise seem to you long in coming? Or did you desire that wrath should descend from your Lord on you, that you broke your promise to me (i.e disbelieving in Allâh and worshipping the calf)?" (86) They said: "We broke not the promise to you, of our own will, but we were made to carry the weight of the ornaments of the [Fir'aun's (Pharaoh)] people, then we cast them (into the fire), and that was what As-Samiri suggested." (87) Then he took out (of the fire) for them (a statue of) a calf which seemed to low. They said: "This is your ilâh (god), and the ilâh (god) of Mûsa (Moses), but [Mûsa (Moses)] has forgotten (his god).'" (88) Did they not see that it could not return them a word (for answer), and that it had no power either to harm them or to do them good? (89) And Hârûn (Aaron) indeed had said to them beforehand: "O my people! You are being tried in this, and verily, your Lord is (Allâh) the Most Gracious, so follow me and obey my order." (90) They said: "We will not stop worshipping it (i.e. the calf), until Mûsa (Moses) returns to us." (91) [Mûsa (Moses)] said: "O Hârûn (Aaron)! What prevented you when you saw them going astray; (92) "That you followed me not (according to my advice to you)? Have you then disobeyed my order?" (93) He [Hârûn (Aaron)] said: "O son of my mother! Seize (me) not by my beard, nor by my head! Verily, I feared lest you should say: 'You have caused a division among the Children of Israel, and you have not respected my word!' " (94) [Mûsa (Moses)] said: "And what is the matter with you. O Samiri? (i.e. why did you do so?)" (95) (Samiri) said: "I saw what they saw not, so I took a handful (of dust) from the (hoof) print of the messenger [Jibril's (Gabriel) horse] and threw it [into the fire in which were put the ornaments of the Fir'aun's (Pharaoh) people, or into the calf]. Thus my inner-self suggested to me." (96) Mûsa (Moses) said: "Then go away! And verily, your (punishment) in this life will be that you will say: "Touch me not (i.e.you will live alone exiled away from mankind); and verily (for a future torment), you have a promise that will not fail. And look at your ilâh (god), to which you have been devoted. We will certainly burn it, and scatter its particles in the sea." (97) Your Ilâh (God) is only Allâh, (the One) Lâ ilâha illa Huwa (none has the right to be worshipped but He). He has full knowledge of all things. (98)

Quran 2:54

وَإِذْ قَالَ مُوسَىٰ لِقَوْمِهِ يَٰقَوْمِ إِنَّكُمْ ظَلَمْتُمْ أَنفُسَكُم بِٱتِّخَاذِكُمُ ٱلْعِجْلَ فَتُوبُوٓاْ إِلَىٰ بَارِئِكُمْ فَٱقْتُلُوٓاْ أَنفُسَكُمْ ذَٰلِكُمْ خَيْرٌ لَّكُمْ عِندَ بَارِئِكُمْ فَتَابَ عَلَيْكُمْ إِنَّهُ هُوَ ٱلتَّوَّابُ ٱلرَّحِيمُ ٥٤

And (remember) when Mûsa (Moses) said to his people: "O my people! Verily, you have wronged yourselves by worshipping the calf. So turn in repentance to your Creator and kill yourselves (the innocent kill the wrongdoers among you), that will be

140

better for you with your Creator." Then He accepted your repentance. Truly, He is the One Who accepts repentance, the Most Merciful. (54)

Quran 2:67-74

وَإِذْ قَالَ مُوسَىٰ لِقَوْمِهِ إِنَّ ٱللَّهَ يَأْمُرُكُمْ أَن تَذْبَحُواْ بَقَرَةً قَالُوٓاْ أَتَتَّخِذُنَا هُزُوًا قَالَ أَعُوذُ بِٱللَّهِ أَنْ أَكُونَ مِنَ ٱلْجَٰهِلِينَ (٦٧) قَالُواْ ٱدْعُ لَنَا رَبَّكَ يُبَيِّن لَّنَا مَا هِيَ قَالَ إِنَّهُ يَقُولُ إِنَّهَا بَقَرَةٌ لَّا فَارِضٌ وَلَا بِكْرٌ عَوَانٌ بَيْنَ ذَٰلِكَ فَٱفْعَلُواْ مَا تُؤْمَرُونَ (٦٨) قَالُواْ ٱدْعُ لَنَا رَبَّكَ يُبَيِّن لَّنَا مَا لَوْنُهَا قَالَ إِنَّهُ يَقُولُ إِنَّهَا بَقَرَةٌ صَفْرَآءُ فَاقِعٌ لَّوْنُهَا تَسُرُّ ٱلنَّٰظِرِينَ (٦٩) قَالُواْ ٱدْعُ لَنَا رَبَّكَ يُبَيِّن لَّنَا مَا هِيَ إِنَّ ٱلْبَقَرَ تَشَٰبَهَ عَلَيْنَا وَإِنَّآ إِن شَآءَ ٱللَّهُ لَمُهْتَدُونَ (٧٠) قَالَ إِنَّهُ يَقُولُ إِنَّهَا بَقَرَةٌ لَّا ذَلُولٌ تُثِيرُ ٱلْأَرْضَ وَلَا تَسْقِى ٱلْحَرْثَ مُسَلَّمَةٌ لَّا شِيَةَ فِيهَا قَالُواْ ٱلْـَٰٔنَ جِئْتَ بِٱلْحَقِّ فَذَبَحُوهَا وَمَا كَادُواْ يَفْعَلُونَ (٧١) وَإِذْ قَتَلْتُمْ نَفْسًا فَٱدَّٰرَٰٔتُمْ فِيهَا وَٱللَّهُ مُخْرِجٌ مَّا كُنتُمْ تَكْتُمُونَ (٧٢) فَقُلْنَا ٱضْرِبُوهُ بِبَعْضِهَا كَذَٰلِكَ يُحْىِ ٱللَّهُ ٱلْمَوْتَىٰ وَيُرِيكُمْ ءَايَٰتِهِ لَعَلَّكُمْ تَعْقِلُونَ (٧٣) ثُمَّ قَسَتْ قُلُوبُكُم مِّنۢ بَعْدِ ذَٰلِكَ فَهِىَ كَٱلْحِجَارَةِ أَوْ أَشَدُّ قَسْوَةً وَإِنَّ مِنَ ٱلْحِجَارَةِ لَمَا يَتَفَجَّرُ مِنْهُ ٱلْأَنْهَٰرُ

141

وَإِنَّ مِنْهَا لَمَا يَشَّقَّقُ فَيَخْرُجُ مِنْهُ ٱلْمَآءُ وَإِنَّ مِنْهَا لَمَا يَهْبِطُ مِنْ خَشْيَةِ ٱللَّهِ وَمَا ٱللَّهُ بِغَٰفِلٍ عَمَّا تَعْمَلُونَ (٧٤)

And (remember) when Mûsa (Moses) said to his people: "Verily, Allâh commands you that you slaughter a cow." They said, "Do you make fun of us?" He said, "I take Allâh's Refuge from being among Al-Jâhilûn (the ignorants or the foolish)." (67) They said, "Call upon your Lord for us that He may make plain to us what it is!" He said, "He says, 'Verily, it is a cow neither too old nor too young, but (it is) between the two conditions', so do what you are commanded." (68) They said, "Call upon your Lord for us to make plain to us its colour." He said, "He says, 'It is a yellow cow, bright in its colour, pleasing to the beholders.' " (69) They said, "Call upon your Lord for us to make plain to us what it is. Verily to us all cows are alike, And surely, if Allâh wills, we will be guided." (70) He [Mûsa (Moses)] said, "He says, 'It is a cow neither trained to till the soil nor water the fields, sound, having no other colour except bright yellow.' " They said, "Now you have brought the truth." So they slaughtered it though they were near to not doing it. (71) And (remember) when you killed a man and fell into dispute among yourselves as to the crime. But Allâh brought forth that which you were hiding. (72) So We said: "Strike him (the dead man) with a piece of it (the cow)." Thus Allâh brings the dead to life and shows you His Ayât (proofs, evidences, verses, lessons, signs, revelations, etc.) so that you may understand. (73) Then, after that, your hearts were hardened and became as stones or even worse in hardness. And indeed, there are stones out of which rivers gush forth, and indeed, there are of them (stones) which split asunder so that water flows from

them, and indeed, there are of them
(stones) which fall down for fear of
Allâh. And Allâh is not unaware of
what you do. (74)

Quran 5:20-25

وَإِذْ قَالَ مُوسَىٰ لِقَوْمِهِ يَٰقَوْمِ ٱذْكُرُواْ نِعْمَةَ ٱللَّهِ عَلَيْكُمْ
إِذْ جَعَلَ فِيكُمْ أَنۢبِيَآءَ وَجَعَلَكُم مُّلُوكًا وَءَاتَىٰكُم مَّا لَمْ
يُؤْتِ أَحَدًا مِّنَ ٱلْعَٰلَمِينَ (٢٠) يَٰقَوْمِ ٱدْخُلُواْ ٱلْأَرْضَ
ٱلْمُقَدَّسَةَ ٱلَّتِى كَتَبَ ٱللَّهُ لَكُمْ وَلَا تَرْتَدُّواْ عَلَىٰٓ أَدْبَارِكُمْ
فَتَنقَلِبُواْ خَٰسِرِينَ (٢١) قَالُواْ يَٰمُوسَىٰٓ إِنَّ فِيهَا قَوْمًا
جَبَّارِينَ وَإِنَّا لَن نَّدْخُلَهَا حَتَّىٰ يَخْرُجُواْ مِنْهَا فَإِن
يَخْرُجُواْ مِنْهَا فَإِنَّا دَٰخِلُونَ (٢٢) قَالَ رَجُلَانِ مِنَ
ٱلَّذِينَ يَخَافُونَ أَنْعَمَ ٱللَّهُ عَلَيْهِمَا ٱدْخُلُواْ عَلَيْهِمُ ٱلْبَابَ
فَإِذَا دَخَلْتُمُوهُ فَإِنَّكُمْ غَٰلِبُونَ وَعَلَى ٱللَّهِ فَتَوَكَّلُوٓاْ إِن
كُنتُم مُّؤْمِنِينَ (٢٣) قَالُواْ يَٰمُوسَىٰٓ إِنَّا لَن نَّدْخُلَهَآ أَبَدًا
مَّا دَامُواْ فِيهَا فَٱذْهَبْ أَنتَ وَرَبُّكَ فَقَٰتِلَآ إِنَّا هَٰهُنَا
قَٰعِدُونَ (٢٤) قَالَ رَبِّ إِنِّى لَآ أَمْلِكُ إِلَّا نَفْسِى وَأَخِى
فَٱفْرُقْ بَيْنَنَا وَبَيْنَ ٱلْقَوْمِ ٱلْفَٰسِقِينَ (٢٥)

And (remember) when Mûsa (Moses)
said to his people: "O my people!
Remember the Favour of Allâh to you,

when He made Prophets among you, made you kings, and gave you what He had not given to any other among the 'Alamîn (mankind and jinn, in the past)." (20) "O my people! Enter the holy land (Palestine) which Allâh has assigned to you, and turn not back (in flight) for then you will be returned as losers." (21) They said: "O Mûsa (Moses)! In it (this holy land) are a people of great strength, and we shall never enter it, till they leave it; when they leave, then we will enter." (22) Two men of those who feared (Allâh and) on whom Allâh had bestowed His Grace (they were Yusha and Kâlab) said: "Assault them through the gate, for when you are in, victory will be yours, and put your trust in Allâh if you are believers indeed." (23) They said: "O Mûsa (Moses)! We shall never enter it as long as they are there. So go you and your Lord and fight you two, we are sitting right here." (24) He [Mûsa (Moses)] said: "O my Lord! I have power only over myself and my brother, so separate us from the people who are the Fâsiqûn (rebellious and disobedient to Allâh)!" (25)

Quran 7:103-142

ثُمَّ بَعَثْنَا مِنْ بَعْدِهِم مُّوسَىٰ بِـَٔايَٰتِنَآ إِلَىٰ فِرْعَوْنَ وَمَلَإِيْهِۦ فَظَلَمُوا۟ بِهَا فَٱنظُرْ كَيْفَ كَانَ عَٰقِبَةُ ٱلْمُفْسِدِينَ (١٠٣) وَقَالَ مُوسَىٰ يَٰفِرْعَوْنُ إِنِّى رَسُولٌ مِّن رَّبِّ ٱلْعَٰلَمِينَ (١٠٤) حَقِيقٌ عَلَىٰٓ أَن لَّآ أَقُولَ عَلَى ٱللَّهِ إِلَّا ٱلْحَقَّ قَدْ جِئْتُكُم بِبَيِّنَةٍ مِّن رَّبِّكُمْ فَأَرْسِلْ مَعِىَ بَنِىٓ إِسْرَٰٓءِيلَ (١٠٥) قَالَ إِن كُنتَ جِئْتَ بِـَٔايَةٍ فَأْتِ بِهَآ إِن كُنتَ مِنَ ٱلصَّٰدِقِينَ (١٠٦) فَأَلْقَىٰ عَصَاهُ فَإِذَا هِىَ ثُعْبَانٌ مُّبِينٌ (١٠٧) وَنَزَعَ يَدَهُۥ فَإِذَا هِىَ بَيْضَآءُ لِلنَّٰظِرِينَ (١٠٨) قَالَ ٱلْمَلَأُ مِن قَوْمِ فِرْعَوْنَ إِنَّ هَٰذَا لَسَٰحِرٌ عَلِيمٌ (١٠٩) يُرِيدُ أَن يُخْرِجَكُم مِّنْ أَرْضِكُمْ فَمَاذَا تَأْمُرُونَ (١١٠) قَالُوٓا۟ أَرْجِهْ وَأَخَاهُ وَأَرْسِلْ فِى ٱلْمَدَآئِنِ حَٰشِرِينَ (١١١) يَأْتُوكَ بِكُلِّ سَٰحِرٍ عَلِيمٍ (١١٢) وَجَآءَ ٱلسَّحَرَةُ فِرْعَوْنَ قَالُوٓا۟ إِنَّ لَنَا لَأَجْرًا إِن كُنَّا نَحْنُ ٱلْغَٰلِبِينَ (١١٣) قَالَ نَعَمْ وَإِنَّكُمْ لَمِنَ

ٱلْمُقَرَّبِينَ (١١٤) قَالُوٓاْ يَٰمُوسَىٰٓ إِمَّآ أَن تُلْقِىَ وَإِمَّآ أَن نَّكُونَ نَحْنُ ٱلْمُلْقِينَ (١١٥) قَالَ أَلْقُواْۖ فَلَمَّآ أَلْقَوْاْ سَحَرُوٓاْ أَعْيُنَ ٱلنَّاسِ وَٱسْتَرْهَبُوهُمْ وَجَآءُو بِسِحْرٍ عَظِيمٍ (١١٦) ۞ وَأَوْحَيْنَآ إِلَىٰ مُوسَىٰٓ أَنْ أَلْقِ عَصَاكَۖ فَإِذَا هِىَ تَلْقَفُ مَا يَأْفِكُونَ (١١٧) فَوَقَعَ ٱلْحَقُّ وَبَطَلَ مَا كَانُواْ يَعْمَلُونَ (١١٨) فَغُلِبُواْ هُنَالِكَ وَٱنقَلَبُواْ صَٰغِرِينَ (١١٩) وَأُلْقِىَ ٱلسَّحَرَةُ سَٰجِدِينَ (١٢٠) قَالُوٓاْ ءَامَنَّا بِرَبِّ ٱلْعَٰلَمِينَ (١٢١) رَبِّ مُوسَىٰ وَهَٰرُونَ (١٢٢) قَالَ فِرْعَوْنُ ءَامَنتُم بِهِۦ قَبْلَ أَنْ ءَاذَنَ لَكُمْۖ إِنَّ هَٰذَا لَمَكْرٌ مَّكَرْتُمُوهُ فِى ٱلْمَدِينَةِ لِتُخْرِجُواْ مِنْهَآ أَهْلَهَاۖ فَسَوْفَ تَعْلَمُونَ (١٢٣) لَأُقَطِّعَنَّ أَيْدِيَكُمْ وَأَرْجُلَكُم مِّنْ خِلَٰفٍ ثُمَّ لَأُصَلِّبَنَّكُمْ أَجْمَعِينَ (١٢٤) قَالُوٓاْ إِنَّآ إِلَىٰ رَبِّنَا مُنقَلِبُونَ (١٢٥) وَمَا تَنقِمُ مِنَّآ إِلَّآ أَنْ ءَامَنَّا بِـَٔايَٰتِ رَبِّنَا لَمَّا جَآءَتْنَاۚ رَبَّنَآ أَفْرِغْ عَلَيْنَا صَبْرًا وَتَوَفَّنَا مُسْلِمِينَ (١٢٦) وَقَالَ ٱلْمَلَأُ مِن قَوْمِ فِرْعَوْنَ أَتَذَرُ مُوسَىٰ وَقَوْمَهُۥ لِيُفْسِدُواْ فِى ٱلْأَرْضِ وَيَذَرَكَ وَءَالِهَتَكَۚ قَالَ سَنُقَتِّلُ أَبْنَآءَهُمْ وَنَسْتَحْىِۦ نِسَآءَهُمْ وَإِنَّا فَوْقَهُمْ قَٰهِرُونَ (١٢٧) قَالَ مُوسَىٰ لِقَوْمِهِ ٱسْتَعِينُواْ بِٱللَّهِ وَٱصْبِرُوٓاْۖ إِنَّ ٱلْأَرْضَ لِلَّهِ يُورِثُهَا مَن يَشَآءُ مِنْ عِبَادِهِۦۖ وَٱلْعَٰقِبَةُ لِلْمُتَّقِينَ (١٢٨) قَالُوٓاْ أُوذِينَا مِن قَبْلِ أَن تَأْتِيَنَا وَمِنۢ بَعْدِ مَا

147

جِئْتَنَا ۚ قَالَ عَسَىٰ رَبُّكُمْ أَن يُهْلِكَ عَدُوَّكُمْ
وَيَسْتَخْلِفَكُمْ فِى ٱلْأَرْضِ فَيَنظُرَ كَيْفَ تَعْمَلُونَ
(١٢٩) وَلَقَدْ أَخَذْنَا ءَالَ فِرْعَوْنَ بِٱلسِّنِينَ وَنَقْصٍ مِّنَ
ٱلثَّمَرَٰتِ لَعَلَّهُمْ يَذَّكَّرُونَ (١٣٠) فَإِذَا جَآءَتْهُمُ
ٱلْحَسَنَةُ قَالُوا۟ لَنَا هَٰذِهِۦ ۖ وَإِن تُصِبْهُمْ سَيِّئَةٌ يَطَّيَّرُوا۟
بِمُوسَىٰ وَمَن مَّعَهُۥٓ ۗ أَلَآ إِنَّمَا طَٰٓئِرُهُمْ عِندَ ٱللَّهِ وَلَٰكِنَّ
أَكْثَرَهُمْ لَا يَعْلَمُونَ (١٣١) وَقَالُوا۟ مَهْمَا تَأْتِنَا بِهِۦ مِنْ
ءَايَةٍ لِّتَسْحَرَنَا بِهَا فَمَا نَحْنُ لَكَ بِمُؤْمِنِينَ
(١٣٢) فَأَرْسَلْنَا عَلَيْهِمُ ٱلطُّوفَانَ وَٱلْجَرَادَ وَٱلْقُمَّلَ
وَٱلضَّفَادِعَ وَٱلدَّمَ ءَايَٰتٍ مُّفَصَّلَٰتٍ فَٱسْتَكْبَرُوا۟ وَكَانُوا۟
قَوْمًا مُّجْرِمِينَ (١٣٣) وَلَمَّا وَقَعَ عَلَيْهِمُ ٱلرِّجْزُ قَالُوا۟
يَٰمُوسَى ٱدْعُ لَنَا رَبَّكَ بِمَا عَهِدَ عِندَكَ ۖ لَئِن كَشَفْتَ عَنَّا
ٱلرِّجْزَ لَنُؤْمِنَنَّ لَكَ وَلَنُرْسِلَنَّ مَعَكَ بَنِىٓ إِسْرَٰٓءِيلَ
(١٣٤) فَلَمَّا كَشَفْنَا عَنْهُمُ ٱلرِّجْزَ إِلَىٰٓ أَجَلٍ هُم بَٰلِغُوهُ
إِذَا هُمْ يَنكُثُونَ (١٣٥) فَٱنتَقَمْنَا مِنْهُمْ فَأَغْرَقْنَٰهُمْ فِى
ٱلْيَمِّ بِأَنَّهُمْ كَذَّبُوا۟ بِـَٔايَٰتِنَا وَكَانُوا۟ عَنْهَا غَٰفِلِينَ
(١٣٦) وَأَوْرَثْنَا ٱلْقَوْمَ ٱلَّذِينَ كَانُوا۟ يُسْتَضْعَفُونَ
مَشَٰرِقَ ٱلْأَرْضِ وَمَغَٰرِبَهَا ٱلَّتِى بَٰرَكْنَا فِيهَا ۖ وَتَمَّتْ
كَلِمَتُ رَبِّكَ ٱلْحُسْنَىٰ عَلَىٰ بَنِىٓ إِسْرَٰٓءِيلَ بِمَا صَبَرُوا۟ ۖ
وَدَمَّرْنَا مَا كَانَ يَصْنَعُ فِرْعَوْنُ وَقَوْمُهُۥ وَمَا كَانُوا۟
يَعْرِشُونَ (١٣٧) وَجَٰوَزْنَا بِبَنِىٓ إِسْرَٰٓءِيلَ ٱلْبَحْرَ

فَأَتَوْاْ عَلَىٰ قَوْمٍ يَعْكُفُونَ عَلَىٰٓ أَصْنَامٍ لَّهُمْ قَالُواْ يَـٰمُوسَى ٱجْعَل لَّنَآ إِلَـٰهًا كَمَا لَهُمْ ءَالِهَةٌ قَالَ إِنَّكُمْ قَوْمٌ تَجْهَلُونَ (١٣٨) إِنَّ هَـٰٓؤُلَآءِ مُتَبَّرٌ مَّا هُمْ فِيهِ وَبَـٰطِلٌ مَّا كَانُواْ يَعْمَلُونَ (١٣٩) قَالَ أَغَيْرَ ٱللَّهِ أَبْغِيكُمْ إِلَـٰهًا وَهُوَ فَضَّلَكُمْ عَلَى ٱلْعَـٰلَمِينَ (١٤٠) وَإِذْ أَنجَيْنَـٰكُم مِّنْ ءَالِ فِرْعَوْنَ يَسُومُونَكُمْ سُوٓءَ ٱلْعَذَابِ يُقَتِّلُونَ أَبْنَآءَكُمْ وَيَسْتَحْيُونَ نِسَآءَكُمْ وَفِى ذَٰلِكُم بَلَآءٌ مِّن رَّبِّكُمْ عَظِيمٌ (١٤١) ۞ وَوَاعَدْنَا مُوسَىٰ ثَلَـٰثِينَ لَيْلَةً وَأَتْمَمْنَـٰهَا بِعَشْرٍ فَتَمَّ مِيقَـٰتُ رَبِّهِ أَرْبَعِينَ لَيْلَةً وَقَالَ مُوسَىٰ لِأَخِيهِ هَـٰرُونَ ٱخْلُفْنِى فِى قَوْمِى وَأَصْلِحْ وَلَا تَتَّبِعْ سَبِيلَ ٱلْمُفْسِدِينَ (١٤٢)

Then after them We sent Mûsa (Moses) with Our Signs to Fir'aun (Pharaoh) and his chiefs, but they wrongfully rejected them. So see how was the end of the Mufsidûn (mischief-makers, corrupters). (103) And Mûsa (Moses) said: "O Fir'aun (Pharaoh)! Verily I am a Messenger from the Lord of the 'Alamîn (mankind, jinn and all that exists). (104) "Proper it is for me that I say nothing concerning Allâh but the truth. Indeed I have come

149

unto you from your Lord with a clear proof. So let the Children of Israel depart along with me." (105) [Fir'aun (Pharaoh)] said: "If you have come with a sign, show it forth, - if you are one of those who tell the truth." (106) Then [Mûsa (Moses)] threw his stick and behold! it was a serpent, manifest! (107) And he drew out his hand, and behold! it was white (with radiance) for the beholders (108) The chiefs of the people of Fir'aun (Pharaoh) said: "This is indeed a well-versed sorcerer; (109) "He wants to get you out of your land, so what do you advise?" (110) They said: "Put him and his brother off (for a time), and send callers to the cities to collect — (111) "That they bring up to you all well-versed sorcerers." (112) And so the sorcerers came to Fir'aun (Pharaoh). They said: "Indeed there will be a (good) reward for us if we are the victors." (113) He said: "Yes, and moreover you will (in

that case) be of the nearest (to me)."
(114) They said: "O Mûsa (Moses)!
Either you throw (first), or shall we have
the (first) throw?" (115) He [Mûsa
(Moses)] said: "Throw you (first)." So
when they threw, they bewitched the
eyes of the people, and struck terror into
them, and they displayed a great magic.
(116) And We reveled to Mûsa (Moses)
(saying): "Throw your stick," and
behold! It swallowed up straight away
all the falsehoods which they showed.
(117) Thus truth was confirmed, and all
that they did was made of no effect.
(118) So they were defeated there and
returned disgraced. (119) And the
sorcerers fell down prostrate. (120) They
said: "We believe in the Lord of the
'Alamîn (mankind, jinn and all that
exists). (121) "The Lord of Mûsa (Moses)
and Hârûn (Aaron)." (122) Fir'aun
(Pharaoh) said: "You have believed in
him [Mûsa (Moses)] before I give you

permission. Surely, this is a plot which you have plotted in the city to drive out its people, but you shall come to know. (123) "Surely, I will cut off your hands and your feet from opposite sides, then I will crucify you all." (124) They said: "Verily, we are returning to our Lord. (125) "And you take vengeance on us only because we believed in the Ayât (proofs, evidences, lessons, signs, etc.) of our Lord when they reached us! Our Lord! pour out on us patience, and cause us to die as Muslims." (126) The chiefs of Fir'aun's (Pharaoh) people said: "Will you leave Mûsa (Moses) and his people to spread mischief in the land, and to abandon you and your gods?" He said: "We will kill their sons, and let live their women, and we have indeed irresistible power over them." (127) Mûsa (Moses) said to his people: "Seek help in Allâh and be patient. Verily, the earth is Allâh's. He gives it as a heritage to whom He wills of His slaves, and the (blessed) end is for the Muttaqûn (pious)." (128) They said: "We (Children of Israel) had suffered troubles before you came to us, and since you have come to us." He said: "It may be that your Lord will destroy your enemy and make you successors on the earth, so that He may see how you act?" (129) And indeed We punished the people of Fir'aun (Pharaoh) with years of drought and shortness of fruits (crops), that they might remember (take heed). (130) But whenever good came to them, they said: "Ours is this." And if evil afflicted them, they ascribed it to evil omens connected with Mûsa (Moses) and those with him. Be informed! Verily, their evil omens are with Allâh but most of them know not. (131) They said [to Mûsa (Moses)]: "Whatever Ayât (proofs, evidences, verses, lessons, signs, revelations, etc.) you may bring to us, to work therewith your sorcery on us, we shall never believe in you." (132) So We sent on them: the flood, the locusts, the lice, the frogs, and the blood: (as a succession of) manifest signs, yet they remained arrogant, and they were of those people who were Mujrimûn (criminals, polytheists sinners). (133) And when the punishment fell on them they said: "O Mûsa (Moses)! Invoke your Lord for us because of His Promise to you. If you remove the punishment from us, we indeed shall believe in you, and we shall let the Children of Israel go with you." (134) But when We removed the punishment from them to a fixed term, which they had to reach, behold! they broke their word! (135) So We took retribution from them. We drowned them in the sea, because they belied Our Ayât (proofs, evidences, verses, lessons, signs, revelations, etc.) and were heedless about them. (136) And We

made the people who were considered
weak to inherit the eastern parts of the
land and the western parts thereof
which We have blessed. And the fair
Word of your Lord was fulfilled for the
Children of Israel, because of their
endurance. And We destroyed
completely all the great works and
buildings which Fir'aun (Pharaoh) and
his people erected (137) And We
brought the Children of Israel (with
safety) across the sea, and they came
upon a people devoted to some of their
idols (in worship). They said: "O Mûsa
(Moses)! Make for us an ilâh (a god) as
they have âlihah (gods)." He said:
"Verily, you are a people who know not
(the Majesty and Greatness of Allâh and
what is obligatory upon you, i.e. to
worship none but Allâh Alone, the One
and the Only God of all that exists)."
(138) [Mûsa (Moses) added:] "Verily,
these people will be destroyed for that

which they are engaged in (idols-worship). And all that they are doing is in vain." (139) He said: "Shall I seek for you an ilâh (a god) other than Allâh, while He has given you superiority over the 'Alamîn (mankind and jinn of your time)." (140) And (remember) when We rescued you from Fir'aun's (Pharaoh) people, who were afflicting you with the worst torment, killing your sons and letting your women live. And in that was a great trial from your Lord. (141) And We appointed for Mûsa (Moses) thirty nights and added (to the period) ten (more), and he completed the term, appointed by his Lord, of forty nights. And Mûsa (Moses) said to his brother Hârûn (Aaron): "Replace me among my people, act in the Right Way (by ordering the people to obey Allâh and to worship Him Alone) and follow not the way of the Mufsidûn (mischief-makers)." (142)

Quran 7:150-157

وَلَمَّا رَجَعَ مُوسَىٰ إِلَىٰ قَوْمِهِ غَضْبَٰنَ أَسِفًا قَالَ بِئْسَمَا خَلَفْتُمُونِى مِنۢ بَعْدِىٓ ۖ أَعَجِلْتُمْ أَمْرَ رَبِّكُمْ ۖ وَأَلْقَى ٱلْأَلْوَاحَ وَأَخَذَ بِرَأْسِ أَخِيهِ يَجُرُّهُۥٓ إِلَيْهِ ۚ قَالَ ٱبْنَ أُمَّ إِنَّ ٱلْقَوْمَ ٱسْتَضْعَفُونِى وَكَادُوا۟ يَقْتُلُونَنِى فَلَا تُشْمِتْ بِىَ ٱلْأَعْدَآءَ وَلَا تَجْعَلْنِى مَعَ ٱلْقَوْمِ ٱلظَّٰلِمِينَ (١٥٠) قَالَ رَبِّ ٱغْفِرْ لِى وَلِأَخِى وَأَدْخِلْنَا فِى رَحْمَتِكَ ۖ وَأَنتَ أَرْحَمُ ٱلرَّٰحِمِينَ (١٥١) إِنَّ ٱلَّذِينَ ٱتَّخَذُوا۟ ٱلْعِجْلَ سَيَنَالُهُمْ غَضَبٌ مِّن رَّبِّهِمْ وَذِلَّةٌ فِى ٱلْحَيَوٰةِ ٱلدُّنْيَا ۚ وَكَذَٰلِكَ نَجْزِى ٱلْمُفْتَرِينَ (١٥٢) وَٱلَّذِينَ عَمِلُوا۟ ٱلسَّيِّـَٔاتِ ثُمَّ تَابُوا۟ مِنۢ بَعْدِهَا وَءَامَنُوٓا۟ إِنَّ رَبَّكَ مِنۢ بَعْدِهَا لَغَفُورٌ رَّحِيمٌ (١٥٣) وَلَمَّا سَكَتَ عَن مُّوسَى ٱلْغَضَبُ أَخَذَ ٱلْأَلْوَاحَ ۖ وَفِى نُسْخَتِهَا هُدًى وَرَحْمَةٌ لِّلَّذِينَ هُمْ لِرَبِّهِمْ يَرْهَبُونَ (١٥٤) وَٱخْتَارَ مُوسَىٰ قَوْمَهُۥ سَبْعِينَ رَجُلًا لِّمِيقَٰتِنَا ۖ فَلَمَّآ أَخَذَتْهُمُ ٱلرَّجْفَةُ قَالَ رَبِّ لَوْ شِئْتَ أَهْلَكْتَهُم مِّن قَبْلُ وَإِيَّٰىَ ۖ أَتُهْلِكُنَا بِمَا فَعَلَ ٱلسُّفَهَآءُ مِنَّآ ۖ إِنْ هِىَ إِلَّا فِتْنَتُكَ تُضِلُّ بِهَا مَن تَشَآءُ وَتَهْدِى مَن تَشَآءُ ۖ أَنتَ وَلِيُّنَا فَٱغْفِرْ لَنَا وَٱرْحَمْنَا ۖ وَأَنتَ خَيْرُ ٱلْغَٰفِرِينَ (١٥٥) ۞ وَٱكْتُبْ لَنَا فِى هَٰذِهِ ٱلدُّنْيَا حَسَنَةً وَفِى ٱلْءَاخِرَةِ إِنَّا هُدْنَآ إِلَيْكَ ۚ قَالَ عَذَابِىٓ أُصِيبُ بِهِۦ مَنْ أَشَآءُ ۖ وَرَحْمَتِى وَسِعَتْ كُلَّ شَىْءٍ ۚ فَسَأَكْتُبُهَا لِلَّذِينَ يَتَّقُونَ وَيُؤْتُونَ

ٱلزَّكَوٰةَ وَٱلَّذِينَ هُم بِـَٔايَـٰتِنَا يُؤْمِنُونَ (١٥٦) ٱلَّذِينَ
يَتَّبِعُونَ ٱلرَّسُولَ ٱلنَّبِىَّ ٱلْأُمِّىَّ ٱلَّذِى يَجِدُونَهُۥ مَكْتُوبًا
عِندَهُمْ فِى ٱلتَّوْرَىٰةِ وَٱلْإِنجِيلِ يَأْمُرُهُم بِٱلْمَعْرُوفِ
وَيَنْهَىٰهُمْ عَنِ ٱلْمُنكَرِ وَيُحِلُّ لَهُمُ ٱلطَّيِّبَـٰتِ وَيُحَرِّمُ
عَلَيْهِمُ ٱلْخَبَـٰٓئِثَ وَيَضَعُ عَنْهُمْ إِصْرَهُمْ وَٱلْأَغْلَـٰلَ ٱلَّتِى
كَانَتْ عَلَيْهِمْ فَٱلَّذِينَ ءَامَنُوا۟ بِهِۦ وَعَزَّرُوهُ وَنَصَرُوهُ
وَٱتَّبَعُوا۟ ٱلنُّورَ ٱلَّذِىٓ أُنزِلَ مَعَهُۥٓ أُو۟لَـٰٓئِكَ هُمُ ٱلْمُفْلِحُونَ
(١٥٧)

And when Mûsa (Moses) returned to his
people, angry and grieved, he said:
"What an evil thing is that which you
have done (i.e. worshipping the calf)
during my absence. Did you hasten and
go ahead as regards the matter of your
Lord (you left His worship)?" And he
threw down the Tablets and seized his
brother by (the hair of) his head and
dragged him towards him. Hârûn
(Aaron) said: "O son of my mother!
Indeed the people judged me weak and
were about to kill me, so make not the
enemies rejoice over me, nor put me

amongst the people who are Zâlimûn (wrong-doers)." (150) Mûsâ (Moses) said: "O my Lord! Forgive me and my brother, and admit us into Your Mercy, for you are the Most Merciful of those who show mercy." (151) Certainly, those who took the calf (for worship), wrath from their Lord and humiliation will come upon them in the life of this world. Thus do We recompense those who invent lies. (152) But those who committed evil deeds and then repented afterwards and believed, verily, your Lord after (all) that is indeed Oft-Forgiving, Most Merciful. (153) And when the anger of Mûsa (Moses) was calmed down, he took up the Tablets, and in their inscription was guidance and mercy for those who fear their Lord. (154) And Mûsa (Moses) chose out of his people seventy (of the best) men for Our appointed time and place of meeting, and when they were seized with a violent earthquake, he said: "O my Lord, if it had been Your Will, You could have destroyed them and me before; would You destroy us for the deeds of the foolish ones among us? It is only Your Trial by which You lead astray whom You will, and keep guided whom You will. You are our Walî (Protector), so forgive us and have Mercy on us, for You are the Best of those who forgive. (155) And ordain for us good in this world, and in the Hereafter. Certainly we have turned unto You." He said: (As to) My Punishment I afflict therewith whom I will and My Mercy embraces all things. That (Mercy) I shall ordain for those who are the Muttaqûn (pious), and give Zakât; and those who believe in Our Ayât (proofs, evidences, verses, lessons, signs and revelations, etc.); (156) Those who follow the Messenger, the Prophet who can neither read nor write (i.e. Muhammad) whom they find written with them in the Taurât (Torah) and the Injeel, - he commands them for Al-Ma'rûf (i.e. Islâmic Monotheism and all that Islâm has ordained); and forbids them from Al-Munkar (i.e. disbelief, polytheism of all kinds, and all that Islâm has forbidden); he allows them as lawful At-Tayyibât (i.e. all good and lawful as regards things, deeds, beliefs, persons, foods), and prohibits them as unlawful Al-Khabâ'ith (i.e. all evil and unlawful as regards things, deeds, beliefs, persons and foods), he releases them from their heavy burdens (of Allâh's Covenant with the children of Israel), and from the fetters (bindings) that were upon them. So those who believe in him (Muhammad), honour him, help him, and follow the light (the Qur'ân) which has been sent down with him, it is they who will be successful. (157)

Quran 14:6-8

وَإِذْ قَالَ مُوسَىٰ لِقَوْمِهِ ٱذْكُرُوا۟ نِعْمَةَ ٱللَّهِ عَلَيْكُمْ إِذْ
أَنجَىٰكُم مِّنْ ءَالِ فِرْعَوْنَ يَسُومُونَكُمْ سُوٓءَ ٱلْعَذَابِ
وَيُذَبِّحُونَ أَبْنَآءَكُمْ وَيَسْتَحْيُونَ نِسَآءَكُمْ وَفِى ذَٰلِكُم
بَلَآءٌ مِّن رَّبِّكُمْ عَظِيمٌ (٦) وَإِذْ تَأَذَّنَ رَبُّكُمْ لَئِن
شَكَرْتُمْ لَأَزِيدَنَّكُمْ وَلَئِن كَفَرْتُمْ إِنَّ عَذَابِى لَشَدِيدٌ
(٧) وَقَالَ مُوسَىٰٓ إِن تَكْفُرُوٓا۟ أَنتُمْ وَمَن فِى ٱلْأَرْضِ
جَمِيعًا فَإِنَّ ٱللَّهَ لَغَنِىٌّ حَمِيدٌ (٨)

And (remember) when Mûsa (Moses)
said to his people: "Call to mind Allâh's
Favour to you, when He delivered you
from Fir'aun's (Pharaoh) people who
were afflicting you with horrible
torment, and were slaughtering your
sons and letting your women live, and
in it was a tremendous trial from your
Lord." (6) And (remember) when your
Lord proclaimed: "If you give thanks
(by accepting Faith and worshipping
none but Allâh), I will give you more (of
My Blessings), but if you are thankless

(i.e. disbelievers), verily! My Punishment is indeed severe." (7) And Mûsa (Moses) said: "If you disbelieve, you and all on earth together, then verily! Allâh is Rich (Free of all needs), Owner of all Praise." (8)

Quran 61:5

وَإِذْ قَالَ مُوسَىٰ لِقَوْمِهِ يَٰقَوْمِ لِمَ تُؤْذُونَنِى وَقَد تَّعْلَمُونَ أَنِّى رَسُولُ ٱللَّهِ إِلَيْكُمْ ۖ فَلَمَّا زَاغُوٓاْ أَزَاغَ ٱللَّهُ قُلُوبَهُمْ ۚ وَٱللَّهُ لَا يَهْدِى ٱلْقَوْمَ ٱلْفَٰسِقِينَ

And (remember) when Mûsa (Moses) said to his people: "O my people! Why do you annoy me while you know certainly that I am the Messenger of Allâh to you? So when they turned away (from the Path of Allâh), Allâh turned their hearts away (from the Right Path). And Allâh guides not the people who are Fâsiqûn (the rebellious, the disobedient to Allâh). (5)

Quran 10:85-89

163

فَقَالُوا۟ عَلَى ٱللَّهِ تَوَكَّلْنَا رَبَّنَا لَا تَجْعَلْنَا فِتْنَةً لِّلْقَوْمِ ٱلظَّـٰلِمِينَ (٨٥) وَنَجِّنَا بِرَحْمَتِكَ مِنَ ٱلْقَوْمِ ٱلْكَـٰفِرِينَ (٨٦) وَأَوْحَيْنَآ إِلَىٰ مُوسَىٰ وَأَخِيهِ أَن تَبَوَّءَا لِقَوْمِكُمَا بِمِصْرَ بُيُوتًا وَٱجْعَلُوا۟ بُيُوتَكُمْ قِبْلَةً وَأَقِيمُوا۟ ٱلصَّلَوٰةَ وَبَشِّرِ ٱلْمُؤْمِنِينَ (٨٧) وَقَالَ مُوسَىٰ رَبَّنَآ إِنَّكَ ءَاتَيْتَ فِرْعَوْنَ وَمَلَأَهُ زِينَةً وَأَمْوَٰلًا فِى ٱلْحَيَوٰةِ ٱلدُّنْيَا رَبَّنَا لِيُضِلُّوا۟ عَن سَبِيلِكَ رَبَّنَا ٱطْمِسْ عَلَىٰ أَمْوَٰلِهِمْ وَٱشْدُدْ عَلَىٰ قُلُوبِهِمْ فَلَا يُؤْمِنُوا۟ حَتَّىٰ يَرَوُا۟ ٱلْعَذَابَ ٱلْأَلِيمَ (٨٨) قَالَ قَدْ أُجِيبَت دَّعْوَتُكُمَا فَٱسْتَقِيمَا وَلَا تَتَّبِعَآنِّ سَبِيلَ ٱلَّذِينَ لَا يَعْلَمُونَ (٨٩)

They(Musa/Moses and Harun/Aaaron) said: "In Allâh we put our trust. Our Lord! Make us not a trial for the folk who are Zâlimûn (polytheists and wrong-doing) (i.e. do not make them overpower us) (85) "And save us by Your Mercy from the disbelieving folk." (86) And We revealed to Mûsa (Moses) and his brother (saying): "Provide dwellings for your people in Egypt, and make your dwellings as places for your worship, and perform As-Salât (Iqâmat-as-Salât), and give glad tidings to the believers." (87) And Mûsa (Moses) said: "Our Lord! You have indeed bestowed on Fir'aun (Pharaoh) and his chiefs splendour and wealth in the life of this world, our Lord! that they may lead men astray from Your Path. Our Lord! Destroy their wealth, and harden their hearts, so that they will not believe until they see the painful torment." (88) Allâh said: "Verily, the invocation of you both is accepted. So you both keep to the Straight Way (i.e. keep on doing good deeds and preaching Allâh's Message with patience), and follow not the path of those who know not (the truth i.e. to believe in the Oneness of Allâh, and also to believe in the Reward of Allâh: Paradise)." (89)

Quran 2:246-251

أَلَمْ تَرَ إِلَى ٱلْمَلَإِ مِنْ بَنِىٓ إِسْرَٰٓءِيلَ مِنْ بَعْدِ مُوسَىٰٓ إِذْ قَالُوا۟ لِنَبِىٍّ لَّهُمُ ٱبْعَثْ لَنَا مَلِكًا نُّقَٰتِلْ فِى سَبِيلِ ٱللَّهِ قَالَ

هَلْ عَسَيْتُمْ إِن كُتِبَ عَلَيْكُمُ ٱلْقِتَالُ أَلَّا تُقَٰتِلُوٱْ قَالُوٱْ وَمَا لَنَآ أَلَّا نُقَٰتِلَ فِى سَبِيلِ ٱللَّهِ وَقَدْ أُخْرِجْنَا مِن دِيَٰرِنَا وَأَبْنَآئِنَا فَلَمَّا كُتِبَ عَلَيْهِمُ ٱلْقِتَالُ تَوَلَّوٱْ إِلَّا قَلِيلاً مِّنْهُمْ وَٱللَّهُ عَلِيمٌ بِٱلظَّٰلِمِينَ (٢٤٦) وَقَالَ لَهُمْ نَبِيُّهُمْ إِنَّ ٱللَّهَ قَدْ بَعَثَ لَكُمْ طَالُوتَ مَلِكًا قَالُوٱْ أَنَّىٰ يَكُونُ لَهُ ٱلْمُلْكُ عَلَيْنَا وَنَحْنُ أَحَقُّ بِٱلْمُلْكِ مِنْهُ وَلَمْ يُؤْتَ سَعَةً مِّنَ ٱلْمَالِ قَالَ إِنَّ ٱللَّهَ ٱصْطَفَٰهُ عَلَيْكُمْ وَزَادَهُ بَسْطَةً فِى ٱلْعِلْمِ وَٱلْجِسْمِ وَٱللَّهُ يُؤْتِى مُلْكَهُ مَن يَشَآءُ وَٱللَّهُ وَاسِعٌ عَلِيمٌ (٢٤٧) وَقَالَ لَهُمْ نَبِيُّهُمْ إِنَّ ءَايَةَ مُلْكِهِ أَن يَأْتِيَكُمُ ٱلتَّابُوتُ فِيهِ سَكِينَةٌ مِّن رَّبِّكُمْ وَبَقِيَّةٌ مِّمَّا تَرَكَ ءَالُ مُوسَىٰ وَءَالُ هَٰرُونَ تَحْمِلُهُ ٱلْمَلَٰئِكَةُ إِنَّ فِى ذَٰلِكَ لَءَايَةً لَّكُمْ إِن كُنتُم مُّؤْمِنِينَ (٢٤٨) فَلَمَّا فَصَلَ طَالُوتُ بِٱلْجُنُودِ قَالَ إِنَّ ٱللَّهَ مُبْتَلِيكُم بِنَهَرٍ فَمَن شَرِبَ مِنْهُ فَلَيْسَ مِنِّى وَمَن لَّمْ يَطْعَمْهُ فَإِنَّهُ مِنِّى إِلَّا مَنِ ٱغْتَرَفَ غُرْفَةً بِيَدِهِ فَشَرِبُوٱْ مِنْهُ إِلَّا قَلِيلاً مِّنْهُمْ فَلَمَّا جَاوَزَهُ هُوَ وَٱلَّذِينَ ءَامَنُوٱْ مَعَهُ قَالُوٱْ لَا طَاقَةَ لَنَا ٱلْيَوْمَ بِجَالُوتَ وَجُنُودِهِ قَالَ ٱلَّذِينَ يَظُنُّونَ أَنَّهُم مُّلَٰقُوٱْ ٱللَّهِ كَم مِّن فِئَةٍ قَلِيلَةٍ غَلَبَتْ فِئَةً كَثِيرَةً بِإِذْنِ ٱللَّهِ وَٱللَّهُ مَعَ ٱلصَّٰبِرِينَ (٢٤٩) وَلَمَّا بَرَزُوٱْ لِجَالُوتَ وَجُنُودِهِ قَالُوٱْ رَبَّنَآ أَفْرِغْ عَلَيْنَا صَبْرًا وَثَبِّتْ أَقْدَامَنَا وَٱنصُرْنَا عَلَى ٱلْقَوْمِ ٱلْكَٰفِرِينَ (٢٥٠) فَهَزَمُوهُم

166

بِإِذْنِ ٱللَّهِ وَقَتَلَ دَاوُۥدُ جَالُوتَ وَءَاتَىٰهُ ٱللَّهُ ٱلْمُلْكَ وَٱلْحِكْمَةَ وَعَلَّمَهُۥ مِمَّا يَشَآءُ ۗ وَلَوْلَا دَفْعُ ٱللَّهِ ٱلنَّاسَ بَعْضَهُم بِبَعْضٍ لَّفَسَدَتِ ٱلْأَرْضُ وَلَـٰكِنَّ ٱللَّهَ ذُو فَضْلٍ عَلَى ٱلْعَٰلَمِينَ (٢٥١)

Have you not thought about the group of the Children of Israel after (the time of) Musâ (Moses)? When they said to a Prophet of theirs, "Appoint for us a king and we will fight in Allâh's Way." He said, "Would you then refrain from fighting, if fighting was prescribed for you?" They said, "Why should we not fight in Allâh's Way while we have been driven out of our homes and our children (families have been taken as captives)?" But when fighting was ordered for them, they turned away, all except a few of them. And Allâh is All-Aware of the Zâlimûn (polytheists and wrong-doers). (246) And their Prophet said to them, "Indeed Allâh has appointed Talût (Saul) as a king over you." They said, "How can he be a king over us when we are fitter than him for the kingdom, and he has not been given enough wealth." He said: "Verily, Allâh has chosen him above you and has increased him abundantly in knowledge and stature. And Allâh grants His Kingdom to whom He wills. And Allâh is All-Sufficient for His creatures' needs, All-Knower." (247) And their Prophet said to them: Verily! The sign of His Kingdom is that there shall come to you At-Tâbût (a wooden box), wherein is Sakinah (peace and reassurance) from your Lord and a remnant of that which Mûsâ (Moses) and Hârûn (Aaron) left behind, carried by the angels. Verily, in this is a sign for you if you are indeed believers. (248) Then when Tâlût (Saul) set out with the army, he said: "Verily! Allâh will try you by a river. So whoever drinks thereof, he is not of me, and whoever tastes it not, he is of me, except him who takes (thereof) in the hollow of his hand." Yet, they drank thereof, all, except a few of them. So when he had crossed it (the river), he and those who believed with him, they said: "We have no power this day against Jâlût (Goliath) and his hosts." But those who knew with certainty that they were to meet their Lord, said: "How often a small group overcame a mighty host by Allâh's Leave?" And Allâh is with As-Sâbirûn (the patient). (249) And when they advanced to meet Jâlût (Goliath) and his forces, they invoked: "Our Lord! Pour forth on us patience, and set firm our feet and make us victorious over the disbelieving people." (250) So they routed them by Allâh's Leave and Dâwûd (David) killed Jâlût (Goliath), and Allâh gave him [Dawûd (David)] the kingdom [after the death of Talût (Saul) and Samuel] and Al¬Hikmah (Prophethood), and taught him of that which He willed. And if Allâh did not check one set of people by means of another, the earth would indeed be full of mischief. But Allâh is full of Bounty to the 'Alamîn (mankind, jinn and all that exists). (251)

Quran 27:15

وَلَقَدْ ءَاتَيْنَا دَاوُۥدَ وَسُلَيْمَـٰنَ عِلْمًا ۖ وَقَالَا ٱلْحَمْدُ لِلَّهِ ٱلَّذِى فَضَّلَنَا عَلَىٰ كَثِيرٍ مِّنْ عِبَادِهِ ٱلْمُؤْمِنِينَ

And indeed We gave knowledge to Dawûd (David) and Sulaimân (Solomon), and they both said: "All the praises and thanks are to Allâh, Who has preferred us above many of His believing slaves!" (15)

Quran 27:15-44

وَلَقَدْ ءَاتَيْنَا دَاوُۥدَ وَسُلَيْمَـٰنَ عِلْمًا ۖ وَقَالَا ٱلْحَمْدُ لِلَّهِ ٱلَّذِى فَضَّلَنَا عَلَىٰ كَثِيرٍ مِّنْ عِبَادِهِ ٱلْمُؤْمِنِينَ (١٥) وَوَرِثَ سُلَيْمَـٰنُ دَاوُۥدَ ۖ وَقَالَ يَـٰٓأَيُّهَا ٱلنَّاسُ عُلِّمْنَا مَنطِقَ ٱلطَّيْرِ وَأُوتِينَا مِن كُلِّ شَىْءٍ ۖ إِنَّ هَـٰذَا لَهُوَ ٱلْفَضْلُ ٱلْمُبِينُ

(١٦) وَحُشِرَ لِسُلَيْمَٰنَ جُنُودُهُۥ مِنَ ٱلْجِنِّ وَٱلْإِنسِ وَٱلطَّيْرِ فَهُمْ يُوزَعُونَ (١٧) حَتَّىٰٓ إِذَآ أَتَوْا۟ عَلَىٰ وَادِ ٱلنَّمْلِ قَالَتْ نَمْلَةٌ يَٰٓأَيُّهَا ٱلنَّمْلُ ٱدْخُلُوا۟ مَسَٰكِنَكُمْ لَا يَحْطِمَنَّكُمْ سُلَيْمَٰنُ وَجُنُودُهُۥ وَهُمْ لَا يَشْعُرُونَ (١٨) فَتَبَسَّمَ ضَاحِكًا مِّن قَوْلِهَا وَقَالَ رَبِّ أَوْزِعْنِىٓ أَنْ أَشْكُرَ نِعْمَتَكَ ٱلَّتِىٓ أَنْعَمْتَ عَلَىَّ وَعَلَىٰ وَٰلِدَىَّ وَأَنْ أَعْمَلَ صَٰلِحًا تَرْضَىٰهُ وَأَدْخِلْنِى بِرَحْمَتِكَ فِى عِبَادِكَ ٱلصَّٰلِحِينَ (١٩) وَتَفَقَّدَ ٱلطَّيْرَ فَقَالَ مَا لِىَ لَآ أَرَى ٱلْهُدْهُدَ أَمْ كَانَ مِنَ ٱلْغَآئِبِينَ (٢٠) لَأُعَذِّبَنَّهُۥ عَذَابًا شَدِيدًا أَوْ لَأَا۟ذْبَحَنَّهُۥٓ أَوْ لَيَأْتِيَنِّى بِسُلْطَٰنٍ مُّبِينٍ (٢١) فَمَكَثَ غَيْرَ بَعِيدٍ فَقَالَ أَحَطتُ بِمَا لَمْ تُحِطْ بِهِۦ وَجِئْتُكَ مِن سَبَإٍۭ بِنَبَإٍ يَقِينٍ (٢٢) إِنِّى وَجَدتُّ ٱمْرَأَةً تَمْلِكُهُمْ وَأُوتِيَتْ مِن كُلِّ شَىْءٍ وَلَهَا عَرْشٌ عَظِيمٌ (٢٣) وَجَدتُّهَا وَقَوْمَهَا يَسْجُدُونَ لِلشَّمْسِ مِن دُونِ ٱللَّهِ وَزَيَّنَ لَهُمُ ٱلشَّيْطَٰنُ أَعْمَٰلَهُمْ فَصَدَّهُمْ عَنِ ٱلسَّبِيلِ فَهُمْ لَا يَهْتَدُونَ (٢٤) أَلَّا يَسْجُدُوا۟ لِلَّهِ ٱلَّذِى يُخْرِجُ ٱلْخَبْءَ فِى ٱلسَّمَٰوَٰتِ وَٱلْأَرْضِ وَيَعْلَمُ مَا تُخْفُونَ وَمَا تُعْلِنُونَ (٢٥) ٱللَّهُ لَآ إِلَٰهَ إِلَّا هُوَ رَبُّ ٱلْعَرْشِ ٱلْعَظِيمِ ۩ (٢٦) ۞ قَالَ سَنَنظُرُ أَصَدَقْتَ أَمْ كُنتَ مِنَ ٱلْكَٰذِبِينَ (٢٧) ٱذْهَب بِّكِتَٰبِى هَٰذَا فَأَلْقِهْ إِلَيْهِمْ ثُمَّ تَوَلَّ عَنْهُمْ فَٱنظُرْ مَاذَا يَرْجِعُونَ (٢٨) قَالَتْ يَٰٓأَيُّهَا ٱلْمَلَؤُا۟ إِنِّىٓ

أُلْقِيَ إِلَيَّ كِتَـٰبٌ كَرِيمٌ ﴿٢٩﴾ إِنَّهُ مِن سُلَيْمَـٰنَ وَإِنَّهُ بِسْمِ ٱللَّهِ ٱلرَّحْمَـٰنِ ٱلرَّحِيمِ ﴿٣٠﴾ أَلَّا تَعْلُواْ عَلَىَّ وَأْتُونِى مُسْلِمِينَ ﴿٣١﴾ قَالَتْ يَـٰٓأَيُّهَا ٱلْمَلَؤُاْ أَفْتُونِى فِى أَمْرِى مَا كُنتُ قَاطِعَةً أَمْرًا حَتَّىٰ تَشْهَدُونِ ﴿٣٢﴾ قَالُواْ نَحْنُ أُوْلُواْ قُوَّةٍ وَأُوْلُواْ بَأْسٍ شَدِيدٍ وَٱلْأَمْرُ إِلَيْكِ فَٱنظُرِى مَاذَا تَأْمُرِينَ ﴿٣٣﴾ قَالَتْ إِنَّ ٱلْمُلُوكَ إِذَا دَخَلُواْ قَرْيَةً أَفْسَدُوهَا وَجَعَلُواْ أَعِزَّةَ أَهْلِهَآ أَذِلَّةً وَكَذَٰلِكَ يَفْعَلُونَ ﴿٣٤﴾ وَإِنِّى مُرْسِلَةٌ إِلَيْهِم بِهَدِيَّةٍ فَنَاظِرَةٌ بِمَ يَرْجِعُ ٱلْمُرْسَلُونَ ﴿٣٥﴾ فَلَمَّا جَآءَ سُلَيْمَـٰنَ قَالَ أَتُمِدُّونَنِ بِمَالٍ فَمَآ ءَاتَـٰنِۦَ ٱللَّهُ خَيْرٌ مِّمَّآ ءَاتَـٰكُم بَلْ أَنتُم بِهَدِيَّتِكُمْ تَفْرَحُونَ ﴿٣٦﴾ ٱرْجِعْ إِلَيْهِمْ فَلَنَأْتِيَنَّهُم بِجُنُودٍ لَّا قِبَلَ لَهُم بِهَا وَلَنُخْرِجَنَّهُم مِّنْهَآ أَذِلَّةً وَهُمْ صَـٰغِرُونَ ﴿٣٧﴾ قَالَ يَـٰٓأَيُّهَا ٱلْمَلَؤُاْ أَيُّكُمْ يَأْتِينِى بِعَرْشِهَا قَبْلَ أَن يَأْتُونِى مُسْلِمِينَ ﴿٣٨﴾ قَالَ عِفْرِيتٌ مِّنَ ٱلْجِنِّ أَنَا۠ ءَاتِيكَ بِهِۦ قَبْلَ أَن تَقُومَ مِن مَّقَامِكَ وَإِنِّى عَلَيْهِ لَقَوِىٌّ أَمِينٌ ﴿٣٩﴾ قَالَ ٱلَّذِى عِندَهُۥ عِلْمٌ مِّنَ ٱلْكِتَـٰبِ أَنَا۠ ءَاتِيكَ بِهِۦ قَبْلَ أَن يَرْتَدَّ إِلَيْكَ طَرْفُكَ فَلَمَّا رَءَاهُ مُسْتَقِرًّا عِندَهُۥ قَالَ هَـٰذَا مِن فَضْلِ رَبِّى لِيَبْلُوَنِىٓ ءَأَشْكُرُ أَمْ أَكْفُرُ وَمَن شَكَرَ فَإِنَّمَا يَشْكُرُ لِنَفْسِهِۦ وَمَن كَفَرَ فَإِنَّ رَبِّى غَنِىٌّ كَرِيمٌ ﴿٤٠﴾ قَالَ نَكِّرُواْ لَهَا عَرْشَهَا نَنظُرْ أَتَهْتَدِىٓ أَمْ تَكُونُ مِنَ ٱلَّذِينَ لَا يَهْتَدُونَ ﴿٤١﴾ فَلَمَّا

جَآءَتْ قِيلَ أَهَـٰكَذَا عَرْشُكِ ۖ قَالَتْ كَأَنَّهُ هُوَ ۚ وَأُوتِينَا
ٱلْعِلْمَ مِن قَبْلِهَا وَكُنَّا مُسْلِمِينَ (٤٢) وَصَدَّهَا مَا كَانَت
تَّعْبُدُ مِن دُونِ ٱللَّهِ ۖ إِنَّهَا كَانَتْ مِن قَوْمٍ كَـٰفِرِينَ
(٤٣) قِيلَ لَهَا ٱدْخُلِى ٱلصَّرْحَ ۖ فَلَمَّا رَأَتْهُ حَسِبَتْهُ لُجَّةً
وَكَشَفَتْ عَن سَاقَيْهَا ۚ قَالَ إِنَّهُ صَرْحٌ مُّمَرَّدٌ مِّن
قَوَارِيرَ ۗ قَالَتْ رَبِّ إِنِّى ظَلَمْتُ نَفْسِى وَأَسْلَمْتُ مَعَ
سُلَيْمَـٰنَ لِلَّهِ رَبِّ ٱلْعَـٰلَمِينَ (٤٤)

And indeed We gave knowledge to
Dawûd (David) and Sulaimân
(Solomon), and they both said: "All the
praises and thanks are to Allâh, Who
has preferred us above many of His
believing slaves!" (15) And Sulaimân
(Solomon) inherited (the knowledge of)
Dawûd (David). He said: "O mankind!
We have been taught the language of
birds, and on us have been bestowed all
things. This, verily, is an evident grace
(from Allâh)." (16) And there were
gathered before Sulaimân (Solomon) his
hosts of jinn and men, and birds, and
they all were set in battle order

173

(marching forward). (17) Till, when they came to the valley of the ants, one of the ants said: "O ants! Enter your dwellings, lest Sulaimân (Solomon) and his hosts should crush you, while they perceive not." (18) So he [Sulaimân (Solomon)] smiled, amused at her speech and said: "My Lord! Grant me the power and ability that I may be grateful for Your Favours which You have bestowed on me and on my parents, and that I may do righteous good deeds that will please You, and admit me by Your Mercy among Your righteous slaves." (19) He inspected the birds, and said: "What is the matter that I see not the hoopoe? Or is he among the absentees? (20) "I will surely punish him with a severe torment, or slaughter him, unless he brings me a clear reason." (21) But the hoopoe stayed not long, he (came up and) said: "I have grasped (the knowledge of a thing) which you have not grasped and I have come to you from Saba' (Sheba) with true news. (22) "I found a woman ruling over them", she has been given all things that could be possessed by any ruler of the earth, and she has a great throne. (23) "I found her and her people worshipping the sun instead of Allâh, and Shaitân (Satan) has made their deeds fair-seeming to them, and has barred them from (Allâh's) Way, so they have no guidance," (24) [As Shaitân (Satan) has barred them from Allâh's Way] so they do not worship (prostrate themselves before) Allâh, Who brings to light what is hidden in the heavens and the earth, and knows what you conceal and what you reveal. (25) Allâh, Lâ ilâha illa Huwa (none has the right to be worshipped but He), the Lord of the Supreme Throne! (26) [Sulaimân (Solomon)] said: "We shall see whether you speak the truth or you are (one) of the liars (27) "Go you with this letter of mine, and deliver it to them, then draw back from them, and see what (answer) they return." (28) She said: "O chiefs! Verily! Here is delivered to me a noble letter, (29) "Verily, It is from Sulaimân (Solomon), and verily, It (reads): In the Name of Allâh, the Most Gracious, the Most Merciful; (30) "Be you not exalted against me, but come to me as Muslims (true believers who submit to Allâh with full submission)' " (31) She said: "O chiefs! Advise me in (this) case of mine. I decide no case till you are present with me (and give me your opinions)." (32) They said: "We have great strength, and great ability for war, but it is for you to command; so think over what you will command." (33) She said: "Verily! Kings, when they enter a town (country), they despoil it, and make the most honourable amongst its people the lowest. And thus they do. (34) "But verily! I am going to send him a present, and see with what (answer) the messengers return." (35) So when (the messengers with the present) came to Sulaimân (Solomon), he said: "Will you help me in wealth? What Allâh has given me is better than that which He has given you! Nay, you rejoice in your gift!" (36) [Then Sulaimân (Solomon) said to the chief of her messengers who brought the present]: "Go back to them. We verily shall come to them with hosts that they cannot resist, and we shall drive them out from there in disgrace, and they will be abased." (37) He said: "O chiefs! Which of you can bring me her throne before they come to me surrendering themselves in obedience?" (38) An Ifrît (strong one) from the jinn said: "I will bring it to you before you rise from your place (council). And verily, I am indeed strong, and trustworthy for such work." (39) One with whom was knowledge of the Scripture said: "I will bring it to you within the twinkling of an eye!" Then when he [Sulaimân (Solomon)] saw it placed before him, he said: "This is by the Grace of my Lord - to test me whether I am grateful or ungrateful! And whoever is grateful, truly, his gratitude is for (the good of) his ownself, and whoever is ungrateful, (he is ungrateful only for the loss of his ownself). Certainly! my Lord is Rich (Free of all wants), Bountiful." (40) He said: "Disguise her throne for her that we may see whether she will be guided (to recognize her throne), or she will be one of those not guided." (41) So when she came, it was said (to her): "Is your throne like this?" She said: "(It is) as though it were the very same." And [Sulaimân (Solomon) said]: "Knowledge was bestowed on us before her, and we were submitted to Allâh (in Islâm as

Muslims before her)." (42) And that which she used to worship besides Allâh has prevented her (from Islâm), for she was of a disbelieving people. (43) It was said to her: "Enter As-Sarh" [(a glass surface with water underneath it) or a palace], but when she saw it, she thought it was a pool, and she (tucked up her clothes) uncovering her legs, Sulaimân (Solomon) said: "Verily, it is Sarh [(a glass surface with water underneath it) or a palace]." She said: "My Lord! Verily, I have wronged myself, and I submit (in Islâm, together with Sulaimân (Solomon), to Allâh, the Lord of the 'Alamîn (mankind, jinn and all that exists)." (44)

Quran 37:123-126

وَإِنَّ إِلْيَاسَ لَمِنَ ٱلْمُرْسَلِينَ (١٢٣) إِذْ قَالَ لِقَوْمِهِ أَلَا تَتَّقُونَ (١٢٤) أَتَدْعُونَ بَعْلاً وَتَذَرُونَ أَحْسَنَ ٱلْخَٰلِقِينَ (١٢٥) ٱللَّهَ رَبَّكُمْ وَرَبَّ ءَابَآئِكُمُ ٱلْأَوَّلِينَ (١٢٦)

And verily, Iliyâs (Elias) was one of the
Messengers (123) When he said to his
people: "Will you not fear Allâh? (124)
"Will you call upon Ba'l (a well- known
idol of his nation whom they used to
worship) and forsake the Best of
creators, (125) "Allâh, your Lord and the
Lord of your forefathers?" (126)

Quran 19:23-33

فَأَجَآءَهَا ٱلْمَخَاضُ إِلَىٰ جِذْعِ ٱلنَّخْلَةِ قَالَتْ يَٰلَيْتَنِى مِتُّ
قَبْلَ هَٰذَا وَكُنتُ نَسْيًا مَّنسِيًّا (٢٣) فَنَادَىٰهَا مِن تَحْتِهَآ
أَلَّا تَحْزَنِى قَدْ جَعَلَ رَبُّكِ تَحْتَكِ سَرِيًّا (٢٤) وَهُزِّىٓ
إِلَيْكِ بِجِذْعِ ٱلنَّخْلَةِ تُسَٰقِطْ عَلَيْكِ رُطَبًا جَنِيًّا
(٢٥) فَكُلِى وَٱشْرَبِى وَقَرِّى عَيْنًا ۖ فَإِمَّا تَرَيِنَّ مِنَ
ٱلْبَشَرِ أَحَدًا فَقُولِىٓ إِنِّى نَذَرْتُ لِلرَّحْمَٰنِ صَوْمًا فَلَنْ
أُكَلِّمَ ٱلْيَوْمَ إِنسِيًّا (٢٦) فَأَتَتْ بِهِۦ قَوْمَهَا تَحْمِلُهُۥ ۖ قَالُوا۟
يَٰمَرْيَمُ لَقَدْ جِئْتِ شَيْئًا فَرِيًّا (٢٧) يَٰٓأُخْتَ هَٰرُونَ مَا
كَانَ أَبُوكِ ٱمْرَأَ سَوْءٍ وَمَا كَانَتْ أُمُّكِ بَغِيًّا
(٢٨) فَأَشَارَتْ إِلَيْهِ ۖ قَالُوا۟ كَيْفَ نُكَلِّمُ مَن كَانَ فِى
ٱلْمَهْدِ صَبِيًّا (٢٩) قَالَ إِنِّى عَبْدُ ٱللَّهِ ءَاتَىٰنِىَ ٱلْكِتَٰبَ
وَجَعَلَنِى نَبِيًّا (٣٠) وَجَعَلَنِى مُبَارَكًا أَيْنَ مَا كُنتُ

وَأَوْصَـٰنِى بِٱلصَّلَوٰةِ وَٱلزَّكَوٰةِ مَا دُمْتُ حَيًّا
(٣١) وَبَرًّا بِوَٰلِدَتِى وَلَمْ يَجْعَلْنِى جَبَّارًا شَقِيًّا
(٣٢) وَٱلسَّلَـٰمُ عَلَىَّ يَوْمَ وُلِدتُّ وَيَوْمَ أَمُوتُ وَيَوْمَ
أُبْعَثُ حَيًّا (٣٣)

And the pains of childbirth drove her to the trunk of a date-palm. She said: "Would that I had died before this, and had been forgotten and out of sight!" (23) Then [the babe 'Īsā (Jesus) or Jibril (Gabriel)] cried unto her from below her, saying: "Grieve not! Your Lord has provided a water stream under you; (24) "And shake the trunk of date-palm towards you, it will let fall fresh ripe-dates upon you." (25) "So eat and drink and be glad, And if you see any human being, say: 'Verily! I have vowed a fast unto the Most Gracious (Allâh) so I shall not speak to any human being this day.'" (26) Then she brought him (the baby) to her people, carrying him. They said: "O Mary! Indeed you have brought a thing Fariyy (a mighty thing). (27) "O sister of Hârûn (Aaron)! Your father was not a man who used to commit adultery, nor your mother was an unchaste woman." (28) Then she pointed to him. They said: "How can we talk to one who is a child in the cradle?" (29) "He ['Īsā (Jesus)] said: Verily! I am a slave of Allâh, He has given me the Scripture and made me a Prophet;" (30) "And He has made me blessed wheresoever I be, and has enjoined on me Salât (prayer), and Zakât, as long as I live." (31) "And dutiful to my mother, and made me not arrogant, unblest. (32) "And Salâm (peace) be upon me the day I was born, and the day I die, and the day I shall be raised alive!" (33)

Quran 3:49-52

وَرَسُولاً إِلَىٰ بَنِىٓ إِسْرَٰٓءِيلَ أَنِّى قَدْ جِئْتُكُم بِـَٔايَةٍ مِّن رَّبِّكُمْ أَنِّىٓ أَخْلُقُ لَكُم مِّنَ ٱلطِّينِ كَهَيْـَٔةِ ٱلطَّيْرِ فَأَنفُخُ فِيهِ فَيَكُونُ طَيْرًا بِإِذْنِ ٱللَّهِ وَأُبْرِئُ ٱلْأَكْمَهَ

وَٱلْأَبْرَصَ وَأُحْىِ ٱلْمَوْتَىٰ بِإِذْنِ ٱللَّهِ وَأُنَبِّئُكُم بِمَا تَأْكُلُونَ وَمَا تَدَّخِرُونَ فِى بُيُوتِكُمْ إِنَّ فِى ذَٰلِكَ لَأَيَةً لَّكُمْ إِن كُنتُم مُّؤْمِنِينَ (٤٩) وَمُصَدِّقًا لِّمَا بَيْنَ يَدَىَّ مِنَ ٱلتَّوْرَىٰةِ وَلِأُحِلَّ لَكُم بَعْضَ ٱلَّذِى حُرِّمَ عَلَيْكُمْ وَجِئْتُكُم بِـَٔايَةٍ مِّن رَّبِّكُمْ فَٱتَّقُوا۟ ٱللَّهَ وَأَطِيعُونِ (٥٠) إِنَّ ٱللَّهَ رَبِّى وَرَبُّكُمْ فَٱعْبُدُوهُ هَٰذَا صِرَٰطٌ مُّسْتَقِيمٌ (٥١) ۞ فَلَمَّآ أَحَسَّ عِيسَىٰ مِنْهُمُ ٱلْكُفْرَ قَالَ مَنْ أَنصَارِىٓ إِلَى ٱللَّهِ قَالَ ٱلْحَوَارِيُّونَ نَحْنُ أَنصَارُ ٱللَّهِ ءَامَنَّا بِٱللَّهِ وَٱشْهَدْ بِأَنَّا مُسْلِمُونَ (٥٢)

And will make him ['Īsā (Jesus)] a Messenger to the Children of Israel (saying): "I have come to you with a sign from your Lord, that I design for you out of clay, a figure like that of a bird, and breathe into it, and it becomes a bird by Allâh's Leave; and I heal him who was born blind, and the leper, and I bring the dead to life by Allâh's Leave. And I inform you of what you eat, and what you store in your houses. Surely, therein is a sign for you, if you believe. (49) And I have come confirming that which was before me of the Taurât (Torah), and to make lawful to you part of what was forbidden to you, and I have come to you with a proof from your Lord. So fear Allâh and obey me. (50) Truly! Allâh is my Lord and your Lord, so worship Him (Alone). This is the Straight Path. (51) Then when 'Īsā (Jesus) came to know of their disbelief, he said: "Who will be my helpers in Allâh's Cause?" Al-Hawâriyyûn (the disciples) said: "We are the helpers of Allâh; we believe in Allâh, and bear witness that we are Muslims (i.e. we submit to Allâh)." (52)

Quran 61:14

يَـٰٓأَيُّهَا ٱلَّذِينَ ءَامَنُوا۟ كُونُوٓا۟ أَنصَارَ ٱللَّهِ كَمَا قَالَ عِيسَى ٱبْنُ مَرْيَمَ لِلْحَوَارِيِّنَ مَنْ أَنصَارِىٓ إِلَى ٱللَّهِ قَالَ ٱلْحَوَارِيُّونَ نَحْنُ أَنصَارُ ٱللَّهِ فَـَٔامَنَت طَّآئِفَةٌ مِّنۢ بَنِىٓ إِسْرَٰٓءِيلَ وَكَفَرَت طَّآئِفَةٌ فَأَيَّدْنَا ٱلَّذِينَ ءَامَنُوا۟ عَلَىٰ عَدُوِّهِمْ فَأَصْبَحُوا۟ ظَـٰهِرِينَ

184

O you who believe! Be you helpers (in the Cause) of Allâh as said 'Īsā (Jesus), son of Maryam (Mary), to the Hawârîyyun (the disciples) : "Who are my helpers (in the Cause) of Allâh?" The Hawârîyyun (the disciples) said: "We are Allâh's helpers" (i.e. we will strive in His Cause!). Then a group of the Children of Israel believed and a group disbelieved. So We gave power to those who believed against their enemies, and they became the victorious (uppermost). (14)

Quran 5:72

لَقَدْ كَفَرَ ٱلَّذِينَ قَالُوٓاْ إِنَّ ٱللَّهَ هُوَ ٱلْمَسِيحُ ٱبْنُ مَرْيَمَ وَقَالَ ٱلْمَسِيحُ يَٰبَنِىٓ إِسْرَٰٓءِيلَ ٱعْبُدُواْ ٱللَّهَ رَبِّى وَرَبَّكُمْ إِنَّهُ مَن يُشْرِكْ بِٱللَّهِ فَقَدْ حَرَّمَ ٱللَّهُ عَلَيْهِ ٱلْجَنَّةَ وَمَأْوَىٰهُ ٱلنَّارُ وَمَا لِلظَّٰلِمِينَ مِنْ أَنصَارٍ

Surely, they have disbelieved who say: "Allâh is the Messiah Īsā (Jesus), son of Maryam (Mary)." But the Messiah

Īsā(Jesus) said: "O Children of Israel!
Worship Allâh, my Lord and your
Lord." Verily, whosoever sets up
partners (in worship) with Allâh, then
Allâh has forbidden Paradise to him,
and the Fire will be his abode. And for
the Zâlimûn (polytheists and wrong-
doers) there are no helpers (72)

Quran 5:112-117

إِذْ قَالَ ٱلْحَوَارِيُّونَ يَـٰعِيسَى ٱبْنَ مَرْيَمَ هَلْ يَسْتَطِيعُ
رَبُّكَ أَن يُنَزِّلَ عَلَيْنَا مَآئِدَةً مِّنَ ٱلسَّمَآءِ ۖ قَالَ ٱتَّقُواْ ٱللَّهَ
إِن كُنتُم مُّؤْمِنِينَ (١١٢) قَالُواْ نُرِيدُ أَن نَّأْكُلَ مِنْهَا
وَتَطْمَئِنَّ قُلُوبُنَا وَنَعْلَمَ أَن قَدْ صَدَقْتَنَا وَنَكُونَ عَلَيْهَا مِنَ
ٱلشَّـٰهِدِينَ (١١٣) قَالَ عِيسَى ٱبْنُ مَرْيَمَ ٱللَّهُمَّ رَبَّنَآ
أَنزِلْ عَلَيْنَا مَآئِدَةً مِّنَ ٱلسَّمَآءِ تَكُونُ لَنَا عِيدًا لِّأَوَّلِنَا
وَءَاخِرِنَا وَءَايَةً مِّنكَ ۖ وَٱرْزُقْنَا وَأَنتَ خَيْرُ ٱلرَّٰزِقِينَ
(١١٤) قَالَ ٱللَّهُ إِنِّى مُنَزِّلُهَا عَلَيْكُمْ ۖ فَمَن يَكْفُرْ بَعْدُ
مِنكُمْ فَإِنِّىٓ أُعَذِّبُهُ عَذَابًا لَّآ أُعَذِّبُهُ أَحَدًا مِّنَ ٱلْعَٰلَمِينَ
(١١٥) وَإِذْ قَالَ ٱللَّهُ يَـٰعِيسَى ٱبْنَ مَرْيَمَ ءَأَنتَ قُلْتَ
لِلنَّاسِ ٱتَّخِذُونِى وَأُمِّىَ إِلَـٰهَيْنِ مِن دُونِ ٱللَّهِ ۖ قَالَ
سُبْحَٰنَكَ مَا يَكُونُ لِىٓ أَنْ أَقُولَ مَا لَيْسَ لِى بِحَقٍّ ۚ إِن

كُنتُ قُلْتُهُ فَقَدْ عَلِمْتَهُ تَعْلَمُ مَا فِى نَفْسِى وَلَآ أَعْلَمُ مَا فِى نَفْسِكَ إِنَّكَ أَنتَ عَلَّمُ ٱلْغُيُوبِ (١١٦) مَا قُلْتُ لَهُمْ إِلَّا مَآ أَمَرْتَنِى بِهِ أَنِ ٱعْبُدُوا ٱللَّهَ رَبِّى وَرَبَّكُمْ وَكُنتُ عَلَيْهِمْ شَهِيدًا مَّا دُمْتُ فِيهِمْ فَلَمَّا تَوَفَّيْتَنِى كُنتَ أَنتَ ٱلرَّقِيبَ عَلَيْهِمْ وَأَنتَ عَلَىٰ كُلِّ شَىْءٍ شَهِيدٌ

(Remember) when Al-Hawârîyyûn (the disciples) said: "O 'Īsā (Jesus), son of Maryam (Mary)! Can your Lord send down to us a table spread (with food) from heaven?" 'Īsā (Jesus) said: "Fear Allâh, if you are indeed believers." (112) They said: "We wish to eat thereof and to satisfy your heart (to be stronger in Faith), and to know that you have indeed told us the truth and that we ourselves be its witnesses." (113) 'Īsā (Jesus), son of Maryam (Mary), said: "O Allâh, our Lord! Send us from heaven a table spread (with food) that there may be for us - for the first and the last of us - a festival and a sign from You; and provide us sustenance, for You are the

Best of sustainers." (114) Allâh said: "I am going to send it down unto you, but if any of you after that disbelieves, then I will punish him with a torment such as I have not inflicted on anyone among (all) the 'Alamîn (mankind and jinn)." (115) And (remember) when Allâh will say (on the Day of Resurrection): "O 'Īsā (Jesus), son of Maryam (Mary)! Did you say unto men: 'Worship me and my mother as two gods besides Allâh?' " He will say: "Glory be to You! It was not for me to say what I had no right (to say). Had I said such a thing, You would surely have known it. You know what is in my inner-self though I do not know what is in Yours, truly, You, only You, are the All-Knower of all that is hidden (and unseen). (116) "Never did I say to them aught except what You (Allâh) did command me to say: 'Worship Allâh, my Lord and your Lord.' And I was a witness over them while I dwelt amongst them, but when You took me up, You were the Watcher over them, and You are a Witness to all things. (117)

Quran 19:36

وَإِنَّ ٱللَّهَ رَبِّى وَرَبُّكُمْ فَٱعْبُدُوهُ هَٰذَا صِرَٰطٌ مُّسْتَقِيمٌ

['Īsā (Jesus) said]: "And verily Allâh is my Lord and your Lord. So worship Him (Alone). That is the Straight Path."

Quran 43:63-64

وَلَمَّا جَآءَ عِيسَىٰ بِٱلْبَيِّنَٰتِ قَالَ قَدْ جِئْتُكُم بِٱلْحِكْمَةِ وَلِأُبَيِّنَ لَكُم بَعْضَ ٱلَّذِى تَخْتَلِفُونَ فِيهِ فَٱتَّقُوا ٱللَّهَ وَأَطِيعُونِ (٦٣) إِنَّ ٱللَّهَ هُوَ رَبِّى وَرَبُّكُمْ فَٱعْبُدُوهُ هَٰذَا صِرَٰطٌ مُّسْتَقِيمٌ (٦٤)

And when 'Īsā (Jesus) came with (Our) clear Proofs, he said: "I have come to you with Al-Hikmah (Prophethood), and in order to make clear to you some of the (points) in which you differ, Therefore fear Allâh and obey me, (63)

189

"Verily, Allâh! He is my Lord (God) and your Lord (God). So worship Him (Alone). This is the (only) Straight Path (i.e. Allâh's religion of true Islâmic Monotheism)." (64)

Quran 61:6

وَإِذْ قَالَ عِيسَى ٱبْنُ مَرْيَمَ يَـٰبَنِىٓ إِسْرَٰٓءِيلَ إِنِّى رَسُولُ ٱللَّهِ إِلَيْكُم مُّصَدِّقًا لِّمَا بَيْنَ يَدَىَّ مِنَ ٱلتَّوْرَٰلةِ وَمُبَشِّرًۢا بِرَسُولٍ يَأْتِى مِنْ بَعْدِى ٱسْمُهُۥٓ أَحْمَدُۖ فَلَمَّا جَاءَهُم بِٱلْبَيِّنَـٰتِ قَالُواْ هَـٰذَا سِحْرٌ مُّبِينٌ

And (remember) when 'Īsā (Jesus), son of Maryam (Mary), said: "O Children of Israel! I am the Messenger of Allâh unto you confirming the Taurât [(Torah) which came] before me, and giving glad tidings of a Messenger to come after me, whose name shall be Ahmed. But when he (Ahmed i.e. Muhammad) came to them with clear proofs, they said: "This is plain magic." (6)

Quran 2:80

وَقَالُواْ لَن تَمَسَّنَا ٱلنَّارُ إِلَّآ أَيَّامًا مَّعْدُودَةً قُلْ أَتَّخَذْتُمْ عِندَ ٱللَّهِ عَهْدًا فَلَن يُخْلِفَ ٱللَّهُ عَهْدَهُ ۖ أَمْ تَقُولُونَ عَلَى ٱللَّهِ مَا لَا تَعْلَمُونَ

And they (Jews) say, "The Fire (i.e. Hell-fire on the Day of Resurrection) shall not touch us but for a few numbered days." Say (O Muhammad to them): "Have you taken a covenant from Allâh, so that Allâh will not break His Covenant? Or is it that you say of Allâh what you know not?

Quran 2:91

وَإِذَا قِيلَ لَهُمْ ءَامِنُواْ بِمَآ أَنزَلَ ٱللَّهُ قَالُواْ نُؤْمِنُ بِمَآ أُنزِلَ عَلَيْنَا وَيَكْفُرُونَ بِمَا وَرَآءَهُ ۥ وَهُوَ ٱلْحَقُّ مُصَدِّقًا لِّمَا مَعَهُمْ قُلْ فَلِمَ تَقْتُلُونَ أَنۢبِيَآءَ ٱللَّهِ مِن قَبْلُ إِن كُنتُم مُّؤْمِنِينَ

And when it is said to them (the Jews), "Believe in what Allâh has sent down," they say, "We believe in what was sent down to us." And they disbelieve in that which came after it, while it is the truth confirming what is with them. Say (O Muhammad to them): "Why then have you killed the Prophets of Allâh aforetime, if you indeed have been believers?"

Quran 2:93-94

وَإِذْ أَخَذْنَا مِيثَٰقَكُمْ وَرَفَعْنَا فَوْقَكُمُ ٱلطُّورَ خُذُواْ مَآ ءَاتَيْنَٰكُم بِقُوَّةٍ وَٱسْمَعُواْ قَالُواْ سَمِعْنَا وَعَصَيْنَا وَأُشْرِبُواْ فِى قُلُوبِهِمُ ٱلْعِجْلَ بِكُفْرِهِمْ قُلْ بِئْسَمَا يَأْمُرُكُم بِهِۦٓ إِيمَٰنُكُمْ إِن كُنتُم مُّؤْمِنِينَ قُلْ إِن كَانَتْ لَكُمُ ٱلدَّارُ ٱلْأَخِرَةُ عِندَ ٱللَّهِ خَالِصَةً مِّن دُونِ ٱلنَّاسِ فَتَمَنَّوُاْ ٱلْمَوْتَ إِن كُنتُمْ صَٰدِقِينَ

And (remember) when We took your covenant and We raised above you the Mount (saying), "Hold firmly to what We have given you and hear (Our Word). They said, "We have heard and disobeyed." And their hearts absorbed (the worship of) the calf because of their disbelief. Say: "Worst indeed is that which your faith enjoins on you if you are believers." (93) Say to (them): "If the home of the Hereafter with Allâh is indeed for you specially and not for others, of mankind, then long for death if you are truthful." (94)

Quran 2:97-98

قُلْ مَن كَانَ عَدُوًّا لِّجِبْرِيلَ فَإِنَّهُ نَزَّلَهُ عَلَىٰ قَلْبِكَ بِإِذْنِ اللَّهِ مُصَدِّقًا لِّمَا بَيْنَ يَدَيْهِ وَهُدًى وَبُشْرَىٰ لِلْمُؤْمِنِينَ مَن كَانَ عَدُوًّا لِّلَّهِ وَمَلَـٰئِكَتِهِ وَرُسُلِهِ وَجِبْرِيلَ وَمِيكَالَ فَإِنَّ اللَّهَ عَدُوٌّ لِّلْكَافِرِينَ

Say (O Muhammad): "Whoever is an enemy to Jibrael (Gabriel) (let him die in his fury), for indeed he has brought it (this Qur'ân) down to your heart by Allâh's Permission, confirming what came before it [i.e. the Taurât (Torah) and the Injeel (Gospel)] and guidance and glad tidings for the believers. (97) "Whoever is an enemy to Allâh, His Angels, His Messengers, Jibrael

193

(Gabriel) and Mikael (Michael), then verily, Allâh is an enemy to the disbelievers."

Quran 2:111

وَقَالُوا۟ لَن يَدْخُلَ ٱلْجَنَّةَ إِلَّا مَن كَانَ هُودًا أَوْ نَصَـٰرَىٰ تِلْكَ أَمَانِيُّهُمْ قُلْ هَاتُوا۟ بُرْهَـٰنَكُمْ إِن كُنتُمْ صَـٰدِقِينَ

And they say, "None shall enter Paradise unless he be a Jew or a Christian." These are their own desires. Say, "Produce your proof if you are truthful."

Quran 2:120

وَلَن تَرْضَىٰ عَنكَ ٱلْيَهُودُ وَلَا ٱلنَّصَـٰرَىٰ حَتَّىٰ تَتَّبِعَ مِلَّتَهُمْ قُلْ إِنَّ هُدَى ٱللَّهِ هُوَ ٱلْهُدَىٰ وَلَئِنِ ٱتَّبَعْتَ أَهْوَآءَهُم بَعْدَ ٱلَّذِى جَآءَكَ مِنَ ٱلْعِلْمِ مَا لَكَ مِنَ ٱللَّهِ مِن وَلِىٍّ وَلَا نَصِيرٍ

Never will the Jews nor the Christians be pleased with you till you follow their religion. Say: "Verily, the Guidance of

Allâh (i.e. Islâmic Monotheism) that is the (only) Guidance." And if you were to follow their (Jews and Christians) desires after what you have received of Knowledge (i.e. the Qur'ân), then you would have against Allâh neither any Walî (protector or guardian) nor any helper.

Quran 2:135-136

وَقَالُواْ كُونُواْ هُودًا أَوْ نَصَٰرَىٰ تَهْتَدُواْۗ قُلْ بَلْ مِلَّةَ إِبْرَٰهِۦمَ حَنِيفًاۖ وَمَا كَانَ مِنَ ٱلْمُشْرِكِينَ

قُولُوٓاْ ءَامَنَّا بِٱللَّهِ وَمَآ أُنزِلَ إِلَيْنَا وَمَآ أُنزِلَ إِلَىٰٓ إِبْرَٰهِۦمَ وَإِسْمَٰعِيلَ وَإِسْحَٰقَ وَيَعْقُوبَ وَٱلْأَسْبَاطِ وَمَآ أُوتِيَ مُوسَىٰ وَعِيسَىٰ وَمَآ أُوتِيَ ٱلنَّبِيُّونَ مِن رَّبِّهِمْ لَا نُفَرِّقُ بَيْنَ أَحَدٍ مِّنْهُمْ وَنَحْنُ لَهُۥ مُسْلِمُونَ

And they say, "Be Jews or Christians, then you will be guided." Say, "Nay, (We follow) only the religion of Ibrâhim (Abraham), Hanifa [Islâmic Monotheism, i.e. to worship none but

Allâh (Alone)], and he was not of Al-Mushrikûn (those who worshipped others along with Allâh)." (135) Say, "We believe in Allâh and that which has been sent down to us and that which has been sent down to Ibrâhim (Abraham), Ismâ'il (Ishmael), Ishâq (Isaac), Ya'qûb (Jacob), and to Al-Asbât [the offspring twelve sons of Ya'qûb (Jacob)], and that which has been given to Mûsa (Moses) and Isâ (Jesus), and that which has been given to the Prophets from their Lord. We make no distinction between any of them, and to Him we have submitted (in Islâm)." (136)

Quran 2:139-140

قُلْ أَتُحَاجُّونَنَا فِى ٱللَّهِ وَهُوَ رَبُّنَا وَرَبُّكُمْ وَلَنَآ أَعْمَٰلُنَا وَلَكُمْ أَعْمَٰلُكُمْ وَنَحْنُ لَهُۥ مُخْلِصُونَ أَمْ تَقُولُونَ إِنَّ إِبْرَٰهِۧمَ وَإِسْمَٰعِيلَ وَإِسْحَٰقَ وَيَعْقُوبَ وَٱلْأَسْبَاطَ كَانُوا۟ هُودًا أَوْ نَصَٰرَىٰٓ قُلْ ءَأَنتُمْ أَعْلَمُ أَمِ ٱللَّهُ وَمَنْ أَظْلَمُ

196

مِمَّن كَتَمَ شَهَٰدَةً عِندَهُۥ مِنَ ٱللَّهِۗ وَمَا ٱللَّهُ بِغَٰفِلٍ عَمَّا تَعۡمَلُونَ

Say (O Muhammad to the Jews and Christians), "Dispute you with us about Allâh while He is our Lord and your Lord? And we are to be rewarded for our deeds and you for your deeds. And we are sincere to Him [in worship and obedience (i.e. we worship Him Alone and none else, and we obey His Orders).]" (139) Or say you that Ibrâhim (Abraham), Ismâ'il (Ishmael), Ishâque (Isaac), Ya'qûb (Jacob) and Al-Asbât [the offspring twelve sons of Ya'qûb (Jacob)] were Jews or Christians? Say, "Do you know better or does Allâh (knows better… that they all were Muslims)? And who is more unjust than he who conceals the testimony [i.e. to believe in Prophet Muhammad when he comes, as is written in their Books.] he has from

Allâh? And Allâh is not unaware of
what you do." (140)

Quran 2:142

سَيَقُولُ ٱلسُّفَهَآءُ مِنَ ٱلنَّاسِ مَا وَلَّىٰهُمْ عَن قِبْلَتِهِمُ ٱلَّتِى
كَانُواْ عَلَيْهَا ۚ قُل لِّلَّهِ ٱلْمَشْرِقُ وَٱلْمَغْرِبُ ۚ يَهْدِى مَن
يَشَآءُ إِلَىٰ صِرَٰطٍ مُّسْتَقِيمٍ

The fools among the people (pagans,
hypocrites, and Jews) will say, "What
has turned them (Muslims) from their
Qiblah [prayer direction (towards
Jerusalem)] to which they were used to
face in prayer." Say "To Allâh belong
both, east and the west. He guides
whom He wills to a Straight Way."

Quran 3:12

قُل لِّلَّذِينَ كَفَرُواْ سَتُغْلَبُونَ وَتُحْشَرُونَ إِلَىٰ جَهَنَّمَ ۚ
وَبِئْسَ ٱلْمِهَادُ

Say to those who disbelieve: "You will
be defeated and gathered together to

Hell, and worst indeed is that place to rest."

Quran 3:20

فَإِنْ حَآجُّوكَ فَقُلْ أَسْلَمْتُ وَجْهِىَ لِلَّهِ وَمَنِ ٱتَّبَعَنِّ وَقُل لِّلَّذِينَ أُوتُوا۟ ٱلْكِتَـٰبَ وَٱلْأُمِّيِّـۧنَ ءَأَسْلَمْتُمْ فَإِنْ أَسْلَمُوا۟ فَقَدِ ٱهْتَدَوا۟ وَّإِن تَوَلَّوْا۟ فَإِنَّمَا عَلَيْكَ ٱلْبَلَـٰغُ وَٱللَّهُ بَصِيرٌ بِٱلْعِبَادِ

So if they dispute with you (Muhammad) say: "I have submitted myself to Allâh (in Islâm), and (so have) those who follow me." And say to those who were given the Scripture (Jews and Christians) and to those who are illiterates (Arab pagans): "Do you (also) submit yourselves (to Allâh in Islâm)?" If they do, they are rightly guided; but if they turn away, your duty is only to convey the Message; and Allâh is All-Seer of (His) slaves

Quran 3:26-27

قُلِ ٱللَّهُمَّ مَٰلِكَ ٱلْمُلْكِ تُؤْتِى ٱلْمُلْكَ مَن تَشَآءُ وَتَنزِعُ ٱلْمُلْكَ مِمَّن تَشَآءُ وَتُعِزُّ مَن تَشَآءُ وَتُذِلُّ مَن تَشَآءُ بِيَدِكَ ٱلْخَيْرُ إِنَّكَ عَلَىٰ كُلِّ شَىْءٍ قَدِيرٌ تُولِجُ ٱلَّيْلَ فِى ٱلنَّهَارِ وَتُولِجُ ٱلنَّهَارَ فِى ٱلَّيْلِ وَتُخْرِجُ ٱلْحَىَّ مِنَ ٱلْمَيِّتِ وَتُخْرِجُ ٱلْمَيِّتَ مِنَ ٱلْحَىِّ وَتَرْزُقُ مَن تَشَآءُ بِغَيْرِ حِسَابٍ

Say: "O Allâh! Possessor of the kingdom, You give the kingdom to whom You will, and You take the kingdom from whom You will, and You endue with honour whom You will, and You humiliate whom You will. In Your Hand is the good. Verily, You are Able to do all things. (26) You make the night to enter into the day, and You make the day to enter into the night (i.e. increase and decrease in the hours of the night and the day during winter and summer), You bring the living out of the dead, and You bring the dead out of the living. And You give wealth and sustenance to whom You will, without limit. (27)

Quran 3:29

قُلْ إِن تُخْفُواْ مَا فِى صُدُورِكُمْ أَوْ تُبْدُوهُ يَعْلَمْهُ ٱللَّهُ وَيَعْلَمُ مَا فِى ٱلسَّمَـٰوَٰتِ وَمَا فِى ٱلْأَرْضِ وَٱللَّهُ عَلَىٰ كُلِّ شَىْءٍ قَدِيرٌ

Say: "Whether you hide what is in your breasts or reveal it, Allâh knows it, and He knows what is in the heavens and what is in the earth. And Allâh is Able to do all things."

Quran 3:31-32

قُلْ إِن كُنتُمْ تُحِبُّونَ ٱللَّهَ فَٱتَّبِعُونِى يُحْبِبْكُمُ ٱللَّهُ وَيَغْفِرْ لَكُمْ ذُنُوبَكُمْ وَٱللَّهُ غَفُورٌ رَّحِيمٌ قُلْ أَطِيعُواْ ٱللَّهَ وَٱلرَّسُولَ فَإِن تَوَلَّوْاْ فَإِنَّ ٱللَّهَ لَا يُحِبُّ ٱلْكَـٰفِرِينَ

Say (O Muhammad to mankind): "If you (really) love Allâh then follow me (i.e. accept Islâmic Monotheism, follow the Qur'ân and the Sunnah), Allâh will love you and forgive you your sins. And Allâh is Oft-Forgiving, Most Merciful." (31) Say (O Muhammad): "Obey Allâh and the Messenger (Muhammad)." But if they turn away, then Allâh does not like the disbelievers (32)

Quran 3:72-73

وَقَالَت طَّآئِفَةٌ مِّنْ أَهْلِ ٱلْكِتَـٰبِ ءَامِنُواْ بِٱلَّذِىٓ أُنزِلَ عَلَى ٱلَّذِينَ ءَامَنُواْ وَجْهَ ٱلنَّهَارِ وَٱكْفُرُوٓاْ ءَاخِرَهُۥ لَعَلَّهُمْ يَرْجِعُونَ وَلَا تُؤْمِنُوٓاْ إِلَّا لِمَن تَبِعَ دِينَكُمْ قُلْ إِنَّ ٱلْهُدَىٰ هُدَى ٱللَّهِ أَن يُؤْتَىٰٓ أَحَدٌ مِّثْلَ مَآ أُوتِيتُمْ أَوْ يُحَآجُّوكُمْ عِندَ رَبِّكُمْ قُلْ إِنَّ ٱلْفَضْلَ بِيَدِ ٱللَّهِ يُؤْتِيهِ مَن يَشَآءُ وَٱللَّهُ وَٰسِعٌ عَلِيمٌ

And a party of the people of the Scripture say: "Believe in the morning in that which is revealed to the believers (Muslims), and reject it at the end of the day, so that they may turn back. (72) And believe no one except the one who follows your religion." Say (O Muhammad): "Verily! Right guidance is the Guidance of Allâh" and do not believe that anyone can receive like that which you have received (of Revelation) except when he follows your religion, otherwise they would engage you in argument before your Lord. Say: "All the bounty is in the Hand of Allâh; He grants to whom He wills. And Allâh is All-Sufficient for His creatures' needs, the All-Knower." (73)

Quran 3:93

كُلُّ ٱلطَّعَامِ كَانَ حِلاًّ لِّبَنِىٓ إِسْرَآءِيلَ إِلَّا مَا حَرَّمَ إِسْرَآءِيلُ عَلَىٰ نَفْسِهِۦ مِن قَبْلِ أَن تُنَزَّلَ ٱلتَّوْرَٰةُۗ قُلْ فَأْتُواْ بِٱلتَّوْرَٰةِ فَٱتْلُوهَآ إِن كُنتُمْ صَٰدِقِينَ

All food was lawful to the Children of Israel, except what Israel made unlawful for himself before the Taurât (Torah) was revealed. Say (O Muhammad): "Bring here the Taurât (Torah) and recite it, if you are truthful."

Quran 3:95

قُلْ صَدَقَ ٱللَّهُ فَٱتَّبِعُوا۟ مِلَّةَ إِبْرَٰهِيمَ حَنِيفًا وَمَا كَانَ مِنَ ٱلْمُشْرِكِينَ

Say: "Allâh has spoken the truth; follow the religion of Ibrâhim (Abraham) Hanifa (Islâmic Monotheism, i.e. he used to worship Allâh Alone), and he was not of Al-Mushrikûn."

Quran 3:98-99

قُلْ يَـٰٓأَهْلَ ٱلْكِتَـٰبِ لِمَ تَكْفُرُونَ بِـَٔايَـٰتِ ٱللَّهِ وَٱللَّهُ شَهِيدٌ عَلَىٰ مَا تَعْمَلُونَ قُلْ يَـٰٓأَهْلَ ٱلْكِتَـٰبِ لِمَ تَصُدُّونَ عَن سَبِيلِ ٱللَّهِ مَنْ ءَامَنَ تَبْغُونَهَا عِوَجًا وَأَنتُمْ شُهَدَآءُ وَمَا ٱللَّهُ بِغَـٰفِلٍ عَمَّا تَعْمَلُونَ

Say: "O people of the Scripture (Jews and Christians)! Why do you reject the Ayât of Allâh (proofs, evidences, verses, lessons, signs, revelations, etc.) while Allâh is Witness to what you do?" (98) Say: "O people of the Scripture (Jews and Christians)! Why do you stop those who have believed, from the Path of

Allâh, seeking to make it seem crooked, while you (yourselves) are witnesses [to Muhammad as a Messenger of Allâh and Islâm (Allâh's Religion, i.e. to worship none but Him Alone)]? And Allâh is not unaware of what you do." (99)

Quran 3:183

ٱلَّذِينَ قَالُوٓاْ إِنَّ ٱللَّهَ عَهِدَ إِلَيْنَآ أَلَّا نُؤْمِنَ لِرَسُولٍ حَتَّىٰ يَأْتِيَنَا بِقُرْبَانٍ تَأْكُلُهُ ٱلنَّارُ قُلْ قَدْ جَآءَكُمْ رُسُلٌ مِّن قَبْلِى بِٱلْبَيِّنَٰتِ وَبِٱلَّذِى قُلْتُمْ فَلِمَ قَتَلْتُمُوهُمْ إِن كُنتُمْ صَٰدِقِينَ

Those (Jews) who said: "Verily, Allâh has taken our promise not to believe in any Messenger unless he brings to us an offering which the fire (from heaven) shall devour." Say: "Verily, there came to you Messengers before me, with clear signs and even with what you speak of; why then did you kill them, if you are truthful?"

Quran 5:17-18

لَّقَدْ كَفَرَ ٱلَّذِينَ قَالُوٓاْ إِنَّ ٱللَّهَ هُوَ ٱلْمَسِيحُ ٱبْنُ مَرْيَمَ
قُلْ فَمَن يَمْلِكُ مِنَ ٱللَّهِ شَيْـًٔا إِنْ أَرَادَ أَن يُهْلِكَ ٱلْمَسِيحَ
ٱبْنَ مَرْيَمَ وَأُمَّهُۥ وَمَن فِى ٱلْأَرْضِ جَمِيعًا وَلِلَّهِ مُلْكُ
ٱلسَّمَـٰوَٰتِ وَٱلْأَرْضِ وَمَا بَيْنَهُمَا يَخْلُقُ مَا يَشَآءُ وَٱللَّهُ
عَلَىٰ كُلِّ شَىْءٍ قَدِيرٌ وَقَالَتِ ٱلْيَهُودُ وَٱلنَّصَـٰرَىٰ نَحْنُ
أَبْنَـٰٓؤُاْ ٱللَّهِ وَأَحِبَّـٰٓؤُهُۥ قُلْ فَلِمَ يُعَذِّبُكُم بِذُنُوبِكُم بَلْ أَنتُم
بَشَرٌ مِّمَّنْ خَلَقَ يَغْفِرُ لِمَن يَشَآءُ وَيُعَذِّبُ مَن يَشَآءُ
وَلِلَّهِ مُلْكُ ٱلسَّمَـٰوَٰتِ وَٱلْأَرْضِ وَمَا بَيْنَهُمَا وَإِلَيْهِ
ٱلْمَصِيرُ

Surely, in disbelief are they who say that
Allâh is the Messiah, son of Maryam
(Mary). Say: "Who then has the least
power against Allâh, if He were to
destroy the Messiah, son of Maryam
(Mary), his mother, and all those who
are on the earth together?" And to Allâh
belongs the dominion of the heavens
and the earth, and all that is between
them. He creates what He wills. And
Allâh is Able to do all things. (17) And

(both) the Jews and the Christians say: "We are the children of Allâh and His loved ones." Say: "Why then does He punish you for your sins?" Nay, you are but human beings, of those He has created, He forgives whom He wills and He punishes whom He wills. And to Allâh belongs the dominion of the heavens and the earth and all that is between them, and to Him is the return (of all).

Quran 5:59-60

قُلْ يَـٰٓأَهْلَ ٱلْكِتَـٰبِ هَلْ تَنقِمُونَ مِنَّآ إِلَّآ أَنْ ءَامَنَّا بِٱللَّهِ وَمَآ أُنزِلَ إِلَيْنَا وَمَآ أُنزِلَ مِن قَبْلُ وَأَنَّ أَكْثَرَكُمْ فَـٰسِقُونَ قُلْ هَلْ أُنَبِّئُكُم بِشَرٍّ مِّن ذَٰلِكَ مَثُوبَةً عِندَ ٱللَّهِ مَن لَّعَنَهُ ٱللَّهُ وَغَضِبَ عَلَيْهِ وَجَعَلَ مِنْهُمُ ٱلْقِرَدَةَ وَٱلْخَنَازِيرَ وَعَبَدَ ٱلطَّـٰغُوتَ أُو۟لَـٰٓئِكَ شَرٌّ مَّكَانًا وَأَضَلُّ عَن سَوَآءِ ٱلسَّبِيلِ

Say: "O people of the Scripture (Jews and Christians)! Do you criticize us for no other reason than that we believe in

Allâh, and in (the revelation) which has been sent down to us and in that which has been sent down before (us), and that most of you are Fâsiqûn [rebellious and disobedient (to Allâh)]?" (59) Say (O Muhammad to the people of the Scripture): "Shall I inform you of something worse than that, regarding the recompense from Allâh: those (Jews) who incurred the Curse of Allâh and His Wrath, those of whom (some) He transformed into monkeys and swines, those who worshipped Tâghût (false deities); such are worse in rank (on the Day of Resurrection in the Hell¬fire), and far more astray from the Right Path (in the life of this world)."

Quran 5:68

قُلْ يَٰٓأَهْلَ ٱلْكِتَٰبِ لَسْتُمْ عَلَىٰ شَىْءٍ حَتَّىٰ تُقِيمُوا۟ ٱلتَّوْرَىٰةَ وَٱلْإِنجِيلَ وَمَآ أُنزِلَ إِلَيْكُم مِّن رَّبِّكُمْ وَلَيَزِيدَنَّ كَثِيرًا مِّنْهُم مَّآ أُنزِلَ إِلَيْكَ مِن رَّبِّكَ طُغْيَٰنًا وَكُفْرًا فَلَا تَأْسَ عَلَى ٱلْقَوْمِ ٱلْكَٰفِرِينَ

Say "O people of the Scripture (Jews and Christians)! You have nothing (as regards guidance) till you act according to the Taurât (Torah), the Injeel, and what has (now) been sent down to you from your Lord (the Qur'ân)." Verily, that which has been sent down to you (Muhammad) from your Lord increases in most of them (their) obstinate rebellion and disbelief. So be not sorrowful over the people who disbelieve.

Quran 5:76-77

قُلْ أَتَعْبُدُونَ مِن دُونِ ٱللَّهِ مَا لَا يَمْلِكُ لَكُمْ ضَرًّا وَلَا نَفْعًا وَٱللَّهُ هُوَ ٱلسَّمِيعُ ٱلْعَلِيمُ قُلْ يَـٰٓأَهْلَ ٱلْكِتَـٰبِ لَا تَغْلُواْ فِى دِينِكُمْ غَيْرَ ٱلْحَقِّ وَلَا تَتَّبِعُوٓاْ أَهْوَآءَ قَوْمٍ قَدْ ضَلُّواْ مِن قَبْلُ وَأَضَلُّواْ كَثِيرًا وَضَلُّواْ عَن سَوَآءِ ٱلسَّبِيلِ

Say (O Muhammad to mankind): "How do you worship besides Allâh something which has no power either to harm or to benefit you? But it is Allâh Who is the All¬Hearer, All¬Knower." (76) Say: "O people of the Scripture (Jews and Christians)! Exceed not the limits in your religion (by believing in something) other than the truth, and do not follow the vain desires of people who went astray before, and who misled many, and strayed from the Right Path." (77)

Quran 6:11-15

الْأَرْضِ ثُمَّ انْظُرُوا كَيْفَ كَانَ عَاقِبَةُ الْمُكَذِّبِينَ

قُلْ لِمَنْ مَا فِي السَّمَاوَاتِ وَالْأَرْضِ ۖ قُلْ لِلَّهِ ۚ كَتَبَ عَلَىٰ نَفْسِهِ الرَّحْمَةَ ۚ لَيَجْمَعَنَّكُمْ إِلَىٰ يَوْمِ الْقِيَامَةِ لَا رَيْبَ فِيهِ ۚ الَّذِينَ خَسِرُوا أَنْفُسَهُمْ فَهُمْ لَا يُؤْمِنُونَ

وَلَهُ مَا سَكَنَ فِي اللَّيْلِ وَالنَّهَارِ ۚ وَهُوَ السَّمِيعُ الْعَلِيمُ

قُلْ أَغَيْرَ اللَّهِ أَتَّخِذُ وَلِيًّا فَاطِرِ السَّمَاوَاتِ وَالْأَرْضِ وَهُوَ يُطْعِمُ وَلَا يُطْعَمُ ۗ قُلْ إِنِّي أُمِرْتُ أَنْ أَكُونَ أَوَّلَ مَنْ أَسْلَمَ ۖ وَلَا تَكُونَنَّ مِنَ الْمُشْرِكِينَ

قُلْ إِنِّي أَخَافُ أَنْ عَصَيْتُ رَبِّي عَذَابَ يَوْمٍ عَظِيمٍ

Say: "Travel in the land and see what was the end of those who rejected truth." (11) Say: "To whom belongs all that is in the heavens and the earth?" Say: "To Allâh. He has prescribed Mercy for Himself. Indeed He will gather you together on the Day of Resurrection, about which there is no doubt. Those who have lost themselves will not believe [in Allâh as being the only Ilâh (God), and Muhammad as being one of His Messengers, and in Resurrection]. (12) And to Him belongs whatsoever exists in the night and the day, and He is the All¬Hearing, the All¬Knowing." (13) Say: "Shall I take as a Walî (helper, protector, Lord or God) any other than Allâh, the Creator of the heavens and the earth? And it is He Who feeds but is not fed." Say: "Verily, I am commanded to be the first of those who submit themselves to Allâh (as Muslims)." And be not you (O Muhammad) of the Mushrikûn (polytheists, pagans, idolaters and disbelievers in the Oneness of Allâh). (14) Say: "I fear, if I disobey my Lord, the torment of a Mighty Day." (15)

Quran 6:19

قُلْ أَىُّ شَىْءٍ أَكْبَرُ شَهَٰدَةً قُلِ ٱللَّهُ شَهِيدٌ بَيْنِى وَبَيْنَكُمْ وَأُوحِىَ إِلَىَّ هَٰذَا ٱلْقُرْءَانُ لِأُنذِرَكُم بِهِۦ وَمَنۢ بَلَغَ أَئِنَّكُمْ لَتَشْهَدُونَ أَنَّ مَعَ ٱللَّهِ ءَالِهَةً أُخْرَىٰ قُل لَّآ أَشْهَدُ قُلْ إِنَّمَا هُوَ إِلَٰهٌ وَٰحِدٌ وَإِنَّنِى بَرِىٓءٌ مِّمَّا تُشْرِكُونَ

Say (O Muhammad): "What thing is the most great in witness?" Say: "Allâh (the Most Great!) is Witness between me and you; this Qur'ân has been revealed to me that I may therewith warn you and whomsoever it may reach. Can you verily bear witness that besides Allâh there are other alihâh (gods)?" Say "I bear no (such) witness!" Say: "But in truth He (Allâh) is the only one Ilâh (God). And truly I am innocent of what you join in worship with Him."

Quran 6:37

وَقَالُواْ لَوْلَا نُزِّلَ عَلَيْهِ ءَايَةٌ مِّن رَّبِّهِۦ ۚ قُلْ إِنَّ ٱللَّهَ قَادِرٌ عَلَىٰٓ أَن يُنَزِّلَ ءَايَةً وَلَـٰكِنَّ أَكْثَرَهُمْ لَا يَعْلَمُونَ

And they said: "Why is not a sign sent down to him from his Lord?" Say: "Allâh is certainly Able to send down a sign, but most of them know not."

Quran 6:40

قُلْ أَرَءَيْتَكُمْ إِنْ أَتَىٰكُمْ عَذَابُ ٱللَّهِ أَوْ أَتَتْكُمُ ٱلسَّاعَةُ أَغَيْرَ ٱللَّهِ تَدْعُونَ إِن كُنتُمْ صَـٰدِقِينَ

Say: "Tell me if Allâh's Torment comes upon you, or the Hour comes upon you, would you then call upon any one other than Allâh? (Reply) if you are truthful!"

Quran 6:46-47

قُلْ أَرَءَيْتُمْ إِنْ أَخَذَ ٱللَّهُ سَمْعَكُمْ وَأَبْصَـٰرَكُمْ وَخَتَمَ عَلَىٰ
قُلُوبِكُم مَّنْ إِلَـٰهٌ غَيْرُ ٱللَّهِ يَأْتِيكُم بِهِ ٱنظُرْ كَيْفَ
نُصَرِّفُ ٱلْـَٔايَـٰتِ ثُمَّ هُمْ يَصْدِفُونَ قُلْ أَرَءَيْتَكُمْ إِنْ
أَتَىٰكُمْ عَذَابُ ٱللَّهِ بَغْتَةً أَوْ جَهْرَةً هَلْ يُهْلَكُ إِلَّا ٱلْقَوْمُ
ٱلظَّـٰلِمُونَ

Say (to the disbelievers): "Tell me, if
Allâh took away your hearing and your
sight, and sealed up your hearts, who is
there - an ilâh (a god) other than Allâh
who could restore them to you?" See
how variously We explain the Ayât
(proofs, evidences, verses, lessons, signs,
revelations, etc.), yet they turn aside.
(46) Say: "Tell me, if the punishment of
Allâh comes to you suddenly (during
the night), or openly (during the day),
will any be destroyed except the
Zâlimûn (polytheists and wrong-doing
people)?" (47)

Quran 6:50

قُل لَّآ أَقُولُ لَكُمْ عِندِى خَزَآئِنُ ٱللَّهِ وَلَآ أَعْلَمُ ٱلْغَيْبَ وَلَآ أَقُولُ لَكُمْ إِنِّى مَلَكٌ ۖ إِنْ أَتَّبِعُ إِلَّا مَا يُوحَىٰٓ إِلَىَّ ۚ قُلْ هَلْ يَسْتَوِى ٱلْأَعْمَىٰ وَٱلْبَصِيرُ ۚ أَفَلَا تَتَفَكَّرُونَ

Say (O Muhammad): "I don't tell you that with me are the treasures of Allâh, nor (that) I know the unseen; nor I tell you that I am an angel. I but follow what is revealed to me." Say: "Are the blind and the one who sees equal? will you not then take thought?"

Quran 6:56-58

قُلْ إِنِّى نُهِيتُ أَنْ أَعْبُدَ ٱلَّذِينَ تَدْعُونَ مِن دُونِ ٱللَّهِ ۚ قُل لَّآ أَتَّبِعُ أَهْوَآءَكُمْ ۙ قَدْ ضَلَلْتُ إِذًا وَمَآ أَنَا۠ مِنَ ٱلْمُهْتَدِينَ قُلْ إِنِّى عَلَىٰ بَيِّنَةٍ مِّن رَّبِّى وَكَذَّبْتُم بِهِ ۚ مَا عِندِى مَا تَسْتَعْجِلُونَ بِهِ ۚ إِنِ ٱلْحُكْمُ إِلَّا لِلَّهِ ۖ يَقُصُّ ٱلْحَقَّ ۖ وَهُوَ خَيْرُ ٱلْفَٰصِلِينَ قُل لَّوْ أَنَّ عِندِى مَا تَسْتَعْجِلُونَ بِهِ لَقُضِىَ ٱلْأَمْرُ بَيْنِى وَبَيْنَكُمْ ۗ وَٱللَّهُ أَعْلَمُ بِٱلظَّٰلِمِينَ

Say: "I have been forbidden to worship those whom you invoke (worship) besides Allâh." Say: "I will not follow

215

your vain desires. If I did, I would go astray, and I would not be one of the rightly guided." (56) Say: "I am on clear proof from my Lord (Islâmic Monotheism), but you deny (the truth that has come to me from Allâh). I have not gotten what you are asking for impatiently (the torment). The decision is only for Allâh, He declares the truth, and He is the Best of judges." (57) Say: "If I had that which you are asking for impatiently (the torment), the matter would have been settled at once between me and you, but Allâh knows best the Zâlimûn (polytheists and wrong¬doers,)." (58)

Quran 6:63-66

قُلْ مَنْ يُنَجِّيكُمْ مِنْ ظُلُمَاتِ الْبَرِّ وَالْبَحْرِ تَدْعُونَهُ
تَضَرُّعًا وَخُفْيَةً لَئِنْ أَنْجَانَا مِنْ هَٰذِهِ لَنَكُونَنَّ مِنَ
الشَّاكِرِينَ قُلِ اللَّهُ يُنَجِّيكُمْ مِنْهَا وَمِنْ كُلِّ كَرْبٍ ثُمَّ أَنْتُمْ
تُشْرِكُونَ قُلْ هُوَ الْقَادِرُ عَلَىٰ أَنْ يَبْعَثَ عَلَيْكُمْ عَذَابًا

مِنْ فَوْقِكُمْ أَوْ مِنْ تَحْتِ أَرْجُلِكُمْ أَوْ يَلْبِسَكُمْ شِيَعًا
وَيُذِيقَ بَعْضَكُمْ بَأْسَ بَعْضٍ ۗ انْظُرْ كَيْفَ نُصَرِّفُ
الْآيَاتِ لَعَلَّهُمْ يَفْقَهُونَ وَكَذَّبَ بِهِ قَوْمُكَ وَهُوَ الْحَقُّ ۚ
قُلْ لَسْتُ عَلَيْكُمْ بِوَكِيلٍ

Say: "Who rescues you from the darkness of the land and the sea (dangers like storms), when you call upon Him in humility and in secret (saying): If He (Allâh) only saves us from this (danger), we shall truly be grateful." (63) Say: "Allâh rescues you from this and from all (other) distresses, and yet you worship others besides Allâh." (64) Say: "He has power to send torment on you from above or from under your feet, or to cover you with confusion in party strife, and make you to taste the violence of one another." See how variously We explain the Ayât (proofs, evidences, lessons, signs, revelations, etc.), so that they may understand. (65) But your people (O

Muhammad) have denied it (the Qur'ân) though it is the truth. Say: "I am not a Wakil (guardian) over you." (66)

Quran 6:71-73

قُلْ أَنَدْعُوا۟ مِن دُونِ ٱللَّهِ مَا لَا يَنفَعُنَا وَلَا يَضُرُّنَا وَنُرَدُّ عَلَىٰٓ أَعْقَابِنَا بَعْدَ إِذْ هَدَىٰنَا ٱللَّهُ كَٱلَّذِى ٱسْتَهْوَتْهُ ٱلشَّيَٰطِينُ فِى ٱلْأَرْضِ حَيْرَانَ لَهُۥٓ أَصْحَٰبٌ يَدْعُونَهُۥٓ إِلَى ٱلْهُدَى ٱئْتِنَا قُلْ إِنَّ هُدَى ٱللَّهِ هُوَ ٱلْهُدَىٰٓ وَأُمِرْنَا لِنُسْلِمَ لِرَبِّ ٱلْعَٰلَمِينَ وَأَنْ أَقِيمُوا۟ ٱلصَّلَوٰةَ وَٱتَّقُوهُ وَهُوَ ٱلَّذِىٓ إِلَيْهِ تُحْشَرُونَ وَهُوَ ٱلَّذِى خَلَقَ ٱلسَّمَٰوَٰتِ وَٱلْأَرْضَ بِٱلْحَقِّ وَيَوْمَ يَقُولُ كُن فَيَكُونُ قَوْلُهُ ٱلْحَقُّ وَلَهُ ٱلْمُلْكُ يَوْمَ يُنفَخُ فِى ٱلصُّورِ عَٰلِمُ ٱلْغَيْبِ وَٱلشَّهَٰدَةِ وَهُوَ ٱلْحَكِيمُ ٱلْخَبِيرُ

Say: "Shall we invoke others besides Allâh (false deities), that can do us neither good nor harm, and shall we turn back on our heels after Allâh has guided us (to true Monotheism)? - like one whom the Shayâtin (devils) have made to go astray, in the land in confusion, his companions calling him

218

to guidance (saying): 'Come to us.' " Say: "Verily, Allâh's Guidance is the only guidance, and we have been commanded to submit (ourselves) to the Lord of the 'Alamîn (mankind, jinn and all that exists); (71) And to perform As-Salât", and to be obedient to Allâh and fear Him, and it is He to Whom you shall be gathered. (72) It is He Who has created the heavens and the earth in truth, and on the Day (i.e. the Day of Resurrection) He will say: "Be!", - and it is! His Word is the truth. His will be the dominion on the Day when the trumpet will be blown. All-Knower of the unseen and the seen. He is the All-Wise, Well-Aware (of all). (73)

Quran 6:90-91

أُو۟لَـٰٓئِكَ ٱلَّذِينَ هَدَى ٱللَّهُ فَبِهُدَىٰهُمُ ٱقْتَدِهْ قُل لَّآ أَسْـَٔلُكُمْ
عَلَيْهِ أَجْرًا إِنْ هُوَ إِلَّا ذِكْرَىٰ لِلْعَـٰلَمِينَ وَمَا قَدَرُوا۟ ٱللَّهَ
حَقَّ قَدْرِهِ إِذْ قَالُوا۟ مَآ أَنزَلَ ٱللَّهُ عَلَىٰ بَشَرٍ مِّن شَىْءٍ
قُلْ مَنْ أَنزَلَ ٱلْكِتَـٰبَ ٱلَّذِى جَآءَ بِهِۦ مُوسَىٰ نُورًا

وَهُدًى لِّلنَّاسِ ۖ تَجْعَلُونَهُ قَرَاطِيسَ تُبْدُونَهَا وَتُخْفُونَ
كَثِيرًا ۖ وَعُلِّمْتُم مَّا لَمْ تَعْلَمُوٓاْ أَنتُمْ وَلَآ ءَابَآؤُكُمْ ۖ قُلِ ٱللَّهُ ۖ
ثُمَّ ذَرْهُمْ فِى خَوْضِهِمْ يَلْعَبُونَ

They are those whom Allâh had guided.
So follow their guidance. Say: "No
reward I ask of you for this (the Qur'ân).
It is only a reminder for the 'Alamîn
(mankind and jinn)." (90) They (the
Jews, Quraish pagans, idolaters) did not
estimate Allâh with an estimation due to
Him when they said: "Nothing did
Allâh send down to any human being
(by revelation)." Say (O Muhammad):
"Who then sent down the Book which
Mûsa (Moses) brought, a light and a
guidance to mankind which you (the
Jews) have made into (separate)
papersheets, disclosing (some of it) and
concealing much. And you (believers in
Allâh and His Messenger Muhammad),
were taught (through the Qur'ân) that
which neither you nor your fathers

knew." Say: "Allâh (sent it down)." Then leave them to play in their vain discussions. (91)

Quran 6:114

أَفَغَيْرَ ٱللَّهِ أَبْتَغِى حَكَمًا وَهُوَ ٱلَّذِىٓ أَنزَلَ إِلَيْكُمُ ٱلْكِتَـٰبَ مُفَصَّلًا ۚ وَٱلَّذِينَ ءَاتَيْنَـٰهُمُ ٱلْكِتَـٰبَ يَعْلَمُونَ أَنَّهُۥ مُنَزَّلٌ مِّن رَّبِّكَ بِٱلْحَقِّ ۖ فَلَا تَكُونَنَّ مِنَ ٱلْمُمْتَرِينَ

[Say (O Muhammad)] "Shall I seek a judge other than Allâh while it is He Who has sent down unto you the Book (the Qur'ân), explained in detail." Those unto whom We gave the Scripture [the Taurât (Torah) and the Injeel (Gospel)] know that it is revealed from your Lord in truth. So be not you of those who doubt.

Quran 6:135

قُلْ يَـٰقَوْمِ ٱعْمَلُوا۟ عَلَىٰ مَكَانَتِكُمْ إِنِّى عَامِلٌ ۖ فَسَوْفَ تَعْلَمُونَ مَن تَكُونُ لَهُۥ عَـٰقِبَةُ ٱلدَّارِ ۗ إِنَّهُۥ لَا يُفْلِحُ ٱلظَّـٰلِمُونَ

Say: "O my people! Work according to your way, surely, I too am working (in my way), and you will come to know for which of us will be the (happy) end in the Hereafter. Certainly the Zâlimûn (polytheists) will not be successful."

Quran 6:143-145

ثَمَـٰنِيَةَ أَزْوَٰجٍۖ مِّنَ ٱلضَّأْنِ ٱثْنَيْنِ وَمِنَ ٱلْمَعْزِ ٱثْنَيْنِۗ قُلْ ءَآلذَّكَرَيْنِ حَرَّمَ أَمِ ٱلْأُنثَيَيْنِ أَمَّا ٱشْتَمَلَتْ عَلَيْهِ أَرْحَامُ ٱلْأُنثَيَيْنِۖ نَبِّئُونِى بِعِلْمٍ إِن كُنتُمْ صَـٰدِقِينَ وَمِنَ ٱلْإِبِلِ ٱثْنَيْنِ وَمِنَ ٱلْبَقَرِ ٱثْنَيْنِۗ قُلْ ءَآلذَّكَرَيْنِ حَرَّمَ أَمِ ٱلْأُنثَيَيْنِ أَمَّا ٱشْتَمَلَتْ عَلَيْهِ أَرْحَامُ ٱلْأُنثَيَيْنِۖ أَمْ كُنتُمْ شُهَدَآءَ إِذْ وَصَّىٰكُمُ ٱللَّهُ بِهَـٰذَاۚ فَمَنْ أَظْلَمُ مِمَّنِ ٱفْتَرَىٰ عَلَى ٱللَّهِ كَذِبًا لِّيُضِلَّ ٱلنَّاسَ بِغَيْرِ عِلْمٍۗ إِنَّ ٱللَّهَ لَا يَهْدِى ٱلْقَوْمَ ٱلظَّـٰلِمِينَ قُل لَّآ أَجِدُ فِى مَآ أُوحِىَ إِلَىَّ مُحَرَّمًا عَلَىٰ طَاعِمٍ يَطْعَمُهُۥٓ إِلَّآ أَن يَكُونَ مَيْتَةً أَوْ دَمًا مَّسْفُوحًا أَوْ لَحْمَ خِنزِيرٍ فَإِنَّهُۥ رِجْسٌ أَوْ فِسْقًا أُهِلَّ لِغَيْرِ ٱللَّهِ بِهِۦۚ فَمَنِ ٱضْطُرَّ غَيْرَ بَاغٍ وَلَا عَادٍ فَإِنَّ رَبَّكَ غَفُورٌ رَّحِيمٌ

Eight pairs; of the sheep two (male and female), and of the goats two (male and female). Say: "Has He forbidden the two males or the two females, or (the young) which the wombs of the two females enclose? Inform me with knowledge if you are truthful." (143) And of the camels two (male and female), and of oxen two (male and female). Say: "Has He forbidden the two males or the two females or (the young) which the wombs of the two females enclose? Or were you present when Allâh ordered you such a thing? Then who does more wrong than one who invents a lie against Allâh, to lead mankind astray without knowledge. Certainly Allâh guides not the people who are Zâlimûn (polytheists and wrong-doers)." (144) Say (O Muhammad): "I find not in that which has been revealed to me anything forbidden to be eaten by one who wishes to eat it, unless it be Maitah (a dead animal) or blood poured forth (by slaughtering or the like), or the flesh of swine (pork) for that surely is impure, or impious (unlawful) meat (of an animal) which is slaughtered as a sacrifice for others than Allâh (or has been slaughtered for idols or on which Allâh's Name has not been mentioned while slaughtering). But whosoever is forced by necessity without wilful disobedience, nor transgressing due limits, (for him) certainly, your Lord is Oft¬Forgiving, Most Merciful." (145)

Quran 6:147-153

فَإِنْ كَذَّبُوكَ فَقُلْ رَبُّكُمْ ذُو رَحْمَةٍ وَاسِعَةٍ وَلَا يُرَدُّ بَأْسُهُ عَنِ الْقَوْمِ الْمُجْرِمِينَ

سَيَقُولُ الَّذِينَ أَشْرَكُوا لَوْ شَاءَ اللَّهُ مَا أَشْرَكْنَا وَلَا آبَاؤُنَا وَلَا حَرَّمْنَا مِنْ شَيْءٍ ۚ كَذَٰلِكَ كَذَّبَ الَّذِينَ مِنْ قَبْلِهِمْ حَتَّىٰ ذَاقُوا بَأْسَنَا ۗ قُلْ هَلْ عِنْدَكُمْ مِنْ عِلْمٍ فَتُخْرِجُوهُ لَنَا ۖ إِنْ تَتَّبِعُونَ إِلَّا الظَّنَّ وَإِنْ أَنْتُمْ إِلَّا تَخْرُصُونَ

قُلْ فَلِلَّهِ الْحُجَّةُ الْبَالِغَةُ ۖ فَلَوْ شَاءَ لَهَدَاكُمْ أَجْمَعِينَ

قُلْ هَلُمَّ شُهَدَاءَكُمُ الَّذِينَ يَشْهَدُونَ أَنَّ اللَّهَ حَرَّمَ هَٰذَا ۖ فَإِن شَهِدُوا فَلَا تَشْهَدْ مَعَهُمْ ۚ وَلَا تَتَّبِعْ أَهْوَاءَ الَّذِينَ كَذَّبُوا بِآيَاتِنَا وَالَّذِينَ لَا يُؤْمِنُونَ بِالْآخِرَةِ وَهُم بِرَبِّهِمْ يَعْدِلُونَ

قُل تَعَالَوْا أَتْلُ مَا حَرَّمَ رَبُّكُمْ عَلَيْكُمْ ۖ أَلَّا تُشْرِكُوا بِهِ شَيْئًا ۖ وَبِالْوَالِدَيْنِ إِحْسَانًا ۖ وَلَا تَقْتُلُوا أَوْلَادَكُم مِّنْ إِمْلَاقٍ ۖ نَّحْنُ نَرْزُقُكُمْ وَإِيَّاهُمْ ۖ وَلَا تَقْرَبُوا الْفَوَاحِشَ مَا ظَهَرَ مِنْهَا وَمَا بَطَنَ ۖ وَلَا تَقْتُلُوا النَّفْسَ الَّتِي حَرَّمَ اللَّهُ إِلَّا بِالْحَقِّ ۚ ذَٰلِكُمْ وَصَّاكُم بِهِ لَعَلَّكُمْ تَعْقِلُونَ

وَلَا تَقْرَبُوا مَالَ الْيَتِيمِ إِلَّا بِالَّتِي هِيَ أَحْسَنُ حَتَّىٰ يَبْلُغَ أَشُدَّهُ ۖ وَأَوْفُوا الْكَيْلَ وَالْمِيزَانَ بِالْقِسْطِ ۖ لَا نُكَلِّفُ نَفْسًا إِلَّا وُسْعَهَا ۖ وَإِذَا قُلْتُمْ فَاعْدِلُوا وَلَوْ كَانَ ذَا قُرْبَىٰ ۖ وَبِعَهْدِ اللَّهِ أَوْفُوا ۚ ذَٰلِكُمْ وَصَّاكُم بِهِ لَعَلَّكُمْ تَذَكَّرُونَ

وَأَنَّ هَٰذَا صِرَاطِي مُسْتَقِيمًا فَاتَّبِعُوهُ ۖ وَلَا تَتَّبِعُوا السُّبُلَ فَتَفَرَّقَ بِكُمْ عَن سَبِيلِهِ ۚ ذَٰلِكُمْ وَصَّاكُم بِهِ لَعَلَّكُمْ تَتَّقُونَ

If they (Jews) belie you (Muhammad) say: "Your Lord is the Owner of Vast Mercy, and never will His Wrath be turned back from the people who are

Mujrimûn (criminals, polytheists, or sinners)." (147) Those who took partners (in worship) with Allâh will say: "If Allâh had willed, we would not have taken partners (in worship) with Him, nor would our fathers, and we would not have forbidden anything (against His Will)." Likewise belied those who were before them, (they argued falsely with Allâh's Messengers), till they tasted Our Wrath. Say: "Have you any knowledge (proof) that you can produce before us? Verily, you follow nothing but guess and you do nothing but lie." (148) Say: "With Allâh is the perfect proof and argument, (i.e. the Oneness of Allâh, the sending of His Messengers and His Books to mankind), had He so willed, He would indeed have guided you all." (149) Say: "Bring forward your witnesses, who can testify that Allâh has forbidden this. Then if they testify, testify not you (O Muhammad) with them. And you should not follow the vain desires of such as treat Our Ayât (proofs, evidences, verses, lessons, signs, revelations, etc.) as falsehoods, and such as believe not in the Hereafter, and they hold others as equal (in worship) with their Lord." (150) Say (O Muhammad): "Come, I will recite what your Lord has prohibited you from: Join not anything in worship with Him; be good and dutiful to your parents; kill not your children because of poverty - We provide sustenance for you and for them; come not near to Al-Fawâhish (shameful sins, illegal sexual intercourse,) whether committed openly or secretly, and kill not anyone whom Allâh has forbidden, except for a just cause (according to Islâmic law). This He has commanded you that you may understand. (151) "And come not near to the orphan's property, except to improve it, until he (or she) attains the age of full strength; and give full measure and full weight with justice. We burden not any person, but that which he can bear. And whenever you give your word (i.e. judge between men or give evidence), say the truth even if a near relative is concerned, and fulfill the Covenant of Allâh, This He commands you, that you may remember. (152) "And verily, this is my Straight Path, so follow it, and follow not (other) paths, for they will separate you away from His Path. This He has ordained for you that you may become Al-Muttaqûn (the pious)." (153)

Quran 6:158

هَلْ يَنظُرُونَ إِلَّآ أَن تَأْتِيَهُمُ ٱلْمَلَـٰٓئِكَةُ أَوْ يَأْتِىَ رَبُّكَ أَوْ يَأْتِىَ بَعْضُ ءَايَـٰتِ رَبِّكَ يَوْمَ يَأْتِى بَعْضُ ءَايَـٰتِ رَبِّكَ لَا يَنفَعُ نَفْسًا إِيمَـٰنُهَا لَمْ تَكُنْ ءَامَنَتْ مِن قَبْلُ أَوْ كَسَبَتْ فِى إِيمَـٰنِهَا خَيْرًا قُلِ ٱنتَظِرُوٓا۟ إِنَّا مُنتَظِرُونَ

Do they then wait for anything other than that the angels should come to them, or that your Lord (Allah) should come, or that some of the Signs of your Lord should come (i.e. portents of the Hour e.g., arising of the sun from the west)! The day that some of the Signs of your Lord do come, no good will it do to a person to believe then, if he believed not before, nor earned good (by performing deeds of righteousness) through his Faith. Say: "Wait you! we (too) are waiting."

Quran 6:161-164

قُلْ إِنَّنِى هَدَىٰنِى رَبِّىٓ إِلَىٰ صِرَٰطٍ مُّسْتَقِيمٍ دِينًا قِيَمًا
مِّلَّةَ إِبْرَٰهِيمَ حَنِيفًا ۚ وَمَا كَانَ مِنَ ٱلْمُشْرِكِينَ قُلْ إِنَّ
صَلَاتِى وَنُسُكِى وَمَحْيَاىَ وَمَمَاتِى لِلَّهِ رَبِّ ٱلْعَٰلَمِينَ
لَا شَرِيكَ لَهُ ۖ وَبِذَٰلِكَ أُمِرْتُ وَأَنَا۠ أَوَّلُ ٱلْمُسْلِمِينَ قُلْ
أَغَيْرَ ٱللَّهِ أَبْغِى رَبًّا وَهُوَ رَبُّ كُلِّ شَىْءٍ ۚ وَلَا تَكْسِبُ
كُلُّ نَفْسٍ إِلَّا عَلَيْهَا ۚ وَلَا تَزِرُ وَازِرَةٌ وِزْرَ أُخْرَىٰ ۚ ثُمَّ
إِلَىٰ رَبِّكُم مَّرْجِعُكُمْ فَيُنَبِّئُكُم بِمَا كُنتُمْ فِيهِ تَخْتَلِفُونَ

Say (O Muhammad): "Truly, my Lord has guided me to a Straight Path, a right religion, the religion of Ibrâhim (Abraham), Hanifa [i.e. the true Islâmic Monotheism - to believe in One God (Allâh i.e. to worship none but Allâh, Alone)] and he was not of Al-Mushrikûn." (161) Say (O Muhammad): "Verily, my Salât (prayer), my sacrifice, my living, and my dying are for Allâh, the Lord of the 'Alamîn (mankind, jinn and all that exists) (162) "He has no partner. And of this I have been commanded, and I am the first of the Muslims." (163) Say: "Shall I seek a lord other than Allâh, while He is the Lord of all things? No person earns any (sin) except against himself (only), and no bearer of burdens shall bear the burden of another. Then unto your Lord is your return, so He will tell you that wherein you have been differing." (164)

Quran 7:28-30

وَإِذَا فَعَلُوا۟ فَٰحِشَةٗ قَالُوا۟ وَجَدْنَا عَلَيْهَآ ءَابَآءَنَا وَٱللَّهُ
أَمَرَنَا بِهَاۗ قُلْ إِنَّ ٱللَّهَ لَا يَأْمُرُ بِٱلْفَحْشَآءِۖ أَتَقُولُونَ عَلَى
ٱللَّهِ مَا لَا تَعْلَمُونَ قُلْ أَمَرَ رَبِّى بِٱلْقِسْطِۖ وَأَقِيمُوا۟
وُجُوهَكُمْ عِندَ كُلِّ مَسْجِدٖ وَٱدْعُوهُ مُخْلِصِينَ لَهُ
ٱلدِّينَۚ كَمَا بَدَأَكُمْ تَعُودُونَ فَرِيقًا هَدَىٰ وَفَرِيقًا حَقَّ
عَلَيْهِمُ ٱلضَّلَٰلَةُۗ إِنَّهُمُ ٱتَّخَذُوا۟ ٱلشَّيَٰطِينَ أَوْلِيَآءَ مِن دُونِ
ٱللَّهِ وَيَحْسَبُونَ أَنَّهُم مُّهْتَدُونَ

And when they commit a Fâhishah (evil deed, going round the Ka'bah in naked state, and every kind of unlawful sexual intercourse), they say: "We found our fathers doing it, and Allâh has commanded it on us." Say: "Nay, Allâh never commands of Fâhishah. Do you say of Allâh what you know not? (28) Say (O Muhammad): My Lord has commanded justice and (said) that you should face Him only (i.e. worship none but Allâh) in every place of worship, in prayers (and not to face other false deities and idols), and invoke Him only making your religion sincere to Him (by not joining in worship any partner to Him and with the intention that you are doing your deeds for Allâh's sake only). As He brought you (into being) in the beginning, so shall you be brought into being [on the Day of Resurrection (in two groups, one as a blessed one (believers), and the other as a wretched one (disbelievers)]. (29) A group He has guided, and a group deserved to be in error; (because) surely they took the Shayâtin (devils) as Auliyâ' (protectors and helpers) instead of Allâh, and think that they are guided. (30)

Quran 7:32-33

قُلْ مَنْ حَرَّمَ زِينَةَ ٱللَّهِ ٱلَّتِىٓ أَخْرَجَ لِعِبَادِهِۦ وَٱلطَّيِّبَـٰتِ مِنَ ٱلرِّزْقِ قُلْ هِىَ لِلَّذِينَ ءَامَنُواْ فِى ٱلْحَيَوٰةِ ٱلدُّنْيَا خَالِصَةً يَوْمَ ٱلْقِيَـٰمَةِ كَذَٰلِكَ نُفَصِّلُ ٱلْأَيَـٰتِ لِقَوْمٍ يَعْلَمُونَ قُلْ إِنَّمَا حَرَّمَ رَبِّىَ ٱلْفَوَٰحِشَ مَا ظَهَرَ مِنْهَا

وَمَا بَطَنَ وَٱلْإِثْمَ وَٱلْبَغْىَ بِغَيْرِ ٱلْحَقِّ وَأَن تُشْرِكُواْ بِٱللَّهِ مَا لَمْ يُنَزِّلْ بِهِۦ سُلْطَٰنًا وَأَن تَقُولُواْ عَلَى ٱللَّهِ مَا لَا تَعْلَمُونَ

Say (O Muhammad): "Who has forbidden the adornment with clothes given by Allâh, which He has produced for His slaves, and At-Taiyyibât [all kinds of Halâl (lawful) things] of food?" Say: "They are, in the life of this world, for those who believe, (and) exclusively for them (believers) on the Day of Resurrection (the disbelievers will not share them)." Thus We explain the Ayât (Islâmic laws) in detail for people who have knowledge. (32) Say (O Muhammad): "(But) the things that my Lord has indeed forbidden are Al-Fawâhish (great evil sins, every kind of unlawful sexual intercourse,) whether committed openly or secretly, sins (of all kinds), unrighteous oppression, joining partners (in worship) with Allâh for which He has given no authority, and saying things about Allâh of which you have no knowledge." (33)

Quran 7:158

قُلْ يَـٰٓأَيُّهَا ٱلنَّاسُ إِنِّى رَسُولُ ٱللَّهِ إِلَيْكُمْ جَمِيعًا ٱلَّذِى لَهُ ، مُلْكُ ٱلسَّمَـٰوَٰتِ وَٱلْأَرْضِ لَآ إِلَـٰهَ إِلَّا هُوَ يُحْىِۦ وَيُمِيتُ فَـَٔامِنُواْ بِٱللَّهِ وَرَسُولِهِ ٱلنَّبِىِّ ٱلْأُمِّىِّ ٱلَّذِى يُؤْمِنُ بِٱللَّهِ وَكَلِمَـٰتِهِۦ وَٱتَّبِعُوهُ لَعَلَّكُمْ تَهْتَدُونَ

Say (O Muhammad): "O mankind! Verily, I am sent to you all as the Messenger of Allâh — to Whom belongs the dominion of the heavens and the earth. Lâ ilâha illa Huwa (none has the right to be worshipped but He); It is He Who gives life and causes death. So believe in Allâh and His Messenger (Muhammad), the Prophet who can neither read nor write (i.e. Muhammad) who believes in Allâh and His Words [(this Qur'ân), the Taurât (Torah) and the Injeel (Gospel) and also Allâh's

Word: "Be!" - and he was, i.e. ʿĪsā (Jesus) son of Maryam (Mary)], and follow him so that you may be guided."

Quran 7:187-188

يَسْـَٔلُونَكَ عَنِ ٱلسَّاعَةِ أَيَّانَ مُرْسَىٰهَا ۖ قُلْ إِنَّمَا عِلْمُهَا عِندَ رَبِّى ۖ لَا يُجَلِّيهَا لِوَقْتِهَآ إِلَّا هُوَ ۚ ثَقُلَتْ فِى ٱلسَّمَـٰوَٰتِ وَٱلْأَرْضِ ۚ لَا تَأْتِيكُمْ إِلَّا بَغْتَةً ۗ يَسْـَٔلُونَكَ كَأَنَّكَ حَفِىٌّ عَنْهَا ۖ قُلْ إِنَّمَا عِلْمُهَا عِندَ ٱللَّهِ وَلَـٰكِنَّ أَكْثَرَ ٱلنَّاسِ لَا يَعْلَمُونَ

قُل لَّآ أَمْلِكُ لِنَفْسِى نَفْعًا وَلَا ضَرًّا إِلَّا مَا شَآءَ ٱللَّهُ ۚ وَلَوْ كُنتُ أَعْلَمُ ٱلْغَيْبَ لَٱسْتَكْثَرْتُ مِنَ ٱلْخَيْرِ وَمَا مَسَّنِىَ ٱلسُّوٓءُ ۚ إِنْ أَنَا۠ إِلَّا نَذِيرٌ وَبَشِيرٌ لِّقَوْمٍ يُؤْمِنُونَ

They ask you about the Hour (Day of Resurrection): "When will be its appointed time?" Say: "The knowledge thereof is with my Lord (Alone). None can reveal its time but He. Heavy is its burden through the heavens and the earth. It shall not come upon you except all of a sudden." They ask you as if you have a good knowledge of it. Say: "The knowledge thereof is with Allâh (Alone) but most of mankind know not." (187) Say (O Muhammad): "I possess no power over benefit or hurt to myself except as Allâh wills. If I had the knowledge of the Ghaib (unseen), I should have secured for myself an abundance of wealth, and no evil should have touched me. I am but a warner, and a bringer of glad tidings unto people who believe." (188)

Quran 7:195-197

أَلَهُمْ أَرْجُلٌ يَمْشُونَ بِهَا ۖ أَمْ لَهُمْ أَيْدٍ يَبْطِشُونَ بِهَا ۖ أَمْ لَهُمْ أَعْيُنٌ يُبْصِرُونَ بِهَا ۖ أَمْ لَهُمْ ءَاذَانٌ يَسْمَعُونَ بِهَا ۗ قُلِ ٱدْعُوا۟ شُرَكَآءَكُمْ ثُمَّ كِيدُونِ فَلَا تُنظِرُونِ

إِنَّ وَلِـِّۧىَ ٱللَّهُ ٱلَّذِى نَزَّلَ ٱلْكِتَـٰبَ ۖ وَهُوَ يَتَوَلَّى ٱلصَّـٰلِحِينَ

وَٱلَّذِينَ تَدْعُونَ مِن دُونِهِۦ لَا يَسْتَطِيعُونَ نَصْرَكُمْ وَلَآ أَنفُسَهُمْ يَنصُرُونَ

236

Have they feet wherewith they walk? Or have they hands wherewith they hold? Or have they eyes wherewith they see? Or have they ears wherewith they hear? Say: "Call your (so-called) partners (of Allâh) and then plot against me, and give me no respite! (195) "Verily, my Walî (Protector, Supporter, and Helper, etc.) is Allâh Who has revealed the Book (the Qur'ân), and He protects (supports and helps) the righteous. (196) "And those whom you call upon besides Him (Allâh) cannot help you nor can they help themselves." (197)

Quran 7:203

وَإِذَا لَمْ تَأْتِهِم بِآيَةٍ قَالُواْ لَوْلَا ٱجْتَبَيْتَهَا قُلْ إِنَّمَآ أَتَّبِعُ مَا يُوحَىٰ إِلَيَّ مِن رَّبِّى هَٰذَا بَصَآئِرُ مِن رَّبِّكُمْ وَهُدًى وَرَحْمَةٌ لِّقَوْمٍ يُؤْمِنُونَ

And if you do not bring them a miracle [according to their (i.e. Quraish-pagans') proposal], they say: "Why have you not

237

brought it?" Say: "I but follow what is revealed to me from my Lord. This (the Qur'ân) is nothing but evidences from your Lord, and a guidance and a mercy for a people who believe."

Quran 9:51-53

قُل لَّن يُصِيبَنَآ إِلَّا مَا كَتَبَ ٱللَّهُ لَنَا هُوَ مَوۡلَىٰنَاۚ وَعَلَى ٱللَّهِ فَلۡيَتَوَكَّلِ ٱلۡمُؤۡمِنُونَ قُلۡ هَلۡ تَرَبَّصُونَ بِنَآ إِلَّا إِحۡدَى ٱلۡحُسۡنَيَيۡنِۖ وَنَحۡنُ نَتَرَبَّصُ بِكُمۡ أَن يُصِيبَكُمُ ٱللَّهُ بِعَذَابٍ مِّنۡ عِندِهِۦ أَوۡ بِأَيۡدِينَاۖ فَتَرَبَّصُوٓاْ إِنَّا مَعَكُم مُّتَرَبِّصُونَ قُلۡ أَنفِقُواْ طَوۡعًا أَوۡ كَرۡهٗا لَّن يُتَقَبَّلَ مِنكُمۡۖ إِنَّكُمۡ كُنتُمۡ قَوۡمٗا فَٰسِقِينَ

Say: "Nothing shall ever happen to us except what Allâh has ordained for us. He is our Maulâ (Lord, Helper and Protector)." And in Allâh let the believers put their trust. (51) Say: "Do you wait for us (anything) except one of the two best things (martyrdom or victory); while we await for you either that Allâh will afflict you with a punishment from Himself or at our hands. So wait, we too are waiting with you." (52) Say: "Spend (in Allâh's Cause) willingly or unwillingly, it will not be accepted from you. Verily, you are ever a people who are Fâsiqûn (rebellious, disobedient to Allâh)." (53)

Quran 9:64-65

يَحۡذَرُ ٱلۡمُنَـٰفِقُونَ أَن تُنَزَّلَ عَلَيۡهِمۡ سُورَةٌ تُنَبِّئُهُم بِمَا فِى قُلُوبِهِمۡۚ قُلِ ٱسۡتَهۡزِءُوٓاْ إِنَّ ٱللَّهَ مُخۡرِجٌ مَّا تَحۡذَرُونَ

وَلَئِن سَأَلۡتَهُمۡ لَيَقُولُنَّ إِنَّمَا كُنَّا نَخُوضُ وَنَلۡعَبُۚ قُلۡ أَبِٱللَّهِ وَءَايَـٰتِهِۦ وَرَسُولِهِۦ كُنتُمۡ تَسۡتَهۡزِءُونَ

The hypocrites fear lest a Sûrah (chapter of the Qur'ân) should be revealed about them, showing them what is in their hearts. Say: "(Go ahead and) mock! But certainly Allâh will bring to light all that you fear." (64) If you ask them (about this), they declare: "We were only talking idly and joking." Say: "Was it at

Allâh, and His Ayât (proofs, evidences, verses, lessons, signs, revelations) and His Messenger that you were mocking?" (65)

Quran 9:94

يَعْتَذِرُونَ إِلَيْكُمْ إِذَا رَجَعْتُمْ إِلَيْهِمْ قُل لَّا تَعْتَذِرُواْ لَن نُّؤْمِنَ لَكُمْ قَدْ نَبَّأَنَا ٱللَّهُ مِنْ أَخْبَارِكُمْ وَسَيَرَى ٱللَّهُ عَمَلَكُمْ وَرَسُولُهُ ۥ ثُمَّ تُرَدُّونَ إِلَىٰ عَلِمِ ٱلْغَيْبِ وَٱلشَّهَدَةِ فَيُنَبِّئُكُم بِمَا كُنْتُمْ تَعْمَلُونَ

They (the hypocrites) will present their excuses to you (Muslims), when you return to them. Say (O Muhammad) "Present no excuses, we shall not believe you. Allâh has already informed us of the news concerning you. Allâh and His Messenger will observe your deeds. In the end you will be brought back to the All-Knower of the unseen and the seen, then He (Allâh) will inform you of what you used to do."

Quran 9:105

وَقُلِ ٱعْمَلُواْ فَسَيَرَى ٱللَّهُ عَمَلَكُمْ وَرَسُولُهُ
وَٱلْمُؤْمِنُونَ ۖ وَسَتُرَدُّونَ إِلَىٰ عَـٰلِمِ ٱلْغَيْبِ وَٱلشَّهَـٰدَةِ
فَيُنَبِّئُكُم بِمَا كُنتُمْ تَعْمَلُونَ

And say (O Muhammad) "Do deeds!
Allâh will see your deeds, and (so will)
His Messenger and the believers. And
you will be brought back to the All-
Knower of the unseen and the seen.
Then He will inform you of what you
used to do."

Quran 10:15-16

وَإِذَا تُتْلَىٰ عَلَيْهِمْ ءَايَاتُنَا بَيِّنَـٰتٍ قَالَ ٱلَّذِينَ لَا يَرْجُونَ
لِقَآءَنَا ٱئْتِ بِقُرْءَانٍ غَيْرِ هَـٰذَآ أَوْ بَدِّلْهُ ۚ قُلْ مَا يَكُونُ لِىَ
أَنْ أُبَدِّلَهُ مِن تِلْقَآئِ نَفْسِىٓ ۖ إِنْ أَتَّبِعُ إِلَّا مَا يُوحَىٰٓ إِلَىَّ ۖ
إِنِّىٓ أَخَافُ إِنْ عَصَيْتُ رَبِّى عَذَابَ يَوْمٍ عَظِيمٍ قُل لَّوْ
شَآءَ ٱللَّهُ مَا تَلَوْتُهُ عَلَيْكُمْ وَلَآ أَدْرَىٰكُم بِهِ ۖ فَقَدْ لَبِثْتُ
فِيكُمْ عُمُرًا مِّن قَبْلِهِ ۚ أَفَلَا تَعْقِلُونَ

And when Our Clear Verses are recited
unto them, those who hope not for their

241

meeting with Us, say: Bring us a Qur'ân other than this, or change it. "Say (O Muhammad): "It is not for me to change it on my own accord; I only follow that which is revealed unto me. Verily, I fear the torment of the Great Day (i.e. the Day of Resurrection). if I were to disobey my Lord." (15) Say (O Muhammad): "If Allâh had so willed, I should not have recited it to you nor would He have made it known to you. Verily, I have stayed amongst you a life time before this. Have you then no sense?" (16)

Quran 10:18

وَيَعْبُدُونَ مِن دُونِ ٱللَّهِ مَا لَا يَضُرُّهُمْ وَلَا يَنفَعُهُمْ وَيَقُولُونَ هَٰؤُلَآءِ شُفَعَٰؤُنَا عِندَ ٱللَّهِ قُلْ أَتُنَبِّـُٔونَ ٱللَّهَ بِمَا لَا يَعْلَمُ فِى ٱلسَّمَٰوَٰتِ وَلَا فِى ٱلْأَرْضِ سُبْحَٰنَهُ وَتَعَٰلَىٰ عَمَّا يُشْرِكُونَ

And they worship besides Allâh things that hurt them not, nor profit them, and

242

they say: "These are our intercessors with Allâh." Say: "Do you inform Allâh of that which He knows not in the heavens and on the earth?" Glorified and Exalted is He above all that which they associate as partners (with Him)!

Quran 10:20-21

وَيَقُولُونَ لَوْلَآ أُنزِلَ عَلَيْهِ ءَايَةٌ مِّن رَّبِّهِ ۖ فَقُلْ إِنَّمَا ٱلْغَيْبُ لِلَّهِ فَٱنتَظِرُوٓاْ إِنِّى مَعَكُم مِّنَ ٱلْمُنتَظِرِينَ وَإِذَآ أَذَقْنَا ٱلنَّاسَ رَحْمَةً مِّنۢ بَعْدِ ضَرَّآءَ مَسَّتْهُمْ إِذَا لَهُم مَّكْرٌ فِىٓ ءَايَاتِنَا ۚ قُلِ ٱللَّهُ أَسْرَعُ مَكْرًا ۚ إِنَّ رُسُلَنَا يَكْتُبُونَ مَا تَمْكُرُونَ

And they say: "How is it that not a sign is sent down on him from his Lord?" Say: "The unseen belongs to Allâh Alone, so wait you, verily I am with you among those who wait (for Allâh's Judgement)." (20) And when We let mankind taste mercy after some adversity has afflicted them, behold! they take to plotting against Our Ayât (proofs, evidences, verses, lessons, signs, revelations, etc.)! Say: "Allâh is more Swift in planning!" Certainly, Our Messengers (angels) record all of that which you plot. (21)

Quran 10:31

قُلْ مَن يَرْزُقُكُم مِّنَ ٱلسَّمَآءِ وَٱلْأَرْضِ أَمَّن يَمْلِكُ ٱلسَّمْعَ وَٱلْأَبْصَـٰرَ وَمَن يُخْرِجُ ٱلْحَىَّ مِنَ ٱلْمَيِّتِ وَيُخْرِجُ ٱلْمَيِّتَ مِنَ ٱلْحَىِّ وَمَن يُدَبِّرُ ٱلْأَمْرَ فَسَيَقُولُونَ ٱللَّهُ فَقُلْ أَفَلَا تَتَّقُونَ

Say: "Who provides for you from the sky and the earth? Or who owns hearing and sight? And who brings out the living from the dead and brings out the dead from the living? And who disposes the affairs?" They will say: "Allâh." Say: "Will you not then be afraid of Allâh's Punishment (for setting up rivals in worship with Allâh)?"

Quran 10:34-35

قُلْ هَلْ مِن شُرَكَآئِكُم مَّن يَبْدَؤُاْ ٱلْخَلْقَ ثُمَّ يُعِيدُهُ ۚ قُلِ
ٱللَّهُ يَبْدَؤُاْ ٱلْخَلْقَ ثُمَّ يُعِيدُهُ ۖ فَأَنَّىٰ تُؤْفَكُونَ قُلْ هَلْ مِن
شُرَكَآئِكُم مَّن يَهْدِىٓ إِلَى ٱلْحَقِّ ۚ قُلِ ٱللَّهُ يَهْدِى لِلْحَقِّ ۗ
أَفَمَن يَهْدِىٓ إِلَى ٱلْحَقِّ أَحَقُّ أَن يُتَّبَعَ أَمَّن لَّا يَهِدِّىٓ إِلَّآ
أَن يُهْدَىٰ ۖ فَمَا لَكُمْ كَيْفَ تَحْكُمُونَ

Say: "Is there of your (Allâh's so-called) partners one that originates the creation and then repeats it?" Say: "Allâh originates the creation and then He repeats it. Then how are you deluded away (from the truth)?" (34) Say: "Is there of your (Allâh's so-called) partners one that guides to the truth?" Say: "It is Allâh Who guides to the truth. Is then He, Who guides to the truth, more worthy to be followed, or he who finds not guidance (himself) unless he is guided? Then, what is the matter with you? How judge you?" (35)

Quran 10:41

وَإِن كَذَّبُوكَ فَقُل لِّى عَمَلِى وَلَكُمْ عَمَلُكُمْ أَنتُم بَرِيٓـُٔونَ مِمَّآ أَعْمَلُ وَأَنَا۠ بَرِىٓءٌ مِّمَّا تَعْمَلُونَ

And if they belie you, say: "For me are my deeds and for you are your deeds! You are innocent of what I do, and I am innocent of what you do!"

Quran 10:49-50

قُل لَّآ أَمْلِكُ لِنَفْسِى ضَرًّا وَلَا نَفْعًا إِلَّا مَا شَآءَ ٱللَّهُ لِكُلِّ أُمَّةٍ أَجَلٌ إِذَا جَآءَ أَجَلُهُمْ فَلَا يَسْتَـْٔخِرُونَ سَاعَةً وَلَا يَسْتَقْدِمُونَ قُلْ أَرَءَيْتُمْ إِنْ أَتَلكُمْ عَذَابُهُۥ بَيَتًا أَوْ نَهَارًا مَّاذَا يَسْتَعْجِلُ مِنْهُ ٱلْمُجْرِمُونَ

Say (O Muhammad): "I have no power over any harm or profit to myself except what Allâh may will. For every Ummah (a community or a nation), there is a term appointed; when their term comes, neither can they delay it nor can they advance it an hour (or a moment)." . (49) Say: "Tell me, - if His torment should come to you by night or by day, - which portion thereof would the Mujrimûn (disbelievers, polytheists, sinners, criminals) hasten on ?" (50)

Quran 10:53

وَيَسْتَنْبِئُونَكَ أَحَقٌّ هُوَ قُلْ إِى وَرَبِّى إِنَّهُ لَحَقٌّ وَمَآ أَنتُم بِمُعْجِزِينَ

And they ask you (O Muhammad) to inform them (saying): "Is it true (i.e. the torment and the establishment of the Hour; - the Day of Resurrection)?" Say: "Yes! By my Lord! It is the very truth! and you cannot escape it!"

Quran 10:58-59

قُلْ بِفَضْلِ ٱللَّهِ وَبِرَحْمَتِهِ فَبِذَٰلِكَ فَلْيَفْرَحُواْ هُوَ خَيْرٌ مِّمَّا يَجْمَعُونَ قُلْ أَرَءَيْتُم مَّآ أَنزَلَ ٱللَّهُ لَكُم مِّن رِّزْقٍ فَجَعَلْتُم مِّنْهُ حَرَامًا وَحَلَٰلاً قُلْ ءَآللَّهُ أَذِنَ لَكُمْ أَمْ عَلَى ٱللَّهِ تَفْتَرُونَ

Say: "In the Bounty of Allâh, and in His Mercy (i.e. Islâm and the Qur'ân); -

therein let them rejoice." That is better than what (the wealth) they amass (58) Say (O Muhammad to these polytheists): "Tell me, what provision Allâh has sent down to you! And you have made of it lawful and unlawful." Say: "Has Allâh permitted you (to do so), or do you invent a lie against Allâh?" (59)

Quran 10:69

قُلْ إِنَّ ٱلَّذِينَ يَفْتَرُونَ عَلَى ٱللَّهِ ٱلْكَذِبَ لَا يُفْلِحُونَ

Say: "Verily, those who invent a lie against Allâh will never be successful"

Quran 10:101-102

قُلِ ٱنظُرُواْ مَاذَا فِى ٱلسَّمَـٰوَٰتِ وَٱلْأَرْضِ وَمَا تُغْنِى ٱلْأَيَـٰتُ وَٱلنُّذُرُ عَن قَوْمٍ لَّا يُؤْمِنُونَ فَهَلْ يَنتَظِرُونَ إِلَّا مِثْلَ أَيَّامِ ٱلَّذِينَ خَلَوْاْ مِن قَبْلِهِمْ قُلْ فَٱنتَظِرُوٓاْ إِنِّى مَعَكُم مِّنَ ٱلْمُنتَظِرِينَ

Say: "Behold all that is in the heavens and the earth," but neither Ayât (proofs, evidences, verses, lessons, signs, revelations, etc.) nor warners benefit those who believe not. (101) Then do they wait for (anything) save for (a destruction) like the days of the men who passed away before them? Say: "Wait then, I am (too) with you among those who wait." (102)

Quran 10:104-106

قُلْ يَـٰٓأَيُّهَا ٱلنَّاسُ إِن كُنتُمْ فِى شَكٍّ مِّن دِينِى فَلَآ أَعْبُدُ ٱلَّذِينَ تَعْبُدُونَ مِن دُونِ ٱللَّهِ وَلَـٰكِنْ أَعْبُدُ ٱللَّهَ ٱلَّذِى يَتَوَفَّىٰكُمْ ۖ وَأُمِرْتُ أَنْ أَكُونَ مِنَ ٱلْمُؤْمِنِينَ وَأَنْ أَقِمْ وَجْهَكَ لِلدِّينِ حَنِيفًا وَلَا تَكُونَنَّ مِنَ ٱلْمُشْرِكِينَ وَلَا تَدْعُ مِن دُونِ ٱللَّهِ مَا لَا يَنفَعُكَ وَلَا يَضُرُّكَ ۖ فَإِن فَعَلْتَ فَإِنَّكَ إِذًا مِّنَ ٱلظَّـٰلِمِينَ

Say (O Muhammad): "O you mankind! If you are in doubt as to my religion (Islâm), then (know that) I will never worship those whom you worship,

249

besides Allâh. But I worship Allâh Who causes you to die, I am commanded to be one of the believers. (104) "And (it is revealed to me): Direct your face entirely towards the religion Hanif (Islâmic Monotheism, i.e. to worship none but Allâh Alone), and never be one of the Mushrikûn (those who ascribe partners to Allâh, polytheists, idolaters, disbelievers in the Oneness of Allâh, and those who worship others along with Allâh). (105) "And invoke not besides Allâh, any that will neither profit you, nor hurt you, but if (in case) you did so, you shall certainly be one of the Zâlimûn (polytheists and wrong-doers)."(106)

Quran 10:108

قُلْ يَٰٓأَيُّهَا ٱلنَّاسُ قَدْ جَآءَكُمُ ٱلْحَقُّ مِن رَّبِّكُمْ فَمَنِ ٱهْتَدَىٰ فَإِنَّمَا يَهْتَدِى لِنَفْسِهِۦ وَمَن ضَلَّ فَإِنَّمَا يَضِلُّ عَلَيْهَا وَمَآ أَنَا۠ عَلَيْكُم بِوَكِيلٍ

Say: "O you mankind! Now truth (i.e. the Qur'ân and Muhammad), has come to you from your Lord. So whosoever receives guidance, he does so for the good of his own self, and whosoever goes astray, he does so to his own loss, and I am not (set) over you as a Wakîl (disposer of affairs to oblige you for guidance)."

Quran 11:13

أَمْ يَقُولُونَ ٱفْتَرَىٰهُۚ قُلْ فَأْتُواْ بِعَشْرِ سُوَرٍ مِّثْلِهِۦ مُفْتَرَيَٰتٍ وَٱدْعُواْ مَنِ ٱسْتَطَعْتُم مِّن دُونِ ٱللَّهِ إِن كُنتُمْ صَٰدِقِينَ

Or they say, "He (Prophet Muhammad) forged it (the Qur'an)." Say: "Bring you then ten forged Sûrahs (chapters) like unto it, and call whomsoever you can, other than Allâh (to your help), if you speak the truth!"

Quran 11:35

أَمْ يَقُولُونَ ٱفْتَرَىٰهُ ۖ قُلْ إِنِ ٱفْتَرَيْتُهُ ۥ فَعَلَىَّ إِجْرَامِى وَأَنَا۠ بَرِىٓءٌ مِّمَّا تُجْرِمُونَ

Or they say: "He (Muhammad) has fabricated it (the Qur'ân)." Say: "If I have fabricated it, upon me be my crimes, but I am innocent of (all) those crimes which you commit."

Quran 11:121-122

وَقُل لِّلَّذِينَ لَا يُؤْمِنُونَ ٱعْمَلُواْ عَلَىٰ مَكَانَتِكُمْ إِنَّا عَٰمِلُونَ وَٱنتَظِرُوٓاْ إِنَّا مُنتَظِرُونَ

And say to those who do not believe: "Act according to your ability and way, We are acting (in our way). (121) And you wait ! We (too) are waiting."(122)

Quran 12:108

قُلْ هَٰذِهِۦ سَبِيلِىٓ أَدْعُوٓاْ إِلَى ٱللَّهِ ۚ عَلَىٰ بَصِيرَةٍ أَنَا۠ وَمَنِ ٱتَّبَعَنِى ۖ وَسُبْحَٰنَ ٱللَّهِ وَمَآ أَنَا۠ مِنَ ٱلْمُشْرِكِينَ

Say (O Muhammad): "This is my way; I invite unto Allâh (i.e. to the Oneness of

Allâh - Islâmic Monotheism) with sure
knowledge, I and whosoever follows me
(also must invite others to Allâh i.e to
the Oneness of Allâh - Islâmic
Monotheism with sure knowledge).
And Glorified and Exalted is Allâh
(above all that they associate as partners
with Him). And I am not of the
Mushrikûn (polytheists, pagans,
idolaters and disbelievers in the
Oneness of Allâh; those who worship
others along with Allâh or set up rivals
or partners to Allâh)."

Quran 13:16

قُلْ مَن رَّبُّ ٱلسَّمَـٰوَٰتِ وَٱلْأَرْضِ قُلِ ٱللَّهُ قُلْ أَفَٱتَّخَذْتُم
مِّن دُونِهِۦٓ أَوْلِيَآءَ لَا يَمْلِكُونَ لِأَنفُسِهِمْ نَفْعًا وَلَا ضَرًّا ۚ
قُلْ هَلْ يَسْتَوِى ٱلْأَعْمَىٰ وَٱلْبَصِيرُ أَمْ هَلْ تَسْتَوِى
ٱلظُّلُمَـٰتُ وَٱلنُّورُ ۗ أَمْ جَعَلُوا۟ لِلَّهِ شُرَكَآءَ خَلَقُوا۟ كَخَلْقِهِۦ
فَتَشَـٰبَهَ ٱلْخَلْقُ عَلَيْهِمْ ۚ قُلِ ٱللَّهُ خَـٰلِقُ كُلِّ شَىْءٍ وَهُوَ
ٱلْوَٰحِدُ ٱلْقَهَّـٰرُ

Say: "Who is the Lord of the heavens and the earth?" Say: "(It is) Allâh." Say: "Have you then taken (for worship) Auliyâ' (protectors) other than Him, such as have no power either for benefit or for harm to themselves?" Say: "Is the blind equal to the one who sees? Or darkness equal to light? Or do they assign to Allâh partners who created the like of His creation, so that the creation (which they made and His creation) seemed alike to them." Say: "Allâh is the Creator of all things, He is the One, the Irresistible."

Quran 13:27

وَيَقُولُ ٱلَّذِينَ كَفَرُواْ لَوْلَآ أُنزِلَ عَلَيْهِ ءَايَةٌ مِّن رَّبِّهِۦ قُلْ إِنَّ ٱللَّهَ يُضِلُّ مَن يَشَآءُ وَيَهْدِىٓ إِلَيْهِ مَنْ أَنَابَ

And those who disbelieve say: "Why is not a sign sent down to him (Muhammad) from his Lord?" Say: "Verily, Allâh sends astray whom He wills and guides unto Himself those who turn to Him in repentance."

Quran 13:30

كَذَٰلِكَ أَرْسَلْنَٰكَ فِىٓ أُمَّةٍ قَدْ خَلَتْ مِن قَبْلِهَآ أُمَمٌ لِّتَتْلُوَا۟ عَلَيْهِمُ ٱلَّذِىٓ أَوْحَيْنَآ إِلَيْكَ وَهُمْ يَكْفُرُونَ بِٱلرَّحْمَٰنِ قُلْ هُوَ رَبِّى لَآ إِلَٰهَ إِلَّا هُوَ عَلَيْهِ تَوَكَّلْتُ وَإِلَيْهِ مَتَابِ

Thus have We sent you (O Muhammad) to a community before whom other communities have passed away, in order that you might recite unto them what We have revealed to you, while they disbelieve in the Most Gracious (Allâh) Say: "He is my Lord! Lâ ilâha illâ Huwa (none has the right to be worshipped but He)! In Him is my trust, and to Him will be my return with repentance."

Quran 13:33

أَفَمَنْ هُوَ قَآئِمٌ عَلَىٰ كُلِّ نَفْسٍ بِمَا كَسَبَتْ وَجَعَلُوا۟ لِلَّهِ شُرَكَآءَ قُلْ سَمُّوهُمْ أَمْ تُنَبِّـُٔونَهُ بِمَا لَا يَعْلَمُ فِى

أَلْأَرْضِ أَم بِظَـٰهِرٍ مِّنَ ٱلْقَوْلِ ۗ بَلْ زُيِّنَ لِلَّذِينَ كَفَرُواْ مَكْرُهُمْ وَصُدُّواْ عَنِ ٱلسَّبِيلِ ۗ وَمَن يُضْلِلِ ٱللَّهُ فَمَا لَهُ ۥ مِنْ هَادٍ

Is then He (Allâh) Who takes charge (guards, maintains, provides) of every person and knows all that he has earned (like any other deities who know nothing)? Yet they ascribe partners to Allâh. Say: "Name them! Is it that you will inform Him of something He knows not in the earth or is it (just) a show of false words." Nay! To those who disbelieved, their plotting is made fairseeming, and they have been hindered from the Right Path, and whom Allâh sends astray, for him, there is no guide.

Quran 13:36

وَٱلَّذِينَ ءَاتَيْنَـٰهُمُ ٱلْكِتَـٰبَ يَفْرَحُونَ بِمَآ أُنزِلَ إِلَيْكَ ۖ وَمِنَ ٱلْأَحْزَابِ مَن يُنكِرُ بَعْضَهُ ۚ قُلْ إِنَّمَآ أُمِرْتُ أَنْ أَعْبُدَ ٱللَّهَ وَلَآ أُشْرِكَ بِهِ ۚ إِلَيْهِ أَدْعُواْ وَإِلَيْهِ مَـَٔابِ

Those to whom We have given the Book (such as 'Abdullâh bin Salâm and other Jews who embraced Islâm), rejoice at what has been revealed unto you (i.e. the Qur'ân), but there are among the Confederates (from the Jews and pagans) those who reject a part thereof. Say (O Muhammad): "I am commanded only to worship Allâh (Alone) and not to join partners with Him. To Him (Alone) I call and to Him is my return."

Quran 13:43

وَيَقُولُ ٱلَّذِينَ كَفَرُواْ لَسْتَ مُرْسَلاً قُلْ كَفَىٰ بِٱللَّهِ شَهِيدًۢا بَيْنِى وَبَيْنَكُمْ وَمَنْ عِندَهُۥ عِلْمُ ٱلْكِتَٰبِ

And those who disbelieved, say: "You (O Muhammad) are not a Messenger." Say: "Sufficient as a witness between me and you is Allâh and those too who have knowledge of the Scripture (such as 'Abdullâh bin Salâm, Salman Al Farsi and other Jews and Christians who embraced Islâm)."

Quran 14:31

قُل لِّعِبَادِيَ ٱلَّذِينَ ءَامَنُواْ يُقِيمُواْ ٱلصَّلَوٰةَ وَيُنفِقُواْ مِمَّا رَزَقْنَٰهُمْ سِرًّا وَعَلَانِيَةً مِّن قَبْلِ أَن يَأْتِىَ يَوْمٌ لَّا بَيْعٌ فِيهِ وَلَا خِلَٰلٌ

Say (O Muhammad) to 'Ibâdî (My slaves) who have believed, that they should perform As-Salât (prayer), and spend in charity out of the sustenance We have given them, secretly and openly, before the coming of a Day on which there will be neither mutual bargaining nor befriending.

Quran 17:42

قُل لَّوْ كَانَ مَعَهُۥ ءَالِهَةٌ كَمَا يَقُولُونَ إِذًا لَّٱبْتَغَوْاْ إِلَىٰ ذِى ٱلْعَرْشِ سَبِيلاً

Say (O Muhammad): "If there had been other âlihah (gods) along with Him as they assert, then they would certainly have sought out a way to the Lord of the Throne (seeking His Pleasures and to be near to Him)

Quran 17:50-51

قُلْ كُونُواْ حِجَارَةً أَوْ حَدِيدًا

أَوْ خَلْقًا مِّمَّا يَكْبُرُ فِى صُدُورِكُمْ فَسَيَقُولُونَ مَن يُعِيدُنَا قُلِ ٱلَّذِى فَطَرَكُمْ أَوَّلَ مَرَّةٍ فَسَيُنْغِضُونَ إِلَيْكَ رُءُوسَهُمْ وَيَقُولُونَ مَتَىٰ هُوَ قُلْ عَسَىٰ أَن يَكُونَ قَرِيبًا

Say (O Muhammad) "Be you stones or iron," (50) "Or some created thing that is yet greater (or harder) in your breasts (thoughts to be resurrected, even then you shall be resurrected)" Then, they will say: "Who shall bring us back (to life)?" Say: "He Who created you first!" Then, they will shake their heads at you and say: "When will that be ?" Say: "Perhaps it is near!" (51)

Quran 17:53

وَقُل لِّعِبَادِى يَقُولُواْ ٱلَّتِى هِىَ أَحْسَنُ إِنَّ ٱلشَّيْطَـٰنَ يَنزَغُ بَيْنَهُمْ إِنَّ ٱلشَّيْطَـٰنَ كَانَ لِلْإِنسَـٰنِ عَدُوًّا مُّبِينًا

And say to My slaves (i.e. the true believers of Islâmic Monotheism) that they should (only) say those words that are the best. (Because) Shaitân (Satan) verily, sows state of conflicit and disagreements among them. Surely, Shaitân (Satan) is to man a plain enemy.

Quran 17:81

وَقُلْ جَآءَ ٱلْحَقُّ وَزَهَقَ ٱلْبَـٰطِلُ إِنَّ ٱلْبَـٰطِلَ كَانَ زَهُوقًا

And say: "Truth (i.e. Islâmic Monotheism or this Qur'ân or Jihâd against polytheists) has come and Bâtil (falsehood, i.e. or polytheism) has vanished. Surely! Bâtil is ever bound to vanish." (81)

Quran 17:84-85

قُلْ كُلٌّ يَعْمَلُ عَلَىٰ شَاكِلَتِهِۦ فَرَبُّكُمْ أَعْلَمُ بِمَنْ هُوَ أَهْدَىٰ سَبِيلاً وَيَسْـَٔلُونَكَ عَنِ ٱلرُّوحِ قُلِ ٱلرُّوحُ مِنْ أَمْرِ رَبِّى وَمَآ أُوتِيتُم مِّنَ ٱلْعِلْمِ إِلَّا قَلِيلاً

Say (O Muhammad to mankind): "Each one does according to Shakilatihi (i.e. his way or his religion or his intentions), and your Lord knows best of him whose path (religion) is right." (84) And they ask you (O Muhammad) concerning the Rûh (the Soul); Say: "The Rûh (the Soul): is one of the things, the knowledge of which is only with my Lord. And of knowledge, you (mankind) have been given only a little." (85)

Quran 17:88

قُل لَّئِنِ ٱجْتَمَعَتِ ٱلْإِنسُ وَٱلْجِنُّ عَلَىٰٓ أَن يَأْتُواْ بِمِثْلِ هَـٰذَا ٱلْقُرْءَانِ لَا يَأْتُونَ بِمِثْلِهِۦ وَلَوْ كَانَ بَعْضُهُمْ لِبَعْضٍ ظَهِيرًا

Say: "If the mankind and the jinn were together to produce the like of this

Qur'ân, they could not produce the like of it, even if they helped one another."

Quran 17:93

أَوْ يَكُونَ لَكَ بَيْتٌ مِّن زُخْرُفٍ أَوْ تَرْقَىٰ فِى ٱلسَّمَاءِ وَلَن نُّؤْمِنَ لِرُقِيِّكَ حَتَّىٰ تُنَزِّلَ عَلَيْنَا كِتَـٰبًا نَّقْرَؤُهُ ۗ قُلْ سُبْحَانَ رَبِّى هَلْ كُنتُ إِلَّا بَشَرًا رَّسُولاً

"Or you have a house of Zukhruf (like silver and pure gold), or you ascend up into the sky, and even then we will put no faith in your ascension until you bring down for us a Book that we would read." Say (O Muhammad): "Glorified (and Exalted) is my Lord [(Allâh) above all that evil they (polytheists) associate with Him]! Am I anything but a man, sent as a Messenger?"

Quran 17:95

قُل لَّوْ كَانَ فِى ٱلْأَرْضِ مَلَـٰئِكَةٌ يَمْشُونَ مُطْمَئِنِّينَ لَنَزَّلْنَا عَلَيْهِم مِّنَ ٱلسَّمَاءِ مَلَكًا رَّسُولاً

Say: "If there were on the earth, angels walking about in peace and security, We should certainly have sent down for them from the heaven an angel as a Messenger."

Quran 17:100

قُل لَّوۡ أَنتُمۡ تَمۡلِكُونَ خَزَآئِنَ رَحۡمَةِ رَبِّىٓ إِذًا لَّأَمۡسَكۡتُمۡ خَشۡيَةَ ٱلۡإِنفَاقِ ۚ وَكَانَ ٱلۡإِنسَـٰنُ قَتُورًا

Say (to the disbelievers): "If you possessed the treasure of the Mercy of my Lord (wealth, money, provision), then you would surely hold back (from spending) for fear of (being exhausted), and man is ever miserly!"

Quran 17:107

قُلۡ ءَامِنُواْ بِهِۦٓ أَوۡ لَا تُؤۡمِنُوٓاْ ۚ إِنَّ ٱلَّذِينَ أُوتُواْ ٱلۡعِلۡمَ مِن قَبۡلِهِۦٓ إِذَا يُتۡلَىٰ عَلَيۡهِمۡ يَخِرُّونَ لِلۡأَذۡقَانِ سُجَّدًا

Say (O Muhammad to them): "Believe in it (the Qur'ân) or do not believe (in it).

263

Verily! those who were given knowledge before it (the Jews and the Christians like 'Abdullâh bin Salâm and Salmân Al-Farsî), when it is recited to them, fall down on their faces in humble prostration." (107)

Quran 17:110-111

قُلِ ٱدْعُوا۟ ٱللَّهَ أَوِ ٱدْعُوا۟ ٱلرَّحْمَٰنَ ۖ أَيًّا مَّا تَدْعُوا۟ فَلَهُ ٱلْأَسْمَآءُ ٱلْحُسْنَىٰ ۚ وَلَا تَجْهَرْ بِصَلَاتِكَ وَلَا تُخَافِتْ بِهَا وَٱبْتَغِ بَيْنَ ذَٰلِكَ سَبِيلًا وَقُلِ ٱلْحَمْدُ لِلَّهِ ٱلَّذِى لَمْ يَتَّخِذْ وَلَدًا وَلَمْ يَكُن لَّهُ ۥ شَرِيكٌ فِى ٱلْمُلْكِ وَلَمْ يَكُن لَّهُ ۥ وَلِىٌّ مِّنَ ٱلذُّلِّ ۖ وَكَبِّرْهُ تَكْبِيرًا

Say (O Muhammad): "Invoke Allâh or invoke the Most Gracious (Allâh), by whatever name you invoke Him (it is the same), for to Him belong the Best Names. And offer your Salât (prayer) neither aloud nor in a low voice, but follow a way between. (110) And say: "All the praises and thanks are to Allâh, Who has not begotten a son (nor offspring), and Who has no partner in (His) Dominion, nor He is low to have a Walî (helper, protector or supporter). And magnify Him with all the magnificence, [Allâhu-Akbar (Allâh is Most Great)]."

Quran 18:29

وَقُلِ ٱلْحَقُّ مِن رَّبِّكُمْ فَمَن شَاءَ فَلْيُؤْمِن وَمَن شَاءَ فَلْيَكْفُرْ إِنَّا أَعْتَدْنَا لِلظَّـٰلِمِينَ نَارًا أَحَاطَ بِهِمْ سُرَادِقُهَا وَإِن يَسْتَغِيثُواْ يُغَاثُواْ بِمَاءٍ كَٱلْمُهْلِ يَشْوِى ٱلْوُجُوهَ بِئْسَ ٱلشَّرَابُ وَسَاءَتْ مُرْتَفَقًا

And say: "The truth is from your Lord." Then whosoever wills, let him believe, and whosoever wills, let him disbelieve. Verily, We have prepared for the Zâlimûn (polytheists and wrong-doers), a Fire whose walls will be surrounding them (disbelievers in the Oneness of Allâh). And if they ask for help (relief, water) they will be granted water like boiling oil, that will scald their faces.

Terrible is the drink, and an evil Murtafaq (dwelling, resting place)!

Quran 18:103-110

قُلْ هَلْ نُنَبِّئُكُم بِٱلْأَخْسَرِينَ أَعْمَـٰلاً ٱلَّذِينَ ضَلَّ سَعْيُهُمْ فِى ٱلْحَيَوٰةِ ٱلدُّنْيَا وَهُمْ يَحْسَبُونَ أَنَّهُمْ يُحْسِنُونَ صُنْعًا أُوْلَـٰئِكَ ٱلَّذِينَ كَفَرُواْ بِـَٔايَـٰتِ رَبِّهِمْ وَلِقَآئِهِۦ فَحَبِطَتْ أَعْمَـٰلُهُمْ فَلَا نُقِيمُ لَهُمْ يَوْمَ ٱلْقِيَـٰمَةِ وَزْنًا ذَٰلِكَ جَزَآؤُهُمْ جَهَنَّمُ بِمَا كَفَرُواْ وَٱتَّخَذُوٓاْ ءَايَـٰتِى وَرُسُلِى هُزُوًا إِنَّ ٱلَّذِينَ ءَامَنُواْ وَعَمِلُواْ ٱلصَّـٰلِحَـٰتِ كَانَتْ لَهُمْ جَنَّـٰتُ ٱلْفِرْدَوْسِ نُزُلاً خَـٰلِدِينَ فِيهَا لَا يَبْغُونَ عَنْهَا حِوَلاً قُل لَّوْ كَانَ ٱلْبَحْرُ مِدَادًا لِّكَلِمَـٰتِ رَبِّى لَنَفِدَ ٱلْبَحْرُ قَبْلَ أَن تَنفَدَ كَلِمَـٰتُ رَبِّى وَلَوْ جِئْنَا بِمِثْلِهِۦ مَدَدًا قُلْ إِنَّمَآ أَنَا۠ بَشَرٌ مِّثْلُكُمْ يُوحَىٰٓ إِلَىَّ أَنَّمَآ إِلَـٰهُكُمْ إِلَـٰهٌ وَٰحِدٌ فَمَن كَانَ يَرْجُواْ لِقَآءَ رَبِّهِۦ فَلْيَعْمَلْ عَمَلاً صَـٰلِحًا وَلَا يُشْرِكْ بِعِبَادَةِ رَبِّهِۦٓ أَحَدًۢا

Say (O Muhammad): "Shall We tell you the greatest losers in respect of (their) deeds? (103) "Those whose efforts have been wasted in this life while they thought that they were acquiring good by their deeds! (104) "They are those

who deny the Ayât (proofs, evidences,
verses, lessons, signs, revelations, etc.)
of their Lord and the Meeting with Him
(in the Hereafter). So their works are in
vain, and on the Day of Resurrection,
We shall assign not weight for them.
(105) "That shall be their recompense,
Hell; because they disbelieved and took
My Ayât (proofs, evidences, verses,
lessons, signs, revelations, etc.) and My
Messengers by way of jest and mockery.
(106) "Verily! those who believe (in the
Oneness of Allâh - Islâmic Monotheism)
and do righteous deeds, shall have the
Gardens of Al-Firdaus (the Paradise) for
their entertainment. (107) "Wherein they
shall dwell (forever). No desire will they
have for removal therefrom." (108) Say
(O Muhammad to mankind). "If the sea
were ink for (writing) the Words of my
Lord, surely, the sea would be
exhausted before the Words of my Lord
would be finished, even if we brought

(another sea) like it for its aid." (109) Say
(O Muhammad): "I am only a man like
you. It has been revealed to me that
your Ilâh (God) is One Ilâh (God — i.e.
Allâh). So whoever hopes for the
Meeting with his Lord, let him work
righteousness and associate none as a
partner in the worship of his Lord."
(110)

Quran 20:135

قُلْ كُلٌّ مُّتَرَبِّصٌ فَتَرَبَّصُوا۟ فَسَتَعْلَمُونَ مَنْ أَصْحَـٰبُ
ٱلصِّرَ ٰطِ ٱلسَّوِىِّ وَمَنِ ٱهْتَدَىٰ

Say: "Each one (believer and disbeliever)
is waiting, so wait you too, and you
shall know who are they that are on the
Straight and Even Path (i.e. Allâh's
religion of Islâmic Monotheism), and
who are they that have let themselves be
guided (on the Right Path).

Quran 21:4

قَالَ رَبِّى يَعْلَمُ ٱلْقَوْلَ فِى ٱلسَّمَآءِ وَٱلْأَرْضِ ۖ وَهُوَ ٱلسَّمِيعُ ٱلْعَلِيمُ

He (Muhammad) said: "My Lord knows (every) word (spoken) in the heavens and on earth. And He is the All-Hearer, the All-Knower."

Quran 21:24

أَمِ ٱتَّخَذُوا۟ مِن دُونِهِۦٓ ءَالِهَةً ۖ قُلْ هَاتُوا۟ بُرْهَٰنَكُمْ ۖ هَٰذَا ذِكْرُ مَن مَّعِىَ وَذِكْرُ مَن قَبْلِى ۗ بَلْ أَكْثَرُهُمْ لَا يَعْلَمُونَ ٱلْحَقَّ ۖ فَهُم مُّعْرِضُونَ

Or have they taken for worship (other) âlihah (gods) besides Him? Say: "Bring your proof:" This (the Qur'ân) is the Reminder for those with me and the Reminder for those before me. But most of them know not the Truth, so they are averse.

Quran 21:42

قُلْ مَن يَكْلَؤُكُم بِٱلَّيْلِ وَٱلنَّهَارِ مِنَ ٱلرَّحْمَـٰنِ ۗ بَلْ هُمْ عَن ذِكْرِ رَبِّهِم مُّعْرِضُونَ

Say: "Who can guard and protect you in the night or in the day from the (punishment of the) Most Gracious (Allâh)?" Nay, but they turn away from the remembrance of their Lord.

Quran 21:45

قُلْ إِنَّمَآ أُنذِرُكُم بِٱلْوَحْىِ ۚ وَلَا يَسْمَعُ ٱلصُّمُّ ٱلدُّعَآءَ إِذَا مَا يُنذَرُونَ

Say (O Muhammad): "I warn you only by the revelation (from Allâh and not by the opinion of the religious scholars and others). But the deaf (who follow the religious scholars and others blindly) will not hear the call, (even) when they are warned [(i.e. one should follow only the Qur'ân and the Sunnah (legal ways, orders, acts of worship, and the statements of Prophet Muhammad, as the Companions of the Prophet did)].

Quran 21:108-111

إِنَّمَا يُوحَىٰ إِلَيَّ أَنَّمَا إِلَٰهُكُمْ إِلَٰهٌ وَاحِدٌ ۖ فَهَلْ أَنْتُمْ مُسْلِمُونَ ۟ فَإِنْ تَوَلَّوْا فَقُلْ آذَنْتُكُمْ عَلَىٰ سَوَاءٍ ۖ وَإِنْ أَدْرِي أَقَرِيبٌ أَمْ بَعِيدٌ مَا تُوعَدُونَ إِنَّهُ يَعْلَمُ الْجَهْرَ مِنَ الْقَوْلِ وَيَعْلَمُ مَا تَكْتُمُونَ وَإِنْ أَدْرِي لَعَلَّهُ فِتْنَةٌ لَكُمْ وَمَتَاعٌ إِلَىٰ حِينٍ

Say (O Muhammad): "It is revealed to me that your Ilâh (God) is only one Ilâh (God - Allâh). Will you then submit to His Will (become Muslims and stop worshipping others besides Allâh)?" (108) But if they (disbelievers, idolaters, Jews, Christians, polytheists) turn away (from Islâmic Monotheism) say (to them O Muhammad): "I give you a notice (of war as) to be known to us all alike. And I know not whether that which you are promised (i.e. the torment or the Day of Resurrection) is near or far." (109)

271

Verily, He (Allâh) knows that which is spoken aloud (openly) and that which you conceal. (110) And I know not, perhaps it may be a trial for you, and an enjoyment for a while. (111)

Quran 22:49

قُلْ يَـٰٓأَيُّهَا ٱلنَّاسُ إِنَّمَآ أَنَا۠ لَكُمْ نَذِيرٌ مُّبِينٌ

Say (O Muhammad): "O mankind! I am (sent) to you only as a plain warner."

Quran 23:84-89

قُلْ لِمَنِ الْأَرْضُ وَمَنْ فِيهَا إِنْ كُنْتُمْ تَعْلَمُونَ سَيَقُولُونَ لِلَّهِ ۚ قُلْ أَفَلَا تَذَكَّرُونَ قُلْ مَنْ رَبُّ السَّمَاوَاتِ السَّبْعِ وَرَبُّ الْعَرْشِ الْعَظِيمِ سَيَقُولُونَ لِلَّهِ ۚ قُلْ أَفَلَا تَتَّقُونَ قُلْ مَنْ بِيَدِهِ مَلَكُوتُ كُلِّ شَيْءٍ وَهُوَ يُجِيرُ وَلَا يُجَارُ عَلَيْهِ إِنْ كُنْتُمْ تَعْلَمُونَ سَيَقُولُونَ لِلَّهِ ۚ قُلْ فَأَنَّىٰ تُسْحَرُونَ

Say: "Whose is the earth and whosoever is therein? If you know!" (84) They will say: "It is Allâh's!" Say: "Will you not then remember?" (85) Say: "Who is (the) Lord of the seven heavens, and (the) Lord of the Great Throne?" (86) They will say: "Allâh." Say: "Will you not then fear Allâh (believe in His Oneness, obey Him, believe in the Resurrection and Recompense for every good or bad deed)?" (87) Say "In Whose Hand is the sovereignty of everything (i.e. treasures of each and everything)? And He protects (all), while against Whom there is no protector, (i.e. if Allâh saves anyone none can punish or harm him, and if Allâh punishes or harms anyone none can save him), if you know?" (88) They will say: "(All that belongs) to Allâh." Say: "How then are you deceived and turn away from the truth?" (89)

Quran 25:15

قُلْ أَذَٰلِكَ خَيْرٌ أَمْ جَنَّةُ ٱلْخُلْدِ ٱلَّتِى وُعِدَ ٱلْمُتَّقُونَ ۚ كَانَتْ لَهُمْ جَزَآءً وَمَصِيرًا

Say: (O Muhammad) "Is that (torment) better or the Paradise of Eternity which is promised to the Muttaqûn (pious and righteous persons)?" It will be theirs as a reward and as a final destination.

Quran 25:57

قُلْ مَآ أَسْـَٔلُكُمْ عَلَيْهِ مِنْ أَجْرٍ إِلَّا مَن شَآءَ أَن يَتَّخِذَ إِلَىٰ رَبِّهِۦ سَبِيلاً

Say: "No reward do I ask of you for this (that which I have brought from my Lord and its preaching), save that whosoever wills, may take a Path to his Lord.

Quran 25:60

وَإِذَا قِيلَ لَهُمُ ٱسْجُدُواْ لِلرَّحْمَٰنِ قَالُواْ وَمَا ٱلرَّحْمَٰنُ أَنَسْجُدُ لِمَا تَأْمُرُنَا وَزَادَهُمْ نُفُورًا

And when it is said to them: "Prostrate yourselves to the Most Gracious (Allâh)! they say: "And what is the Most

Gracious? Shall we fall down in prostration to that which you command us?" And it increases in them only aversion

Quran 25:77

قُلْ مَا يَعْبَؤُاْ بِكُمْ رَبِّى لَوْلَا دُعَآؤُكُمْ فَقَدْ كَذَّبْتُمْ فَسَوْفَ يَكُونُ لِزَامًا

Say (O Muhammad to the disbelievers): "My Lord pays attention to you only because of your invocation to Him. But now you have indeed denied (Him). So the torment will be yours forever (permanent punishment)."

Quran 26:216

فَإِنْ عَصَوْكَ فَقُلْ إِنِّى بَرِىٓءٌ مِّمَّا تَعْمَلُونَ

Then if they disobey you (Muhammad), say: "I am innocent of what you do."

Quran 27:59

قُلِ ٱلْحَمْدُ لِلَّهِ وَسَلَامٌ عَلَىٰ عِبَادِهِ ٱلَّذِينَ ٱصْطَفَىٰٓ ءَآللَّهُ خَيْرٌ أَمَّا يُشْرِكُونَ

Say: "Praise and thanks are to Allâh, and peace be on His slaves whom He has chosen (for His Message)! Is Allâh better, or (all) that you ascribe as partners (to Him)?" (Of course, Allâh is Better)

Quran 27:64-65

أَمَّن يَبْدَؤُاْ ٱلْخَلْقَ ثُمَّ يُعِيدُهُۥ وَمَن يَرْزُقُكُم مِّنَ ٱلسَّمَآءِ وَٱلْأَرْضِ أَءِلَٰهٌ مَّعَ ٱللَّهِ قُلْ هَاتُواْ بُرْهَٰنَكُمْ إِن كُنتُمْ صَٰدِقِينَ قُل لَّا يَعْلَمُ مَن فِى ٱلسَّمَٰوَٰتِ وَٱلْأَرْضِ ٱلْغَيْبَ إِلَّا ٱللَّهُ وَمَا يَشْعُرُونَ أَيَّانَ يُبْعَثُونَ

Is not He (better than your so-called gods) Who originates creation, and shall thereafter repeat it, and Who provides for you from heaven and earth? Is there any ilâh (god) with Allâh? Say, "Bring forth your proofs, if you are truthful." (64) Say: "None in the heavens and the earth knows the Ghaib (unseen) except Allâh, nor can they perceive when they shall be resurrected." (65)

Quran 27:69

قُلْ سِيرُواْ فِى ٱلْأَرْضِ فَٱنظُرُواْ كَيْفَ كَانَ عَٰقِبَةُ ٱلْمُجْرِمِينَ

Say to them "Travel in the land and see how has been the end of the Mujrimun (criminals, those who denied Allâh's Messengers and disobeyed Allâh)."

Quran 27:72

قُلْ عَسَىٰٓ أَن يَكُونَ رَدِفَ لَكُم بَعْضُ ٱلَّذِى تَسْتَعْجِلُونَ

Say: "Perhaps that which you wish to hasten on, may be close behind you"

Quran 27:92-93

وَأَنْ أَتْلُوَ الْقُرْآنَ ۖ فَمَنِ اهْتَدَىٰ فَإِنَّمَا يَهْتَدِي لِنَفْسِهِ ۖ وَمَنْ ضَلَّ فَقُلْ إِنَّمَا أَنَا مِنَ الْمُنْذِرِينَ

277

وَقُلِ الْحَمْدُ لِلَّهِ سَيُرِيكُمْ آيَاتِهِ فَتَعْرِفُونَهَا ۚ وَمَا رَبُّكَ بِغَافِلٍ عَمَّا تَعْمَلُونَ

And that I should recite the Qur'ân, then whosoever receives guidance, receives it for the good of his ownself, and whosoever goes astray, say (to him): "I am only one of the warners." (92) And say "All the praises and thanks are to Allâh. He will show you His Ayât (signs, in yourselves, and in the universe or punishments), and you shall recognize them. And your Lord is not unaware of what you do." (93)

Quran 28:49

قُلْ فَأْتُوا بِكِتَابٍ مِّنْ عِندِ اللَّهِ هُوَ أَهْدَىٰ مِنْهُمَا أَتَّبِعْهُ إِن كُنْتُمْ صَادِقِينَ

Say (to them, O Muhammad): "Then bring a Book from Allâh, which is a better guide than these two [the Taurât

(Torah) and the Qur'ân], that I may follow it, if you are truthful."

Quran 28:71-72

قُلْ أَرَءَيْتُمْ إِن جَعَلَ ٱللَّهُ عَلَيْكُمُ ٱلَّيْلَ سَرْمَدًا إِلَىٰ يَوْمِ
ٱلْقِيَـٰمَةِ مَنْ إِلَـٰهٌ غَيْرُ ٱللَّهِ يَأْتِيكُم بِضِيَآءٍ ۖ أَفَلَا
تَسْمَعُونَ قُلْ أَرَءَيْتُمْ إِن جَعَلَ ٱللَّهُ عَلَيْكُمُ ٱلنَّهَارَ
سَرْمَدًا إِلَىٰ يَوْمِ ٱلْقِيَـٰمَةِ مَنْ إِلَـٰهٌ غَيْرُ ٱللَّهِ يَأْتِيكُم
بِلَيْلٍ تَسْكُنُونَ فِيهِ ۚ أَفَلَا تُبْصِرُونَ

Say: "Tell me! If Allâh made the night continuous for you till the Day of Resurrection, which ilâh (god) besides Allâh could bring you light? Will you not then hear?" (71) Say: "Tell me! If Allâh made the day continuous for you till the Day of Resurrection, which ilâh (god) besides Allâh could bring you night wherein you rest? Will you not then see?" (72)

Quran 28:85

إِنَّ ٱلَّذِى فَرَضَ عَلَيْكَ ٱلْقُرْءَانَ لَرَآدُّكَ إِلَىٰ مَعَادٍۚ قُل رَّبِّىٓ أَعْلَمُ مَن جَآءَ بِٱلْهُدَىٰ وَمَنْ هُوَ فِى ضَلَٰلٍ مُّبِينٍ

Verily, He Who has given you (O Muhammad) the Qur'an (i.e. ordered you to act on its laws and to preach it to others) will surely bring you back to the Ma'âd (place of return, either to Makkah in this life or to Paradise after your death, etc.). Say: "My Lord is Aware of him who brings guidance, and of him who is in manifest error."

Quran 29:20

قُلْ سِيرُواْ فِى ٱلْأَرْضِ فَٱنظُرُواْ كَيْفَ بَدَأَ ٱلْخَلْقَۚ ثُمَّ ٱللَّهُ يُنشِئُ ٱلنَّشْأَةَ ٱلْءَاخِرَةَۚ إِنَّ ٱللَّهَ عَلَىٰ كُلِّ شَىْءٍ قَدِيرٌ

Say: "Travel in the land and see how (Allâh) originated the creation, and then Allâh will bring forth the creation of the Hereafter (i.e. resurrection after death). Verily, Allâh is Able to do all things."

Quran 29:46

وَلَا تُجَـٰدِلُوٓاْ أَهْلَ ٱلْكِتَـٰبِ إِلَّا بِٱلَّتِى هِىَ أَحْسَنُ إِلَّا ٱلَّذِينَ ظَلَمُواْ مِنْهُمْۖ وَقُولُوٓاْ ءَامَنَّا بِٱلَّذِىٓ أُنزِلَ إِلَيْنَا وَأُنزِلَ إِلَيْكُمْ وَإِلَـٰهُنَا وَإِلَـٰهُكُمْ وَٰحِدٌ وَنَحْنُ لَهُۥ مُسْلِمُونَ

And argue not with the people of the Scripture (Jews and Christians), unless it be in (a way) that is better (with good words and in good manner, inviting them to Islâmic Monotheism with His Verses), except with such of them as do wrong, and say (to them): "We believe in that which has been revealed to us and revealed to you; our Ilâh (God) and your Ilâh (God) is One (i.e. Allâh), and to Him we have submitted (as Muslims)."

Quran 29:50

وَقَالُواْ لَوْلَآ أُنزِلَ عَلَيْهِ ءَايَـٰتٌ مِّن رَّبِّهِۦۖ قُلْ إِنَّمَا ٱلْأَيَـٰتُ عِندَ ٱللَّهِ وَإِنَّمَآ أَنَا۠ نَذِيرٌ مُّبِينٌ

And they say: "Why are not signs sent down to him from his Lord? Say: "The signs are only with Allâh, and I am only a plain warner."

Quran 29:52

قُلْ كَفَىٰ بِٱللَّهِ بَيْنِى وَبَيْنَكُمْ شَهِيدًا يَعْلَمُ مَا فِى ٱلسَّمَـٰوَٰتِ وَٱلْأَرْضِ وَٱلَّذِينَ ءَامَنُوا۟ بِٱلْبَـٰطِلِ وَكَفَرُوا۟ بِٱللَّهِ أُو۟لَـٰٓئِكَ هُمُ ٱلْخَـٰسِرُونَ

Say (to them O Muhammad): "Sufficient is Allâh for a witness between me and you. He knows what is in the heavens and on earth." And those who believe in Bâtil (all false deities other than Allâh), and disbelieve in Allâh and (in His Oneness), it is they who are the losers.

Quran 29:63

وَلَئِن سَأَلْتَهُم مَّن نَّزَّلَ مِنَ ٱلسَّمَآءِ مَآءً فَأَحْيَا بِهِ ٱلْأَرْضَ مِنۢ بَعْدِ مَوْتِهَا لَيَقُولُنَّ ٱللَّهُ قُلِ ٱلْحَمْدُ لِلَّهِ بَلْ أَكْثَرُهُمْ لَا يَعْقِلُونَ

And If you were to ask them: "Who sends down water from the sky, and gives life therewith to the earth after its death?" they will surely reply: "Allâh." Say: "All the praises and thanks are to Allâh!" Nay! Most of them have no sense.

Quran 30:42

قُلْ سِيرُواْ فِى ٱلْأَرْضِ فَٱنظُرُواْ كَيْفَ كَانَ عَٰقِبَةُ ٱلَّذِينَ مِن قَبْلُ كَانَ أَكْثَرُهُم مُّشْرِكِينَ

Say (O Muhammad): "Travel in the land and see what was the end of those before (you)! Most of them were Mushrikûn (polytheists, idolaters, disbelievers in the Oneness of Allah)."

Quran 31:25

وَلَئِن سَأَلْتَهُم مَّنْ خَلَقَ ٱلسَّمَٰوَٰتِ وَٱلْأَرْضَ لَيَقُولُنَّ ٱللَّهُ قُلِ ٱلْحَمْدُ لِلَّهِ بَلْ أَكْثَرُهُمْ لَا يَعْلَمُونَ

And if you ask them: "Who has created the heavens and the earth," they will certainly say: "Allâh." Say: "All the praises and thanks be to Allâh!" But most of them know not.

Quran 32:11

قُلْ يَتَوَفَّىٰكُم مَّلَكُ ٱلْمَوْتِ ٱلَّذِى وُكِّلَ بِكُمْ ثُمَّ إِلَىٰ رَبِّكُمْ تُرْجَعُونَ

Say: "The angel of death, who is set over you, will take your souls, Then you shall be brought to your Lord."

Quran 34:3

وَقَالَ ٱلَّذِينَ كَفَرُوا۟ لَا تَأْتِينَا ٱلسَّاعَةُ قُلْ بَلَىٰ وَرَبِّى لَتَأْتِيَنَّكُمْ عَٰلِمِ ٱلْغَيْبِ لَا يَعْزُبُ عَنْهُ مِثْقَالُ ذَرَّةٍ فِى ٱلسَّمَٰوَٰتِ وَلَا فِى ٱلْأَرْضِ وَلَآ أَصْغَرُ مِن ذَٰلِكَ وَلَآ أَكْبَرُ إِلَّا فِى كِتَٰبٍ مُّبِينٍ

Those who disbelieve say: "The Hour will not come to us." Say: "Yes, by my Lord, the All¬Knower of the unseen, it

will come to you." not even the weight
of an atom (or a small ant) or less than
that or greater, escapes His Knowledge
in the heavens or in the earth, but it is in
a Clear Book (Al¬Lauh Al¬Mahfûz).

Quran 34:22

قُلِ ٱدْعُواْ ٱلَّذِينَ زَعَمْتُم مِّن دُونِ ٱللَّهِ لَا يَمْلِكُونَ
مِثْقَالَ ذَرَّةٍ فِى ٱلسَّمَٰوَٰتِ وَلَا فِى ٱلْأَرْضِ وَمَا لَهُمْ
فِيهِمَا مِن شِرْكٍ وَمَا لَهُۥ مِنْهُم مِّن ظَهِيرٍ

Say: "Call upon those whom you assert
(to be associate gods) besides Allâh,
they possess not even an atom's (or a
small ant's) weight either in the heavens
or on the earth, nor have they any share
in either, nor there is for Him any
supporter from among them.

Quran 34:24-27

قُلْ مَن يَرْزُقُكُم مِّنَ ٱلسَّمَٰوَٰتِ وَٱلْأَرْضِ قُلِ ٱللَّهُ وَإِنَّا
أَوْ إِيَّاكُمْ لَعَلَىٰ هُدًى أَوْ فِى ضَلَٰلٍ مُّبِينٍ قُل لَّا
تُسْـَٔلُونَ عَمَّآ أَجْرَمْنَا وَلَا نُسْـَٔلُ عَمَّا تَعْمَلُونَ قُلْ

285

يَجْمَعُ بَيْنَنَا رَبُّنَا ثُمَّ يَفْتَحُ بَيْنَنَا بِٱلْحَقِّ وَهُوَ ٱلْفَتَّاحُ ٱلْعَلِيمُ قُلْ أَرُونِىَ ٱلَّذِينَ أَلْحَقْتُم بِهِۦ شُرَكَآءَ كَلَّا بَلْ هُوَ ٱللَّهُ ٱلْعَزِيزُ ٱلْحَكِيمُ

Say "Who gives you provision from the heavens and the earth?" Say: "Allâh, And verily, (either) we or you are rightly guided or in plain error." (24) Say "You will not be asked about our sins, nor shall we be asked of what you do." (25) Say: "Our Lord will assemble us all together (on the Day of Resurrection), then He will judge between us with truth. And He is the Just judge, the All-Knower of the true state of affairs." (26): "Show me those whom you have joined with Him as partners. Nay (there are not at all any partners with Him)! But He is Allâh (Alone), the All¬Mighty, the All¬Wise." (27)

Quran 34:30

قُل لَّكُم مِّيعَادُ يَوْمٍ لَّا تَسْتَأْخِرُونَ عَنْهُ سَاعَةً وَلَا تَسْتَقْدِمُونَ

Say (O Muhammad): "The appointment to you is for a Day, which you cannot put back for an hour (or a moment) nor put forward."

Quran 34:36

قُلْ إِنَّ رَبِّى يَبْسُطُ ٱلرِّزْقَ لِمَن يَشَآءُ وَيَقْدِرُ وَلَٰكِنَّ أَكْثَرَ ٱلنَّاسِ لَا يَعْلَمُونَ

Say (O Muhammad): "Verily, my Lord enlarges the provision to whom He wills and restricts, but most men know not."

Quran 34:39

قُلْ إِنَّ رَبِّى يَبْسُطُ ٱلرِّزْقَ لِمَن يَشَآءُ مِنْ عِبَادِهِۦ وَيَقْدِرُ لَهُۥ ۚ وَمَآ أَنفَقْتُم مِّن شَىْءٍ فَهُوَ يُخْلِفُهُۥ ۖ وَهُوَ خَيْرُ ٱلرَّٰزِقِينَ

Say: "Truly, my Lord enlarges the provision for whom He wills of His slaves, and (also) restricts (it) for him,

287

and whatsoever you spend of anything
(in Allâh's Cause), He will replace it.
And He is the Best of providers."

Quran 34:46-50

قُلْ إِنَّمَا أَعِظُكُم بِوَاحِدَةٍ أَنْ تَقُومُوا لِلَّهِ مَثْنَىٰ وَفُرَادَىٰ
ثُمَّ تَتَفَكَّرُوا مَا بِصَاحِبِكُم مِنْ جِنَّةٍ إِنْ هُوَ إِلَّا نَذِيرٌ
لَكُم بَيْنَ يَدَيْ عَذَابٍ شَدِيدٍ قُلْ مَا سَأَلْتُكُم مِنْ أَجْرٍ
فَهُوَ لَكُمْ إِنْ أَجْرِيَ إِلَّا عَلَى اللَّهِ وَهُوَ عَلَىٰ كُلِّ
شَيْءٍ شَهِيدٌ قُلْ إِنَّ رَبِّي يَقْذِفُ بِالْحَقِّ عَلَّامُ الْغُيُوبِ
قُلْ جَاءَ الْحَقُّ وَمَا يُبْدِئُ الْبَاطِلُ وَمَا يُعِيدُ قُلْ إِنْ
ضَلَلْتُ فَإِنَّمَا أَضِلُّ عَلَىٰ نَفْسِي وَإِنِ اهْتَدَيْتُ فَبِمَا
يُوحِي إِلَيَّ رَبِّي إِنَّهُ سَمِيعٌ قَرِيبٌ

Say (to them O Muhammad): "I exhort
you to one (thing) only: that you stand
up for Allâh's sake in pairs and singly,
and reflect (within yourselves the life
history of the Prophet): there is no
madness in your companion
(Muhammad), He is only a warner to
you in face of a severe torment." (46) Say
(O Muhammad): "Whatever wage I

288

might have asked of you is yours. My wage is from Allâh only. and He is a Witness over all things." (47) Say (O Muhammad): "Verily! my Lord sends down (Revelation and makes apparent) the truth (i.e. this Revelation that had come to me), the All¬Knower of the Ghaib (unseen). (48) Say (O Muhammad): "Al-Haqq (the truth the Qur'ân and Allâh's Revealation) has come, and Al¬Bâtil [falsehood - Iblîs (Satan)] can neither create anything nor resurrect (anything)." (49) Say: "If (even) I go astray, I shall stray only to my own loss. But if I remain guided, it is because of the Revealation of my Lord to me. Truly, He is All¬Hearer, Ever Near (to all things)."

Quran 35:40

قُلْ أَرَءَيْتُمْ شُرَكَآءَكُمُ ٱلَّذِينَ تَدْعُونَ مِن دُونِ ٱللَّهِ أَرُونِى مَاذَا خَلَقُوا۟ مِنَ ٱلْأَرْضِ أَمْ لَهُمْ شِرْكٌ فِى

ٱلسَّمَـٰوَٰتِ أَمْ ءَاتَيْنَـٰهُمْ كِتَـٰبًا فَهُمْ عَلَىٰ بَيِّنَتٍ مِّنْهُ بَلْ إِن يَعِدُ ٱلظَّـٰلِمُونَ بَعْضُهُم بَعْضًا إِلَّا غُرُورًا

Say: "Tell me or inform me (what) do you think about your (so¬called) partner¬gods to whom you call upon besides Allâh? show me, what they have created of the earth? Or have they any share in the heavens? Or have We given them a Book, so that they act on clear proof therefrom? Nay, the Zâlimûn (polytheists and wrong¬doers) promise one another nothing but delusions."

Quran 36:79

قُلْ يُحْيِيهَا ٱلَّذِىٓ أَنشَأَهَآ أَوَّلَ مَرَّةٍ وَهُوَ بِكُلِّ خَلْقٍ عَلِيمٌ

Say: "He will give life to them Who created them for the first time! And He is the All-Knower of every creation!"

Quran 37:11

فَٱسْتَفْتِهِمْ أَهُمْ أَشَدُّ خَلْقًا أَم مَّنْ خَلَقْنَآ إِنَّا خَلَقْنَـٰهُم مِّن طِينٍ لَّازِبٍ

Then ask them (i.e. these polytheists, O Muhammad): "Are they stronger as creation, or those (others like the heavens and the earth and the mountains) whom We have created?" Verily, We created them of a sticky clay.

Quran 37:15-18

وَقَالُوٓا۟ إِنْ هَـٰذَآ إِلَّا سِحْرٌ مُّبِينٌ أَءِذَا مِتْنَا وَكُنَّا تُرَابًا وَعِظَـٰمًا أَءِنَّا لَمَبْعُوثُونَ أَوَءَابَآؤُنَا ٱلْأَوَّلُونَ قُلْ نَعَمْ وَأَنتُمْ دَٰخِرُونَ

And they say: "This is nothing but evident magic! (15) "When we are dead and have become dust and bones, shall we (then) verily be resurrected? (16) "And also our fathers of old?" (17) Say: "Yes, and you shall then be humiliated." (18)

Quran 37:149-150

291

فَٱسْتَفْتِهِمْ أَلِرَبِّكَ ٱلْبَنَاتُ وَلَهُمُ ٱلْبَنُونَ أَمْ خَلَقْنَا ٱلْمَلَـٰٓئِكَةَ إِنَـٰثًا وَهُمْ شَـٰهِدُونَ

Now ask them (O Muhammad): "Are there (only) daughters for your Lord and sons for them?" (149) Or did We create the angels female while they were witnesses? (150)

Quran 38:65-70

قُلْ إِنَّمَا أَنَا مُنْذِرٌ ۖ وَمَا مِنْ إِلَٰهٍ إِلَّا اللَّهُ الْوَاحِدُ الْقَهَّارُ رَبُّ السَّمَاوَاتِ وَالْأَرْضِ وَمَا بَيْنَهُمَا الْعَزِيزُ الْغَفَّارُ قُلْ هُوَ نَبَأٌ عَظِيمٌ أَنْتُمْ عَنْهُ مُعْرِضُونَ مَا كَانَ لِيَ مِنْ عِلْمٍ بِالْمَلَإِ الْأَعْلَىٰ إِذْ يَخْتَصِمُونَ إِنْ يُوحَىٰ إِلَيَّ إِلَّا أَنَّمَا أَنَا نَذِيرٌ مُبِينٌ

Say (O Muhammad): "I am only a warner and there is no Ilâh (God) except Allâh (none has the right to be worshipped but Allâh) the One, the Irresistible, (65) "The Lord of the heavens and the earth and all that is between them, the All-Mighty, the Oft-

Forgiving." (66) Say: "That (this Qur'ân) is a great news, (67) "From which you turn away! (68) "I had no knowledge of the chiefs (angels) on high when they were disputing and discussing (about the creation of Adam). (69) "Only this has been revealed to me, that I am a plain warner." (70)

Quran 38:86-88

قُلْ مَا أَسْأَلُكُمْ عَلَيْهِ مِنْ أَجْرٍ وَمَا أَنَا مِنَ الْمُتَكَلِّفِينَ إِنْ هُوَ إِلَّا ذِكْرٌ لِلْعَالَمِينَ وَلَتَعْلَمُنَّ نَبَأَهُ بَعْدَ حِينٍ

Say (O Muhammad): "No wage do I ask of you for this (the Qur'ân), nor am I one of the Mutakallifûn (those who pretend and fabricate things which do not exist). (86) "It (this Qur'ân) is only a Reminder for all the 'Alamîn (mankind and jinn). (87) "And you shall certainly know the truth of it after a while." (88)

Quran 39:8-15

وَإِذَا مَسَّ الْإِنْسَانَ ضُرٌّ دَعَا رَبَّهُ مُنِيبًا إِلَيْهِ ثُمَّ إِذَا خَوَّلَهُ نِعْمَةً مِنْهُ نَسِيَ مَا كَانَ يَدْعُو إِلَيْهِ مِنْ قَبْلُ وَجَعَلَ لِلَّهِ أَنْدَادًا لِيُضِلَّ عَنْ سَبِيلِهِ ۚ قُلْ تَمَتَّعْ بِكُفْرِكَ قَلِيلًا ۖ إِنَّكَ مِنْ أَصْحَابِ النَّارِ أَمَّنْ هُوَ قَانِتٌ آنَاءَ اللَّيْلِ سَاجِدًا وَقَائِمًا يَحْذَرُ الْآخِرَةَ وَيَرْجُو رَحْمَةَ رَبِّهِ ۗ قُلْ هَلْ يَسْتَوِي الَّذِينَ يَعْلَمُونَ وَالَّذِينَ لَا يَعْلَمُونَ ۗ إِنَّمَا يَتَذَكَّرُ أُولُو الْأَلْبَابِ قُلْ يَا عِبَادِ الَّذِينَ آمَنُوا اتَّقُوا رَبَّكُمْ ۚ لِلَّذِينَ أَحْسَنُوا فِي هَٰذِهِ الدُّنْيَا حَسَنَةٌ ۗ وَأَرْضُ اللَّهِ وَاسِعَةٌ ۗ إِنَّمَا يُوَفَّى الصَّابِرُونَ أَجْرَهُمْ بِغَيْرِ حِسَابٍ قُلْ إِنِّي أُمِرْتُ أَنْ أَعْبُدَ اللَّهَ مُخْلِصًا لَهُ الدِّينَ وَأُمِرْتُ لِأَنْ أَكُونَ أَوَّلَ الْمُسْلِمِينَ قُلْ إِنِّي أَخَافُ إِنْ عَصَيْتُ رَبِّي عَذَابَ يَوْمٍ عَظِيمٍ قُلِ اللَّهَ أَعْبُدُ مُخْلِصًا لَهُ دِينِي فَاعْبُدُوا مَا شِئْتُمْ مِنْ دُونِهِ ۗ قُلْ إِنَّ الْخَاسِرِينَ الَّذِينَ خَسِرُوا أَنْفُسَهُمْ وَأَهْلِيهِمْ يَوْمَ الْقِيَامَةِ ۗ أَلَا ذَٰلِكَ هُوَ الْخُسْرَانُ الْمُبِينُ

And when some hurt touches man, he cries to his Lord (Allâh Alone), turning to Him in repentance, but when He bestows a favor upon him from Himself, he forgets that for which he cried for before, and he sets up rivals to Allâh, in

order to mislead others from His Path.
Say: "Take pleasure in your disbelief for
a while: surely, you are (one) of the
dwellers of the Fire!" (8) Is one who is
obedient to Allâh, prostrating himself or
standing (in prayer) during the hours of
the night, fearing the Hereafter and
hoping for the Mercy of his Lord (like
one who disbelieves)? Say: "Are those
who know equal to those who know
not?" It is only men of understanding
who will remember (i.e. get a lesson
from Allâh's Signs and Verses). (9) Say
(O Muhammad): "O My slaves who
believe (in the Oneness of Allâh Islâmic
— Monotheism), be afraid of your Lord
(Allâh) and keep your duty to Him.
Good is (the reward) for those who do
good in this world, and Allâh's earth is
spacious (so if you cannot worship
Allâh at a place, then go to another)!
Only those who are patient shall receive
their reward in full, without reckoning."

(10) Say (O Muhammad): "Verily, I am commanded to worship Allâh (Alone) by obeying Him and doing religious deeds sincerely for His sake only. (11) "And I am commanded (this) in order that I may be the first of those who submit themselves to Allâh (in Islâm) as Muslims." (12) Say (O Muhammad): "Verily, if I disobey my Lord, I am afraid of the torment of a great Day." (13) Say (O Muhammad) "Allâh Alone I worship by doing religious deeds sincerely for His sake only (and not to show off, and not to set up rivals with Him in worship)." (14) So worship what you like besides Him. Say (O Muhammad): "The losers are those who will lose themselves and their families on the Day of Resurrection. Verily, that will be a manifest loss!" (15)

Quran 39:38-40

وَلَئِنْ سَأَلْتَهُمْ مَنْ خَلَقَ السَّمَاوَاتِ وَالْأَرْضَ لَيَقُولُنَّ
اللَّهُ ۚ قُلْ أَفَرَأَيْتُمْ مَا تَدْعُونَ مِنْ دُونِ اللَّهِ إِنْ أَرَادَنِيَ
اللَّهُ بِضُرٍّ هَلْ هُنَّ كَاشِفَاتُ ضُرِّهِ أَوْ أَرَادَنِي بِرَحْمَةٍ
هَلْ هُنَّ مُمْسِكَاتُ رَحْمَتِهِ ۚ قُلْ حَسْبِيَ اللَّهُ ۖ عَلَيْهِ
يَتَوَكَّلُ الْمُتَوَكِّلُونَ قُلْ يَا قَوْمِ اعْمَلُوا عَلَىٰ مَكَانَتِكُمْ
إِنِّي عَامِلٌ ۖ فَسَوْفَ تَعْلَمُونَ مَنْ يَأْتِيهِ عَذَابٌ يُخْزِيهِ
وَيَحِلُّ عَلَيْهِ عَذَابٌ مُقِيمٌ

And verily, if you ask them: "Who
created the heavens and the earth?"
Surely, they will say: "Allâh (has created
them)." Say: "Tell me then, the things
that you invoke besides Allâh, if Allâh
intended some harm for me, could they
remove His harm, or if He (Allâh)
intended some mercy for me, could they
withhold His Mercy?" Say : "Sufficient
for me is Allâh; in Him those who trust
(i.e. believers) must put their trust." (38)
Say: (O Muhammad) "O My people!
Work according to your way, I am
working (according to my way). Then
you will come to know, (39) "To whom

comes a disgracing torment, and on whom descends an everlasting torment." (40)

Quran 39:43-44

أَمِ ٱتَّخَذُواْ مِن دُونِ ٱللَّهِ شُفَعَآءَ قُلْ أَوَلَوْ كَانُواْ لَا يَمْلِكُونَ شَيْئًا وَلَا يَعْقِلُونَ قُل لِّلَّهِ ٱلشَّفَـٰعَةُ جَمِيعًا لَّهُۥ مُلْكُ ٱلسَّمَـٰوَٰتِ وَٱلْأَرْضِ ثُمَّ إِلَيْهِ تُرْجَعُونَ

Have they taken (others) as intercessors besides Allâh? Say: "Even if they have power over nothing whatever and have no intelligence?" (43) Say: "To Allâh belongs all intercession. His is the Sovereignty of the heavens and the earth, Then to Him you shall be brought back." (44)

Quran 39:64

قُلْ أَفَغَيْرَ ٱللَّهِ تَأْمُرُوٓنِّىٓ أَعْبُدُ أَيُّهَا ٱلْجَـٰهِلُونَ

Say: "Do you order me to worship other than Allâh? O you fools!"

Quran 40:66

قُلْ إِنِّى نُهِيتُ أَنْ أَعْبُدَ ٱلَّذِينَ تَدْعُونَ مِن دُونِ ٱللَّهِ لَمَّا
جَآءَنِىَ ٱلْبَيِّنَـٰتُ مِن رَّبِّى وَأُمِرْتُ أَنْ أُسْلِمَ لِرَبِّ
ٱلْعَـٰلَمِينَ

Say (O Muhammad): "I have been
forbidden to worship those whom you
worship besides Allâh, since there have
come to me evidences from my Lord,
and I am commanded to submit (in
Islâm) to the Lord of the 'Alamîn
(mankind, jinn and all that exists).

Quran 41:6

قُلْ إِنَّمَآ أَنَا۠ بَشَرٌ مِّثْلُكُمْ يُوحَىٰٓ إِلَىَّ أَنَّمَآ إِلَـٰهُكُمْ إِلَـٰهٌ
وَٰحِدٌ فَٱسْتَقِيمُوٓا۟ إِلَيْهِ وَٱسْتَغْفِرُوهُ ۗ وَوَيْلٌ لِّلْمُشْرِكِينَ

Say (O Muhammad): "I am only a
human being like you. It is revealed to
me that your Ilâh (God) is One Ilâh
(God - Allâh), therefore take Straight
Path to Him (with true Faith — Islâmic
Monotheism) and obedience to Him,

and seek forgiveness of Him. And woe to Al-Mushrikûn (the polytheists, idolaters, disbelievers in the Oneness of Allâh).

Quran 41:9

قُلْ أَئِنَّكُمْ لَتَكْفُرُونَ بِالَّذِى خَلَقَ ٱلْأَرْضَ فِى يَوْمَيْنِ وَتَجْعَلُونَ لَهُۥ أَندَادًا ۚ ذَٰلِكَ رَبُّ ٱلْعَٰلَمِينَ

Say: "Do you verily disbelieve in Him Who created the earth in two Days And you set up rivals (in worship) with Him? That is the Lord of the 'Alamîn (mankind, jinn and all that exists).

Quran 41:44

وَلَوْ جَعَلْنَٰهُ قُرْءَانًا أَعْجَمِيًّا لَّقَالُوا۟ لَوْلَا فُصِّلَتْ ءَايَٰتُهُۥ ۖ ءَا۬عْجَمِيٌّ وَعَرَبِىٌّ ۗ قُلْ هُوَ لِلَّذِينَ ءَامَنُوا۟ هُدًى وَشِفَآءٌ ۖ وَٱلَّذِينَ لَا يُؤْمِنُونَ فِىٓ ءَاذَانِهِمْ وَقْرٌ وَهُوَ عَلَيْهِمْ عَمًى ۚ أُو۟لَٰٓئِكَ يُنَادَوْنَ مِن مَّكَانٍۭ بَعِيدٍ

And if We had sent this as a Qur'ân in a foreign language (other than Arabic), they would have said: "Why are not its Verses explained in detail (in our language)? What! (A Book) not in Arabic and (the Messenger) an Arab?" Say: "It is for those who believe, a guide and a healing. And as for those who disbelieve, there is heaviness (deafness) in their ears, and it (the Qur'ân) is blindness for them. They are those who are called from a place far away (so they neither listen nor understand).

Quran 41:52

قُلْ أَرَءَيْتُمْ إِن كَانَ مِنْ عِندِ ٱللَّهِ ثُمَّ كَفَرْتُم بِهِۦ مَنْ أَضَلُّ مِمَّنْ هُوَ فِى شِقَاقٍ بَعِيدٍ

Say: "Tell me, if it (the Qur'ân) is from Allâh, and you disbelieve in it, who is more astray than one who is in opposition far away (from Allâh's Right Path and His obedience).

Quran 42:23

ذَٰلِكَ ٱلَّذِى يُبَشِّرُ ٱللَّهُ عِبَادَهُ ٱلَّذِينَ ءَامَنُوا۟ وَعَمِلُوا۟ ٱلصَّٰلِحَٰتِ ۗ قُل لَّآ أَسْـَٔلُكُمْ عَلَيْهِ أَجْرًا إِلَّا ٱلْمَوَدَّةَ فِى ٱلْقُرْبَىٰ ۗ وَمَن يَقْتَرِفْ حَسَنَةً نَّزِدْ لَهُۥ فِيهَا حُسْنًا ۚ إِنَّ ٱللَّهَ غَفُورٌ شَكُورٌ

That is (the Paradise) whereof Allâh gives glad tidings to His slaves who believe (in the Oneness of Allâh — Islâmic Monotheism) and do righteous good deeds. Say: "No reward do I ask of you for this except to be kind to me for my kinship with you." And whoever earns a good righteous deed, We shall give him an increase of good in respect thereof. Verily, Allâh is Oft-Forgiving, Most Ready to appreciate (the deeds of those who are obedient to Him).

Quran 43:81

قُلْ إِن كَانَ لِلرَّحْمَٰنِ وَلَدٌ فَأَنَا۠ أَوَّلُ ٱلْعَٰبِدِينَ

Say (O Muhammad): "If the Most Gracious (Allâh) had a son (or children as you pretend), then I am the first of Allâh's worshippers [who deny and refute this claim (and the first to believe in Allâh Alone and testify He has no children)]."

Quran 43:88-89

وَقِيلِهِۦ يَٰرَبِّ إِنَّ هَٰٓؤُلَآءِ قَوْمٌ لَّا يُؤْمِنُونَ

فَٱصْفَحْ عَنْهُمْ وَقُلْ سَلَٰمٌ فَسَوْفَ يَعْلَمُونَ

(And Allâh has knowledge) of (Prophet Muhammad's) saying: "O my Lord! Verily, these are a people who believe not!" (88) So turn away from them (O Muhammad), and say: Salâm (peace)! But they will come to know. (89)

Quran 45:26

قُلِ ٱللَّهُ يُحْيِيكُمْ ثُمَّ يُمِيتُكُمْ ثُمَّ يَجْمَعُكُمْ إِلَىٰ يَوْمِ ٱلْقِيَٰمَةِ لَا رَيْبَ فِيهِ وَلَٰكِنَّ أَكْثَرَ ٱلنَّاسِ لَا يَعْلَمُونَ

Say: "Allâh gives you life, then causes you to die, then He will assemble you on the Day of Resurrection about which there is no doubt. But most of mankind know not."

Quran 46:4

قُلْ أَرَءَيْتُم مَّا تَدْعُونَ مِن دُونِ ٱللَّهِ أَرُونِى مَاذَا خَلَقُوا۟ مِنَ ٱلْأَرْضِ أَمْ لَهُمْ شِرْكٌ فِى ٱلسَّمَٰوَٰتِ ۖ ٱئْتُونِى بِكِتَٰبٍ مِّن قَبْلِ هَٰذَآ أَوْ أَثَٰرَةٍ مِّنْ عِلْمٍ إِن كُنتُمْ صَٰدِقِينَ

Say (O Muhammad to these pagans): "Think you about all that you invoke besides Allâh? Show me. What have they created of the earth? Or have they a share in (the creation of) the heavens? Bring me a Book (revealed before this), or some trace of knowledge (in support of your claims), if you are truthful!"

Quran 46:8-10

أَمْ يَقُولُونَ ٱفْتَرَىٰهُ ۖ قُلْ إِنِ ٱفْتَرَيْتُهُ فَلَا تَمْلِكُونَ لِى مِنَ ٱللَّهِ شَيْـًٔا ۖ هُوَ أَعْلَمُ بِمَا تُفِيضُونَ فِيهِ ۖ كَفَىٰ بِهِۦ شَهِيدًۢا بَيْنِى وَبَيْنَكُمْ ۖ وَهُوَ ٱلْغَفُورُ ٱلرَّحِيمُ قُلْ مَا كُنتُ

304

بِدْعًا مِّنَ ٱلرُّسُلِ وَمَآ أَدْرِى بِى وَلَا يُفْعَلُ مَا وَلَا بِكُمْ إِنَّ
أَتَّبِعُ إِلَّا مَا يُوحَىٰ إِلَيَّ وَمَآ أَنَا۠ إِلَّا نَذِيرٌ مُّبِينٌ قُلْ
أَرَءَيْتُمْ إِن كَانَ مِنْ عِندِ ٱللَّهِ وَكَفَرْتُم بِهِ ۖ وَشَهِدَ شَاهِدٌ
مِّنْ بَنِىٓ إِسْرَٰٓءِيلَ عَلَىٰ مِثْلِهِ ۦ فَـَٔامَنَ وَٱسْتَكْبَرْتُمْ ۚ إِنَّ
ٱللَّهَ لَا يَهْدِى ٱلْقَوْمَ ٱلظَّٰلِمِينَ

Or say they: "He (Muhammad) has fabricated it." Say: "If I have fabricated it? still you have no power to support me against Allâh. He knows best of what you say among yourselves concerning it (i.e. this Qur'ân)! Sufficient is He as a witness between me and you! And He is the Oft-Forgiving, the Most Merciful." (8) Say (O Muhammad):"I am not a new thing among the Messengers (of Allâh) (i.e. I am not the first Messenger) nor do I know what will be done with me or with you. I only follow that which is revealed to me, and I am but a plain warner." (9) Say: "Tell me! If this (Qur'ân) is from Allâh and you deny it, and a witness from among the

Children of Israel ('Abdullâh bin Salâm) testifies that [this Qur'ân is from Allâh (like the Taurât (Torah)], and he believed (embraced Islâm) while you are too proud (to believe)." Verily, Allâh guides not the people who are Zâlimûn (polytheists, disbelievers and wrong-doers). (10)

Quran 49:14

قَالَتِ ٱلْأَعْرَابُ ءَامَنَّاۖ قُل لَّمْ تُؤْمِنُوا۟ وَلَٰكِن قُولُوٓا۟ أَسْلَمْنَا وَلَمَّا يَدْخُلِ ٱلْإِيمَٰنُ فِى قُلُوبِكُمْۖ وَإِن تُطِيعُوا۟ ٱللَّهَ وَرَسُولَهُۥ لَا يَلِتْكُم مِّنْ أَعْمَٰلِكُمْ شَيْـًٔاۚ إِنَّ ٱللَّهَ غَفُورٌ رَّحِيمٌ

The bedouins say: "We believe." Say: "You believe not but you only say, 'We have surrendered (in Islâm),' for Faith has not yet entered your hearts. But if you obey Allâh and His Messenger, He will not decrease anything in reward for your deeds. Verily, Allâh is Oft-Forgiving, Most Merciful."

Quran 49:16-17

قُلْ أَتُعَلِّمُونَ ٱللَّهَ بِدِينِكُمْ وَٱللَّهُ يَعْلَمُ مَا فِى ٱلسَّمَـٰوَٰتِ
وَمَا فِى ٱلْأَرْضِ وَٱللَّهُ بِكُلِّ شَىْءٍ عَلِيمٌ يَمُنُّونَ عَلَيْكَ
أَنْ أَسْلَمُوا قُل لَّا تَمُنُّوا عَلَىَّ إِسْلَـٰمَكُم بَلِ ٱللَّهُ يَمُنُّ
عَلَيْكُمْ أَنْ هَدَىٰكُمْ لِلْإِيمَـٰنِ إِن كُنتُمْ صَـٰدِقِينَ

Say: "Will you inform Allâh of your
religion While Allâh knows all that is in
the heavens and all that is in the earth,
and Allâh is All-Aware of everything.
(16) They regard as favor to you (O
Muhammad) that they have embraced
Islâm. Say: "Count not your Islâm as a
favor to me. Nay, but Allâh has
conferred a favor upon you, that He has
guided you to the Faith, if you indeed
are true.

Quran 56:49-55

قُلْ إِنَّ الْأَوَّلِينَ وَالْآخِرِينَ لَمَجْمُوعُونَ إِلَىٰ مِيقَاتِ
يَوْمٍ مَعْلُومٍ ثُمَّ إِنَّكُمْ أَيُّهَا الضَّالُّونَ الْمُكَذِّبُونَ لَآكِلُونَ

307

مِنْ شَجَرٍ مِنْ زَقُّومٍ فَمَالِئُونَ مِنْهَا الْبُطُونَ فَشَارِبُونَ عَلَيْهِ مِنَ الْحَمِيمِ فَشَارِبُونَ شُرْبَ الْهِيمِ

Say (O Muhammad): "(Yes) verily, those of old, and those of later times. (49) "All will surely be gathered together for appointed Meeting of a known Day. (50) "Then moreover, verily, you the erring-ones, the deniers (of Resurrection)! (51) "You verily will eat of the trees of Zaqqûm. (52) "Then you will fill your bellies therewith, (53) "And drink boiling water on top of it. (54) "And you will drink (that) like thirsty camels!" (55)

Quran 62:6

قُلْ يَـٰٓأَيُّهَا ٱلَّذِينَ هَادُوٓاْ إِن زَعَمْتُمْ أَنَّكُمْ أَوْلِيَآءُ لِلَّهِ مِن دُونِ ٱلنَّاسِ فَتَمَنَّوُاْ ٱلْمَوْتَ إِن كُنتُمْ صَـٰدِقِينَ

Say: "O you Jews! If you pretend that you are friends of Allâh, to the exclusion of (all) other mankind, then long for death if you are truthful."

Quran 62:8

قُلْ إِنَّ ٱلْمَوْتَ ٱلَّذِى تَفِرُّونَ مِنْهُ فَإِنَّهُ مُلَـٰقِيكُمْ ثُمَّ تُرَدُّونَ إِلَىٰ عَـٰلِمِ ٱلْغَيْبِ وَٱلشَّهَـٰدَةِ فَيُنَبِّئُكُم بِمَا كُنتُمْ تَعْمَلُونَ

Say: "Verily, the death from which you flee will surely meet you, then you will be sent back to (Allâh), the All-Knower of the unseen and the seen, and He will tell you what you used to do."

Quran 64:7

زَعَمَ ٱلَّذِينَ كَفَرُوٓا۟ أَن لَّن يُبْعَثُوا۟ قُلْ بَلَىٰ وَرَبِّى لَتُبْعَثُنَّ ثُمَّ لَتُنَبَّؤُنَّ بِمَا عَمِلْتُمْ وَذَٰلِكَ عَلَى ٱللَّهِ يَسِيرٌ

The disbelievers pretend that they will never be resurrected (for the Account). Say: "Yes! By my Lord, you will certainly be resurrected, then you will be informed of (and recompensed for) what you did, and that is easy for Allâh.

Quran 67:23-30

قُلْ هُوَ الَّذِي أَنْشَأَكُمْ وَجَعَلَ لَكُمُ السَّمْعَ وَالْأَبْصَارَ
وَالْأَفْئِدَةَ ۖ قَلِيلًا مَا تَشْكُرُونَ قُلْ هُوَ الَّذِي ذَرَأَكُمْ فِي
الْأَرْضِ وَإِلَيْهِ تُحْشَرُونَ وَيَقُولُونَ مَتَىٰ هَٰذَا الْوَعْدُ إِنْ
كُنْتُمْ صَادِقِينَ قُلْ إِنَّمَا الْعِلْمُ عِنْدَ اللَّهِ وَإِنَّمَا أَنَا نَذِيرٌ
مُبِينٌ فَلَمَّا رَأَوْهُ زُلْفَةً سِيئَتْ وُجُوهُ الَّذِينَ كَفَرُوا وَقِيلَ
هَٰذَا الَّذِي كُنْتُمْ بِهِ تَدَّعُونَ قُلْ أَرَأَيْتُمْ إِنْ أَهْلَكَنِيَ اللَّهُ
وَمَنْ مَعِيَ أَوْ رَحِمَنَا فَمَنْ يُجِيرُ الْكَافِرِينَ مِنْ عَذَابٍ
أَلِيمٍ قُلْ هُوَ الرَّحْمَٰنُ آمَنَّا بِهِ وَعَلَيْهِ تَوَكَّلْنَا ۖ فَسَتَعْلَمُونَ
مَنْ هُوَ فِي ضَلَالٍ مُبِينٍ قُلْ أَرَأَيْتُمْ إِنْ أَصْبَحَ مَاؤُكُمْ
غَوْرًا فَمَنْ يَأْتِيكُمْ بِمَاءٍ مَعِينٍ

Say it is He Who has created you, and
endowed you with hearing (ears),
seeing (eyes), and hearts. Little thanks
you give. (23) Say: "It is He Who has
created you from the earth, and to Him
shall you be gathered (in the
Hereafter)." (24) They say: "When will
this promise (i.e. the Day of
Resurrection) come to pass if you are
telling the truth?" (25) Say (O
Muhammad): "The knowledge (of its
exact time) is with Allâh only, and I am

only a plain warner." (26) But when they will see it (the torment on the Day of Resurrection) approaching, the faces of those who disbelieve will change and turn black with sadness and in grief and it will be said (to them): "This is (the promise) which you were calling for!" (27) Say (O Muhammad): "Tell me! If Allâh destroys me, and those with me, or He bestows His Mercy on us — who can save the disbelievers from a painful torment?" (28) Say: "He is the Most Gracious (Allâh), in Him we believe, and in Him we put our trust. So you will come to know who is it that is in manifest error." (29) Say (O Muhammad): "Tell me! If (all) your water were to sink away, who then can supply you with flowing (spring) water?" (30)

Quran 72:20-22

قُلْ إِنَّمَآ أَدْعُواْ رَبِّى وَلَا أُشْرِكُ بِهِۦٓ أَحَدًا

قُلْ إِنِّى لَآ أَمْلِكُ لَكُمْ ضَرًّا وَلَا رَشَدًا

قُلْ إِنِّى لَن يُجِيرَنِى مِنَ ٱللَّهِ أَحَدٌ وَلَنْ أَجِدَ مِن دُونِهِۦ مُلْتَحَدًا

Say (O Muhammad): "I invoke only my Lord (Allâh Alone), and I associate none as partners along with Him." (20) Say: "It is not in my power to cause you harm, or to bring you to the Right Path." (21) Say (O Muhammad): "None can protect me from Allâh's punishment (if I were to disobey Him), nor can I find refuge except in Him. (22)

Quran 72:25

قُلْ إِنْ أَدْرِىٓ أَقَرِيبٌ مَّا تُوعَدُونَ أَمْ يَجْعَلُ لَهُۥ رَبِّىٓ أَمَدًا

Say (O Muhammad): "I know not whether (the punishment) which you are promised is near or whether my Lord will appoint for it a distant term

Quran 109:1-6

قُلْ يَـٰٓأَيُّهَا ٱلْكَـٰفِرُونَ لَآ أَعْبُدُ مَا تَعْبُدُونَ وَلَآ أَنتُمْ عَـٰبِدُونَ مَآ أَعْبُدُ وَلَآ أَنَا۠ عَابِدٌ مَّا عَبَدتُّمْ وَلَآ أَنتُمْ عَـٰبِدُونَ مَآ أَعْبُدُ لَكُمْ دِينُكُمْ وَلِىَ دِينِ

Say: "O disbelievers! (1) "I worship not that which you worship, (2) "Nor will you worship that which I worship. (3) "And I shall not worship that which you are worshipping. (4) "Nor will you worship that which I worship. (5) "To you be your religion, and to me my religion (Islâmic Monotheism)." (6)

Quran 112:1-4

قُلْ هُوَ ٱللَّهُ أَحَدٌ ٱللَّهُ ٱلصَّمَدُ لَمْ يَلِدْ وَلَمْ يُولَدْ وَلَمْ يَكُن لَّهُۥ كُفُوًا أَحَدٌۢ

Say: "He is Allâh, (the) One. (1) "Allâh-us-Samad [Allâh the Self-Sufficient Master, Whom all creatures need and who needs none, (He neither eats nor drinks)]. (2) "He begets not, nor was He begotten; (3) "And there is nothing co-equal or comparable unto Him." (4)

Quran 3:64

قُلْ يَـٰٓأَهْلَ ٱلْكِتَـٰبِ تَعَالَوْاْ إِلَىٰ كَلِمَةٍ سَوَآءٍ بَيْنَنَا وَبَيْنَكُمْ أَلَّا نَعْبُدَ إِلَّا ٱللَّهَ وَلَا نُشْرِكَ بِهِۦ شَيْـًٔا وَلَا يَتَّخِذَ بَعْضُنَا بَعْضًا أَرْبَابًا مِّن دُونِ ٱللَّهِ فَإِن تَوَلَّوْاْ فَقُولُواْ ٱشْهَدُواْ بِأَنَّا مُسْلِمُونَ

Say: "O people of the Scripture (Jews and Christians): Come to a word that is just between us and you, that we worship none but Allâh (Alone), and that we associate no partners with Him, and that none of us shall take others as lords besides Allâh. Then, if they turn away, say: "Bear witness that we are Muslims."

Quran 3:61

فَمَنْ حَآجَّكَ فِيهِ مِنْ بَعْدِ مَا جَآءَكَ مِنَ ٱلْعِلْمِ فَقُلْ تَعَالَوْاْ نَدْعُ أَبْنَآءَنَا وَأَبْنَآءَكُمْ وَنِسَآءَنَا وَنِسَآءَكُمْ

وَأَنفُسَنَا وَأَنفُسَكُمْ ثُمَّ نَبْتَهِلْ فَنَجْعَل لَّعْنَتَ ٱللَّهِ عَلَى ٱلْكَـٰذِبِينَ

Then whoever disputes with you concerning him ['Īsā (Jesus)] after (all this) knowledge that has come to you, [i.e. 'Īsā (Jesus)] being a slave of Allâh, and having no share in Divinity) say: (O Muhammad) "Come, let us call our sons and your sons, our women and your women, ourselves and yourselves - then we pray and invoke (sincerely) the Curse of Allâh upon those who lie."

Quran 3:119

هَـٰٓأَنتُمْ أُوْلَآءِ تُحِبُّونَهُمْ وَلَا يُحِبُّونَكُمْ وَتُؤْمِنُونَ بِٱلْكِتَـٰبِ كُلِّهِ وَإِذَا لَقُوكُمْ قَالُوٓاْ ءَامَنَّا وَإِذَا خَلَوْاْ عَضُّواْ عَلَيْكُمُ ٱلْأَنَامِلَ مِنَ ٱلْغَيْظِ قُلْ مُوتُواْ بِغَيْظِكُمْ إِنَّ ٱللَّهَ عَلِيمُۢ بِذَاتِ ٱلصُّدُورِ

Lo! You are the ones who love them but they love you not, and you believe in all the Scriptures. And when they meet

315

you, they say, "We believe". But when they are alone, they bite the tips of their fingers at you in rage. Say: "Perish in your rage. Certainly, Allâh knows what is in the breasts (all the secrets)." (119)

Quran 2:285

ءَامَنَ ٱلرَّسُولُ بِمَآ أُنزِلَ إِلَيْهِ مِن رَّبِّهِ وَٱلْمُؤْمِنُونَ كُلٌّ ءَامَنَ بِٱللَّهِ وَمَلَـٰٓئِكَتِهِ وَكُتُبِهِ وَرُسُلِهِ لَا نُفَرِّقُ بَيْنَ أَحَدٍ مِّن رُّسُلِهِ وَقَالُواْ سَمِعْنَا وَأَطَعْنَا غُفْرَانَكَ رَبَّنَا وَإِلَيْكَ ٱلْمَصِيرُ

The Messenger (Muhammad) believes in what has been sent down to him from his Lord, and (so do) the believers. Each one believes in Allâh, His Angels, His Books, and His Messengers. (They say), "We make no distinction between one another of His Messengers" and they say, "We hear, and we obey. (We seek) Your Forgiveness, our Lord, and to You is the return (of all)." (285)